The Business Bible

Victoria Devine is transforming the way millennials think about money. With a background in behavioural psychology and chart-topping podcasts, *She's on the Money* and *The Business Bible*, Victoria understands what makes her generation tick and she knows how to make hard-to-understand concepts fun, fresh and relatable.

Now retired from her role as an award-winning financial adviser, Victoria is a co-director and founder of Zella Money, an award-winning mortgage-broking business, and a financial columnist for *The Age* and *Sydney Morning Herald*. She has been a guest speaker at events and featured in publications such as *The Financial Standard*, *Vogue*, ABC News, RMIT Future of Financial Planning, Mamamia, *Elle* magazine, Yahoo Finance and many more. She was also named on the *Forbes* 30 Under 30 Asia list for 2021.

Victoria's number one bestselling first book, *She's on the Money*, won the ABIA General Non-fiction Book of the Year 2022 and the Best Personal Finance & Investment Book of the Year at the 2021 Business Book Awards. If you can't find her, chances are she's at home with an oat latte in one hand and her Old English sheepadoodle, Lucy, in the other.

shesonthemoney.com.au
@shesonthemoneyaus
@ShesontheMoneyAUS

Also by Victoria Devine

She's on the Money
Investing with She's on the Money
She's on the Money Budget Journal
Property with She's on the Money
Money Diaries with She's on the Money

The Business Bible

Victoria Devine

How to build a successful business – and a life you love

PENGUIN BOOKS

UK | USA | Canada | Ireland | Australia
India | New Zealand | South Africa | China

Penguin Books is part of the Penguin Random House group of companies
whose addresses can be found at global.penguinrandomhouse.com

First published by Penguin Books in 2024

Cover and text design by George Saad © Penguin Random House Australia Pty Ltd
Author photograph by Miranda Stokkel
Typeset in 10.5/17 pt FreightText Pro by Midland Typesetters, Australia

Printed and bound in Australia by Griffin Press, an accredited
ISO AS/NZS 14001 Environmental Management Systems printer

A catalogue record for this
book is available from the
National Library of Australia

ISBN 978 1 76134 774 0

penguin.com.au

We at Penguin Random House Australia acknowledge that Aboriginal and Torres Strait Islander
peoples are the Traditional Custodians and the first storytellers of the lands on which we live and
work. We honour Aboriginal and Torres Strait Islander peoples' continuous connection to Country,
waters, skies and communities. We celebrate Aboriginal and Torres Strait Islander stories, traditions
and living cultures; and we pay our respects to Elders past and present.

As the author of this book I'd like to acknowledge and pay respect to Australia's Aboriginal and Torres Strait Islander peoples, the traditional custodians of lands, waterways and skies across Australia. I'd like to particularly acknowledge the Wurundjeri people of the Kulin Nation who are the traditional custodians of the land on which I was able to write this book. I pay my respects to Elders past and present, and I share my friendship and kindness.

For Harvey,
May you always dream boldly, lead with kindness
and know that anything is possible.

Prologue

Welcome, friends, to your Business Bible, in which I share everything I've learnt about setting up and running a successful business. Consider it your invitation to the world of business ownership – a world where flexibility, independence and financial rewards await!

It's my goal with this book to help you design your dream lifestyle as an entrepreneur and find satisfaction and success in the world of business ownership, all while staying true to your personal values and goals. I truly believe it's possible for anyone to start a business that serves their passion and purpose so they can build a future for themselves, and the world, that they're proud of.

For those who don't know me yet, I'm a born-and-bred Tassie girl who grew up in Melbourne, which is where I've started and built two multi-million-dollar businesses of my own from scratch. My biggest business success story is my finance education platform, She's on the Money (SOTM, amongst friends) – you may know me from one of my podcasts (hello, listeners!). SOTM is built on my core belief that it's possible for *anyone*, no matter where they're starting from, to build an ideal future life for themselves once they've gained a money education. And my first business baby, Zella Money, is a financial advice business that I founded back in 2015, before SOTM came to life – I'm still Zella's managing director, and these days our focus is on home loans and asset finance.

They're two very different businesses, but across both, my teams and I are tirelessly driven by our mission of empowering others to make smarter money decisions every day. We want to instil in our clients and listeners the confidence they need to be able to change their financial situation for the better, however that may look for them.

One incredible way to revolutionise your financial future is by starting, growing and sustaining a business of your own, if it's something that appeals to you – and you're up for the challenge! Entrepreneurship opens doors that simply aren't accessible when you're working in a salaried position for somebody else's company. There's a lot to get excited about – and we're going to think blue-sky in this book but also step through the fine detail, to get you totally clear and prepared for what lies ahead on your path.

What kind of business is this book about, you ask? Well, I know from my daily interactions with the SOTM community that many of you have tried-and-tested side hustles that you're keen to take full time, while the go-getters among us are dreaming of our small biz goals becoming Canva-style unicorns. And I'm all for that, friend! If this handy guide sees some of us shooting high and landing among the highest of stars, yay for us all! But to give us clear focus and match up with most people's aspirations and realities in the here and now, we're going to zoom our attention in on businesses with less than 20 staff, operating in one of the most beautiful places on the planet – this being the government's definition of 'small business in Australia'[1] (well, maybe I added the 'most beautiful' part but you know I'm not wrong).

That's not to say this book won't be inspiring for *anyone* who wants to run *any kind* of enterprise the world over. I also know, since we get regular feedback from listeners across the globe, that for the most part the ideas and info we share are translatable no matter where you live or how wealthy you may (or may not) feel. So take heart that a good chunk, if not most, of this book will be practical, useful and inspiring to you, too! Plus, the gold in these pages is as much about self-empowerment and general financial wizardry as practical guidance.

Your financial success and future business success are about self-belief, and knowledge, and more than a little hard graft. And that applies to everyone, no matter where you're from, or what type or size of business you want to run. You'll see it echoed in the interviews I've gathered with my entrepreneurial pals from across different industries. Whether you're looking at micro, small or large business, Australian or international, bricks-and-mortar or digital, manufacturing or service, the words in this book are designed to guide us all. Everyone is welcome and we're all taking this journey together.

That means, at times in these pages we'll go deep on ideas and concerns that may feel a little irrelevant, depending on what kind of biz you're in. If that's the case, take what's on the page as a general guide and use our good friend Google to unearth any details more specific to you. Or skip ahead to the next bit that's useful. This book doesn't have to be read in chronological order (although, of course, it can be). But I've designed it so you can dip in and out, referring to the info at different times and different stages, depending on what you need. End of financial year? Come back and revise your bookkeeping. Sales a little flat? Flick through the marketing sections. Bringing on a new partner? Perhaps it's time to revise your structure.

Like life, business is not set-and-forget but an ongoing, ever-evolving concern. How big or small it becomes is up to you. The only rule I have is: make it yours and make it sing. Okay? I'll be cheering for you!

My business journey - so far

Before we start writing *your* business story together, let me briefly take you back to the beginning and retrace my path so you know where I'm coming from. When I look back, I feel I've achieved a lot and I'm really proud of it, but also I worked really hard to get here – and sometimes I don't honestly know how I did it.

I kicked off my career in organisational psychology, having studied that at uni, and started working as a cultural engagement consultant. I was curious to discover that I was always having the same conversations with employees when we discussed workplace culture: everything kept coming back to money. A lot of the time, this wasn't actually a workplace issue. There was a missing link – something or someone that could help people meet their financial potential. That's when I felt the spark of my new passion: I wanted to transform other people's relationships with money and make a real impact on their lives.

So, I took the big leap into the financial advice world, with all the study that requires. I began working in a wealth practice, doing an accelerated MBA alongside, and before long I decided I wanted to start my own financial advice business. It was hard to find the hours in the day – I'd be getting up at 4.30 am to go to the gym, smashing my bullet coffee (who was I?!) and at my desk by 6.30 or 7 am so I could get a uni assignment done or work on my fledgling business idea for a couple of hours before starting my full-time job. Then I'd have uni three or four evenings a week from 6 pm till 9 or 10 pm. Some of my units I was able to take as four-day intensives – those were wildly exhausting! – which meant I was able to complete my MBA in just under two years. Helpful too, because I was so fired up with all I was learning, I became eager to start putting it all into practice.

While I finished up my MBA I enrolled in my finance diploma – thankfully, that was all online and self-paced. But still, my weekends were taken up with more assignments and working on my business. Because I felt so passionate, I was willing to sacrifice time with family and friends – there were many gatherings, brunches and holidays with girlfriends I had to say no to in the name of building my business. And I wasn't born into a family with intergenerational wealth who could kickstart my business – it all came down to yours truly. But to me it was worth it. I was a woman on a mission!

The day finally came when I was ready to launch full time into my wealth business, which I'd named Zella, after my beautiful grandmother who was a big influence on me growing up. As a strong woman she was the perfect inspiration for a company designed to empower and uplift women.

One of my first challenges was building out my client base – after all, I couldn't just steal the clients from my previous company. So I kicked off a series of lunch-and-learn sessions at various law firms and other corporates in Melbourne's CBD, figuring those would be a great way to reach and connect with people on the corporate career ladder who wanted some financial guidance. The sessions covered the basics of financial literacy and I had so many women come along that I decided to call it She's on the Money. Over the next year or two it started to gather pace, so in 2017 I decided to create a Facebook group where everyone who attended my workshops could connect, and I could share the materials from the sessions along with extra activities for people to complete. I remember the day in 2019 when we hit 1700 people in the group – I was like, *This is wild!*

Based on feedback from that group I decided to start a podcast, and pretty quickly it blew up. I realised I was really on to something: there was a need and a demand that I was helping people with. And because of the podcast and the community in my Facebook group, my wealth business started to grow – it all helped new clients to find me. So Zella Money and SOTM kind of grew together, to the point where I was able to start hiring staff and create two teams of people who supported me so I could reduce my hours and take the pressure off a little.

It was such a thrilling (and challenging) time of growth, and then, in September 2022, I decided I wanted a family in the not-too-distant future and it was time to get some balance back. So I kept building SOTM but sold off the wealth-business side of Zella and shifted its focus purely to mortgage broking, which had been just a small component of our work previously. As I write this, I've stepped back somewhat from the day-to-day of running Zella (the fabulous team there have it covered) and I'm still loving what I do at SOTM, but I also have the *very* important job of being mum to my gorgeous Harvey. Family time is incredibly important, so I'm thinking more than ever about the sustainability of both businesses into the future as new chapters unfold.

Of course, that's not the end of my story – it's really just the beginning. And I know I was very fortunate in having a great trajectory, so much opportunity and an element of 'right place, right time' for sure. But I'll also say there was a whole lot of legwork, more than I (and many other people) anticipated before I was in the thick of it!

The real point I'd like to make here is that was *my* journey – yours will look different and be beautifully unique to you. Along the way, my choices and priorities reflected me and my values, and while I made plenty of mistakes and would do many things differently if given a second chance, I'm also proud that I approached it all as only I could: as me. I urge you to do the same.

There's a contribution to the world that only *you* can make. What's lighting you up? What really matters to you? What's the mark you'd like to leave? In this book we'll answer those questions and more, to clarify your vision and create your one-of-a-kind roadmap for business success.

Let's get into it!

Chapter One

Putting the 'you' in small business

Do you dream of total independence in your career, running your own show and building something of your very own? Are you craving more flexibility in your working hours? Do you have a passion that's unfulfilled in your day job, one that you wish you could turn into an income stream? Or are you looking to open up your earning potential way beyond your current salary and build a financial asset that could one day be sold or passed down the generations?

An impressive number of Australians are embracing the entrepreneurial spirit and choosing to be self-employed. There are around 2.6 million actively trading businesses in the Australian economy.

The Australian Bureau of Statistics (ABS) defines a business as 'small' if it has fewer than 20 employees, and by this measure, 97.3 per cent of businesses in Australia are small businesses.[1] More often than not, these businesses are run, financed and operated by just the owner alone – 1.6 million (62.1 per cent) have no employees at all.[2]

Another common definition of small business used by the Australian Taxation Office (ATO) are those businesses with a turnover of $10 million or less.[3] Using this definition, 98 per cent of Australian businesses are small businesses. The vast majority (92 per cent) of these have a turnover of less than $2 million. On those figures, friends, I think we can safely call Australia the land of the solopreneur!

Could this be you? By the end of this chapter, you'll know for sure if it's an adventure you want to set out on. In this opening section we'll explore the journey of deciding to become self-employed. We'll weigh the pros and cons of self-employment and discuss the personal traits that often lead to success. We'll cover the essential skills, experience and support needed to thrive. Finally, we'll have an honest conversation about the risks involved.

So, if you're considering taking the plunge into self-employment, keep reading. This chapter is your guide to understanding what you need to succeed as a small business owner and seeing whether you have what it takes. Are you ready?

Your business-money story

Before we jump into the hows of running a business, let's take a look at the whys. First, why does Australia have such a high rate of small business ownership, and is becoming a small business owner right for you? And second, if you *do* see yourself being a proud business owner, then let's unearth your deeper purpose and the real 'why' behind your motivations, as this is what will keep you going even when times get tough.

Is running a business for me?

Despite it being so popular, running your own business is not ideal for everyone. Entrepreneurship is a gamble, possibly the biggest legal one you can take. When it's your business, then *everything* – good and bad, including paying the bills, not to mention your own salary – is completely down to you. So before you get too excited about jumping all-in, let's consider the pros and cons of running your own show versus working for the man.

THE PROS AND CONS OF SELF-EMPLOYMENT

When you're self-employed, you call the shots. You get to decide when, where and how you work. No more being bogged down by company policies – you're the boss! This autonomy allows you to pursue projects that truly excite you. You can enjoy more flexibility in your days and take extended breaks or travel while you're working. Many people love the thrill of leadership and building a team from the ground up. Plus, there's the potential for unlimited profits – the harder and smarter you work, the more you can earn.

But let's keep it real – there are downsides, too. Financial uncertainty is a big one. Without a guaranteed or steady income, budgeting can be tough. When you run your own business, if you haven't made a sale all week, if you're too sick to go to work, if the coffee machine blows up or your manufacturer stops trading, then no-one's going to fly in and save you. Your rent won't get paid by some magical money tree in the sky, my friend, no. As an entrepreneur, you'll also wear many hats, from marketing guru to accountant, which can be stressful and require new skills. And taking time off – or even switching off – is a challenge when you're the one responsible for everything.

THE PROS AND CONS OF HAVING A CONVENTIONAL JOB

On the flip side, having a job provides structure and stability (especially in a permanent role). Your salary, hours and benefits (like superannuation, holiday pay and sick leave), are all laid out for you. This can offer a sense of security, knowing you have a steady income regardless of other ventures. It's often easier to set clear boundaries between work and home, and you don't have to shoulder the responsibility of supporting the livelihoods of employees, or the bigger financial and legal ramifications of owning a business.

However, jobs can be stressful, with demanding workloads, tight deadlines and lack of clarity leading to burnout. Set schedules can limit your freedom, long commutes can drain your time and finances, and a lack of autonomy over your tasks can make work feel unfulfilling. Your earning capacity and career trajectory also tend to be limited by your role, the priorities of your company management and the employment market.

HOW TO CHOOSE?!

Both paths have their pros and cons. It ultimately comes down to what works best for you, based on your circumstances and goals. If you're after flexibility and autonomy with some financial security, entrepreneurship might be your calling. Sure, it can be risky, but the more you know and the better you plan, the less likely you are to end up so far under water you can't surface. Besides, as we've all learnt from recent years, there's no such thing as certainty or guarantees, even in the everyday world. So if you have a dream, why not start making a plan to back yourself? With a little help from this book, supported by the cheer squad that is the SOTM community, and your own hard work, who knows where your ideas could take you!

Find your entrepreneurial edge

Despite the potential challenges and uncertainty, many of us choose to take the big leap to working for ourselves. Australia is regularly described as an entrepreneurial nation and it's fair to say that small businesses are the backbone of our economy and the labour force. The well-recognised Australian attributes of a spirit of independence, a DIY attitude and the courage to give things a go 'are strongly demonstrated in the data', suggests research firm McCrindle, with almost nine in ten businesses (88 per cent) employing four people or fewer and 86 per cent of Gen Z wanting to work in something they started themselves (either solely or as a side hustle) to combat the cost of living, achieve financial goals or develop a temporary income system.[4]

I'd like to think that SOTM's corner of the conversation has more than a little something to do with this, too. Our annual community surveys regularly show that a good many of us side-hustle in all kinds of ventures. Those of you who are regular listeners to our podcast or who have bought previous books in the series, such as *Money Diaries*, will know of the many stories among our community members – women who've made tens of thousands of dollars through business and investment ventures like property, coffee carts, Etsy stores, upcycling and OnlyFans, to name just a few.

With the rise of the gig economy, social media and peer-to-peer platforms like eBay, Facebook Marketplace, Etsy and Depop, and drop-shipping via Instagram and TikTok, it's easier than ever to make coin selling your old clothes and experimental creations, or to hire out your brain or brawn (or both!) in an effort to build up your bank account.

But at what moment does a side hustle become more? When do you decide to turn your bit-on-the-side into a fully-fledged business? And more importantly, what's your driving force to do so?

What's your motivation?

If you've picked up this book, chances are you've hit that magical turning point – or, at least, you're thinking about it. The time has come for your casual part-time pocket-money earner to put on its big-girl pants. You've decided to turn your side-bit into a main character, or you've built up enough experience in your field to strike out on your own.

But why? What about working for yourself has inspired you?

External motivations

In general, the entrepreneurial drive is motivated by necessity and/or opportunity.[5] Perhaps you've seen a gap in the market and decided to create an opportunity for yourself, or maybe you've inherited an idea or business, or perhaps the sheer instability of corporate life and global economics has created a situation where you feel more confident backing yourself than putting your time into someone else's show. For many, it boils down to the allure of independence and liberation from corporate restraints, plus the chance to put your skills to the test and show the world what you're made of.

Sounds great, right? Until it isn't. Whatever your reason, the reality is, it's not going to be easy. To make good on their dreams, entrepreneurs take major financial risks, work long hours and practically torture themselves trying to stay afloat and build a business from the ground up. If you think about it, it's a downright harrowing ordeal. So why would anybody want to go through with it? What do you stand to gain from the whole experience?

MONEY

Let's be real – of course money is a significant motivator. The potential to become uber-rich draws many people to entrepreneurship. We hear stories about Tammy Hembrow (Saski Collection) and Zoë Foster Blake (Go-To skincare) and it seems like anyone with a cute tush or good idea can become an overnight millionaire. While this obviously isn't true, it *is* possible for a dedicated entrepreneur with a solid idea and great timing to make more money than they ever would in a traditional job. There's nothing wrong with pursuing wealth, but if it's your only motivation you might get frustrated if you don't see profits right away or the timing of the market just isn't in your favour.

POWER

The desire for control is a strong motivator. As the boss of your own organisation you get to enact your vision and make all the decisions, from hiring to strategic direction. If you've been frustrated by poor leadership in previous jobs this can be incredibly appealing. However, with great power comes great responsibility. The pressure of making all the decisions can be intense. But it also means you have the privilege of being captain of your ship and steering your business towards success.

DREAM TEAMS

Some people thrive in a collaborative environment. They love the energy of team-based problem-solving and the joy of achieving goals together. As an entrepreneur you get to build your own team from scratch.

You choose your partners, mentors and employees, creating a work environment that suits you perfectly. Your team can become like a family (though beware, like any family, there will be disagreements!), and the satisfaction of building something together can be incredibly rewarding.

AUTONOMY

Some people dive into entrepreneurship because they're tired of the rigid demands of traditional work. High-level positions often come with long hours catering to bosses, board members and clients, and a rinse-and-repeat cycle of responsibilities. Yawn! On paper, at least, it seems that being your own boss frees you from these restraints. You can determine your own hours, work from wherever you want, set your own goals and focus attention on your chosen priorities. However, the reality is that entrepreneurship is demanding, especially in the early stages. You might find yourself working harder and longer than ever before. But ultimately, the freedom can make it worthwhile.

LEGACY

For some people, entrepreneurship is about more than money or experience – it's about leaving a lasting legacy. They want to create something meaningful that will outlast them, whether it's becoming the face of a brand, earning a bit of fame, passing the business on to future generations or leaving the world a better place because of their contribution. This motivation is powerful because it offers a sense of purpose that extends beyond immediate rewards.

OVER TO YOU

The more driven you are, the better you'll handle the inevitable challenges. Before you dive into entrepreneurship, take a moment to understand what you want out of the experience. Knowing your motivations will help you stay satisfied and resilient in the long run.

Using these prompts, think about and write down your motivations:

» I am motivated by . . .

» because . . .

If you have more than one motivation, can you identify which is the most important?

Internal motivations

Often, when we first start to dream of personal business success, we can become excited by and focus on the external successes of others – particularly, these days, in the influencer space. I mean, who wouldn't want to be paid to travel round the world, wear stunning clothes, jewellery and make-up, and be regularly sent gifts to model while eating out and partying at someone else's expense? Pick me, pick me!

The truth is, though, it's more likely that they've made it that far through sheer hard work, perseverance and commitment to their deeper purpose. One post a week for a year, does not a success story make. No, there may be a lot more happening behind the scenes than you realise. (Just read some of the stories in this book and you'll begin to see what I mean.)

You see, while all these external markers of success are amazing – yes they are! – the real key to both success and satisfaction in business (and in life) is focusing on what truly lights you up inside: your 'why'. Over the long term, those who do an activity for its inherent satisfaction

– the fun or challenge – rather than for chasing its external rewards tend to get better results. Aligning your strengths with what internally motivates you is where you'll find your sweet spot – the magical 'why' that will keep you powering through the dark days and long nights.

Assuming you choose the path of small business ownership, you will almost certainly face some challenges along the way. In part that's what you've signed up for, right – less 'boring certainty' and more 'high risk, high reward'? At times that decision will feel like the worst one you've ever made and you'll wish yourself back in the safe, cosy cubicle corner you escaped from. In these moments you'll need to turn to your 'why' – your bigger purpose.

If all you're chasing are external rewards your small business may ultimately end up feeling like all you're doing is fulfilling someone else's dreams: your advertisers', your customers', your staffs'. People often forget that in business you're ultimately still at the mercy of market forces. But if you can tap into your intrinsic motivation – the drive burning inside – you'll keep going no matter what.

When your inner light is fired up, if things beyond your control prevent you from reaching those external markers of success, you'll still have a reason to keep going strong. This is the secret sauce for all successful entrepreneurs. So let's look at some common intrinsic motivators.

MAKING A DIFFERENCE

Many business ideas are driven by the goal of solving a problem or making the world a better place. The desire to make a positive impact is incredibly powerful. Take locally grown business Koh, for instance. It was developed by two Bondi-based dads wanting to create cleaning products that worked and, more importantly, were safe for their families and the planet. It's become a hugely successful multi-million-dollar global company that's still propelled by its purpose to keep the world both clean and green.[6]

A SENSE OF ACCOMPLISHMENT

Not many things in life push you to find out what you're *really* capable of as much as running your own business does. Being tested to your limits and coming out stronger rewards you with a sense of achievement and fulfilment that no-one can take away from you. As Steve Jobs' widow, Laurene Powell Jobs, shared as an addendum to his 2005 Stanford speech, Steve used to say: 'Your work is going to fill a large part of your life and the only way to be truly satisfied is to do what you believe is great work. And the only way to do great work is to love what you do. If you haven't found it yet – keep looking.'[7]

FINDING PERSONAL MEANING

Tech guru and venture capitalist Guy Kawasaki urges entrepreneurs to focus on making meaning, not money. He believes that if your goal is to grow your company just to sell it off or take it public and cash out, you're setting yourself up for failure. Do it for the meaning it brings, he says – for example, improving quality of life, righting a wrong, keeping a good thing alive.[8] Building something you believe in can also enrich your life and give you a meaningful reason to get out of bed in the morning.

GROWTH AND LIFE EXPERIENCE

To thrive as an entrepreneur, you can't afford to stand still. The best entrepreneurs love the journey just as much as the destination. They're curious about the path ahead of them, even if it's strewn with risks, challenges and setbacks, and they want to put themselves in the way of that experience to see what happens. They have an insatiable thirst for learning that not only helps their business but also fuels their personal growth in terms of skills and knowledge and greater self-understanding. This synergy creates a sweet spot that maximises their impact.

I recently started my business as a celebrant: I conduct wedding ceremonies and complete the legal documentation of marriages in Australia. My business is aimed at couples who, like me, are in their mid-thirties and live in the inner suburbs of Melbourne, and who usually work in the corporate sector and want their ceremony to be fun and memorable. My aim is to bring calm on people's wedding day.

The reason I started working as a celebrant is that I decided I wanted a side hustle. The corporate life has its perks, but I didn't want my income to be limited to what someone else decides I earn.

A rewarding part of my job is that I get as much business as the amount of effort I put in. I like this because my life is busy, so I can take on as much work as I need.

What people may not expect is the amount of admin involved in being a celebrant. I work on my own so I oversee it all and deal with a lot of serious legal information. I'm still in the early stages of my business, but I have an accountant who helped set up my invoicing and business banking and advised me about what things I need and what can wait.

To be a celebrant you need to be part of an association, and I'm a member of the Celebrant Society. They're amazing; their motto is 'community over competition', which I love. I've found the society helpful, thoughtful and caring, especially for a role that's quite isolating. I also have a group chat with a few of the girls I did my celebrant course with.

I've learnt, so far, that you get out of a side hustle what you put into it. Success doesn't happen overnight.

MY WHY

Personally, I've long had a sense of purpose around female empowerment and self-fulfilment. I always knew that although my mostly female client base was smart, they just hadn't been given the financial education that men get. I made it my mission to fix that. That was the difference I set out to make with both Zella and She's on the Money.

I'm also hardwired to chase a sense of accomplishment and growth. I've never been one to sit still and I'm always looking for new ways to innovate. I love the idea of taking something old and making it relevant for today's audiences. That's what I've done in each of my businesses, whether they're listener-focused or client-focused, and even in my more recent adventures in property. I like to build on ideas that have been proven (no need to reinvent the wheel) yet put my own spin on them: a fresh take for fresh eyes and ears.

So what's going to drive you? What will get you out of bed, even on the toughest of days? What will keep you in the game when all your cards have fallen? Find your 'why' – your intrinsic motivation – and use it to power you forward as we learn the ins and outs of building a business from scratch.

OVER TO YOU

Reflect on your 'why' and write it down, being as specific as possible. If you find this difficult, visualise the future: what have you achieved and how do you feel?

Once you're clear on your why, put it somewhere visible. Let it be your daily inspiration as your business dreams take flight.

Let's get personal

Now that you've completed the important task of figuring out what's powering your business journey, it's time to take a fresh look at who's behind the wheel: you! First, let's help you get clear on your values, then evaluate your skills, and finally, look at who and what support systems you have in place to keep you strong. This will give you alignment between where you want to go and how you're going to get there.

Get clear on your values

I really encourage you to work out what your personal values are, if you don't know already. Why? Because your business is about to become a huge part of your life and if it clashes with the values you hold dear you're likely to experience some major friction. You can't have everything all at once and compromises will need to be made along the way. Gain a strong understanding of your 'happy life' non-negotiables – be they family time, travel, adventure or creativity – so that when you're inevitably faced with a tough decision about what to prioritise, your values can guide you. There are lots of fantastic tools out there for figuring out your values, so I'd make a bet that doing this will bring benefits in other parts of your life, too.

OVER TO YOU Do a values exercise to identify your top five core values — for you as a person, not for your business (yet). Pin them up somewhere or save them in your phone to refer back to any time you're struggling to figure out how best to proceed with something while staying true to yourself.

Take an honest look in the mirror

Identifying your current strengths and weaknesses is a slightly uncomfortable but incredibly important exercise. One thing that's helped make my businesses successful is being clear on what I'm great at, and equally clear on what I'm less good at.

Like most small business owners, in the beginning I had to do everything. That included creating the She's on the Money logo using PowerPoint and building my teaching materials using templates I bought off Etsy. (When we're bootstrapping, friends, we can't be ultra-choosy.) Through the start-up phase my guidelines were 'near enough is good enough' and 'perfect is the enemy of done'. In the early days the most important thing is doing whatever it takes to get up and running. So you start by testing your concept while at the same time bringing in money – whatever you need to do to get the ball rolling.

Then, as my businesses grew and began to make a little extra money that I could plough back in to help them grow, I used those funds to outsource things that others could do better – graphic design, repeatable aspects of content creation and finally, even though I'd qualified as a financial adviser, an accountant to oversee the financials. I mean, I love my spreadsheets and I'm very across them, but the intricacies of Australian tax law are not my bag – so I chose to give that one to the experts.

I was also very aware of building a business around the things I'm best at. I have a master's in psychology and a business degree, and combining those two things with my lived experiences during my student days of terrible girl-math, overspending and budget blowouts meant I was in the best position to create courses in financial education for women my age.

And yes, I wanted all those things listed on the previous pages – like money, freedom and self-expression. To get those for myself required developing *a lot* of self-honesty and self-awareness. In fact, I'd go so far as to argue that these might just be *the most* important things you'll gain from your entrepreneurial journey, delivering riches well beyond the money tree.

You see, when working for others you can hide behind the corporation's practices and policies and use them as excuses for your own shortcomings or failures. But when you work for yourself you do that at your own peril. If you don't front up and own your challenges and downfalls you'll never be able to fix them. And if you fail to fix them, well, it's *your* business that's going to fail. It's not always necessary to be the person who has all the answers, but you should know where to find that person – and get them involved.

With that in mind, in order to know what kind of business you might be good at, where your skills or knowledge may be lacking and, most importantly, whether you're up to the task of taking on what could be the biggest challenge of your life, it's time to take a personal inventory. Once you have a clear picture of your situation you can start thinking about how best to use your personal capital (your unique combination of skills, traits and connections), to create a balanced life. After all, building a successful business is ultimately part of designing a life that you love – and that's what we're all here for, right?

WHAT DO YOU BRING TO THE TABLE?

When you're going for a job, you write up a resumé. When you're planning to start your own business, it's equally important to draw up a list of your skills, knowledge, experience and attributes and match these against what's required to run your business, both for today and in the future. While you may have to don multiple hats in the early stages of your business venture, by mapping out the skills and knowledge needed over the long term you can plan ahead for who to hire and when.

While this task may sound like overkill for a solopreneur operation, taking moments like this to work 'on' your business rather than 'in' it is critical for your long-term success and survival. Stepping outside the everyday to look down on your workflow with an objective eye can help alert you to potential risks and roadblocks and direct you to a safer path. Doing this activity now may also help you identify people you know who could help you, whether as a one-off or on an ongoing basis.

OVER TO YOU } Following the example laid out in the table on page 26, map your business requirements against your current skills, noting where you may have gaps and identifying people who could help you. Be honest with yourself — it will help prevent difficulties down the track.

Take this example of a bakery business. The owner has strong skills in the baking and other food prep areas but recognises that tax, branding, marketing and social media are not their strong points – better to outsource those from day one.

Task – skill/knowledge	Can I do this? Or someone else?
1. Baking bread	Yes, me.
2. Baking cakes and sweets	Yes, me – though need to build repertoire.
3. Decorating cakes and sweets	Sort of me – definitely need to improve skills (or hire a specialist).
4. Baking meat pies/rolls	Yes, me.
5. Making sandwiches	Yes, me. Would like to hire a sandwich hand eventually.
6. Sandwich ingredients prep	Yes, me. Would like to hire a sandwich hand eventually.
7. Making coffee	Will need to hire for opening. Maybe they could stay on after morning rush to help prep sandwich ingredients?
8. Goods delivery	Need to hire – use hubby to start with.
9. Ordering stock	Yes, me.
10. Bookkeeping and accounts	Yes, me – to start with. Would like to outsource this eventually.
11. EOFY tax	External tax agent.
12. Council permits	Yes, me – to start with.
13. Logo and branding	Cousin Anne.
14. Advertising and marketing	Anne to set up templates, me to continue.

Task – skill/knowledge	Can I do this? Or someone else?
15. Social media accounts	Anne to set up templates, me to continue. Perhaps Tristan will take over?
16. Community advocacy	Yes, me – to start with.

Who's got your back?

Believing in your concept and maintaining a positive attitude are crucial, but as someone who has experienced the highs and lows of entrepreneurship I can tell you that the first years in business can be incredibly challenging. As well as assessing your core skills and the knowledge you need for running the business, it's essential to identify and strengthen your support systems.

What safety nets do you have in place for these scenarios?

a) You're sleep-deprived and hungry from late nights spent writing business plans, reviewing finances, creating marketing strategies and networking, yet the fridge is bare.

b) You're sick and stressed, which unfortunately happens more often than you'd like, yet still have commitments you need to show up for. (I once did an interview with a high fever because I couldn't miss the media exposure.)

c) You're out of money, out of money, out of money.

d) All of the above.

Planning ahead for these situations is crucial and, as with life, your relationships and contacts may well be the key to keeping you and your business alive. So let's look closer at these critical considerations for shoring up your support network.

PARTNER SUPPORT

If you're in a relationship, ensure your partner believes in your ability and is willing to support you emotionally (and possibly, at times, financially). Determine how much time and money you are both willing to sacrifice.

FAMILY PLANNING

If you want to start a family or already have kids, be mindful of the time and energy required during your offspring's formative years – and by that I mean both your human dependants and your business baby. (I waited until my businesses were firmly established and able to run somewhat autonomously before I opted to have Harvey. While many in our community do have young families and run businesses, personally there's no way I could have managed both in infancy at the same time!)

FRIENDS AND FAMILY

Whether you're single or not, talk to your friends and family about being there for you when you need to be in multiple places at once. If you're very fortunate (and/or a great manager), you may well find that your employees become friends and like family – but that doesn't mean you can or should take advantage of anyone to get your business to where it needs to be. I'd also advise you to think carefully before more formally employing a friend or family member. While this can work for some, if you don't think you can make it happen without significantly impacting your relationship, ask yourself if it's really worth it.

BUSINESS MENTOR

Find someone who has expertise in your industry and is willing to offer you their advice. Don't underestimate having the friendly ear of someone who's been through what you're going through and fully understands the ups and downs. While your nearest and dearest will love you, they may not always get it or be able to offer helpful advice.

DELEGATION

Don't try to do it all! Hire good employees or contractors, get a good accountant, and maybe even employ a housekeeper to handle the chores you can't manage after a long workday.

Look after yourself

The demands of running a business can take a toll on your physical and mental health if you don't manage stress effectively. Surviving the first few years until your business finds an even flow can be make or break. And realistically, you don't want to be running a sprint – you're in this for the long haul, right? As such, approach setting up and running your business like a marathon (not that I'd personally be keen for that, but you get the gist) and put things in place to keep you healthy over the long run.

EXERCISE

Make time for physical activity to re-energise your body and mind. It doesn't have to be a real marathon, but (sadly for me) running to Star-bucks for a double espresso doesn't count either!

SLEEP

In your business journey it's beyond important to rest and recharge along the way. Even when you feel like the to-do list is never-ending, keeping sleep a high priority will mean you're much better equipped to go the distance. You need it to keep your brain firing so you can make good decisions, show up well rested for important business meetings, maintain good relationships, tap into your creativity, and so much more.

SOCIAL TIME

I'll be the first to admit that I sacrificed a lot of this in the early days of Zella and SOTM, and I really do understand why socialising often goes straight on the backburner when you're setting out as an entrepreneur. But it's a powerful way to fill your cup and re-energise, let off steam, reconnect with loved ones, have fun and remind yourself there's more to life than business.

PROFESSIONAL SUPPORT

Regular sessions with a business mentor and/or therapist can provide valuable advice and a listening ear. It's not a sign of weakness; it's a sign of taking personal responsibility.

PERSPECTIVE

Learn to laugh and enjoy the journey as much as possible! Your personal capital will help you navigate the tough days and ultimately lead your business to tremendous success. First and foremost you must invest in yourself, as without you there is no business.

Small business is a big responsibility

Whether you're operating as a solopreneur, microbusiness or small business, you will have to answer to people other than yourself. I know, I know, I did say earlier that one of the big motivations of working for yourself is being your own boss and calling the shots – and that's true, but only to a degree. Ultimately, even if you don't have staff, you have customers (and potentially investors, if not the bank) to answer to, not to mention being able to feed and house yourself. Running a small business is no small venture. Even if it's just you, there's *a lot* you're responsible for.

MEG'S BUSINESS STORY

I had been doing socials on the side for other business owners (or within my job role) for close to 13 years and I was starting to get approached more and more by people who wanted me to do it for them too. But I had to turn them away as my part-time job was the priority. One day I said to my hubby, 'What if I just go all in and see what happens? I can always get another job!' The next day I quit my part-time job and gave four weeks' notice.

My first week self-employed I was on cloud nine thinking I was living the dream, then I lost four clients and thought, *What have I done?*

Fast forward and I've now been freelancing full time for two years (11 years as a side hustle). A lot has changed, mainly the way I manage my boundaries – saying no, not checking or responding to emails outside of work hours, and not sharing my phone number.

Looking back, I actually wouldn't change a thing. Without the hard and shitty times (or clients), I wouldn't have grown within my business or known what boundaries I needed to implement.

Take care of these

With that in mind, here are a couple of things that are really important to take care of and my suggestions on how you could do that.

IT'S ALL IN THE TIMING

Did I mention that you won't have a lot of spare time in the first few years of running your business? You have to get clever about making time work in your favour – find ways to stretch and bend it, to get more out of it. One of those ways is to make the clock do double time. Have a scheduled phone call? Take it while you're out walking so you can get in some daily exercise. Travelling to a meeting? Pop on a podcast (I hear *She's on the Money* is good) and expand your education. Brainstorm required? Provide lunch so you can eat, connect and create simultaneously. A lot of the success in small business comes from working smarter (as you simply won't be able to work any harder than you already are). What clever ways can you make time work for you?

KEEP YOUR EYE ON THE MONEY

At the end of the day, you're working for yourself to earn money – ideally, a lot of it. And it's almost guaranteed you'll owe people money too: creditors and investors, stockists and service providers to name a few. As such, it's critical that you set up and run good business accounts. If this is something you find boring then it's imperative you prioritise getting someone on board to assist you. While some of us may feel okay with living our everyday lives budget-free (I am definitely not one of those people!), that's not going to fly in the world of business. We'll get into exactly what reports you need a bit later but for now, just know that if you're not prepared to stay on top of your bookkeeping and accounts it's highly likely that running your own business may not be your jam.

In fact, on that, it's shocking to me how many 'entrepreneurs' start their businesses without a solid grasp of finances, too busy dreaming about future millions instead of focusing on today. Cash is your oxygen.

How much do you have to keep your business alive? Do you have enough to cover a year's worth of rent and overheads? If this is your first rodeo, it's here's where you're most likely to stumble. Before you go all in, ensure you can withstand the inevitable start-up financial bleed that happens before you start turning a profit.

I often see new entrepreneurs making one of two mistakes:

» **Underfunding**: They haven't raised enough capital and only have about six months' worth of funds. They dream up perfect scenarios, but soon enough reality hits and a few months in, they run out of cash.

» **Overfunding**: They have so much funding that they don't develop the necessary skills to generate revenue. They focus on raising the next round of funding instead of building a profitable business.

Starting a new business, especially one requiring up-front financial investment, drains money. You need to be practical about what it takes to cover necessities like rent, supplies and inventory. If you miss conducting due diligence up front you're setting yourself up for failure. Don't worry, I've got your back here – we'll talk about financing in a lot more detail in Chapter 5.

STAY IN TOUCH

As we touched on in the previous section, your support network could be the make or break of your small business career. If you expect them to look after you then you have an equal responsibility to take care of your relationships with them. In the first few years you won't have a lot of spare time or money, so that means finding other ways in which you can continue to show them how important they are to you. Get creative: send handwritten cards/letters, schedule catch-ups (in person or remote), send memes and pics, exchange voice notes, send gifts that remind you of them, walk and talk – and be sure to ask about what's going on in *their* lives.

STAY TRUE

Finally, your word is your bond. One of the most important things my dad taught me is that a promise is a promise. When that promise is to yourself it's even more important to honour it. It can be easy to sacrifice your own needs when other things seem more urgent or important, but sticking to your guns becomes critical when it's your livelihood at risk.

You and your business are yoked, so every decision you make – both for you and for it – affects you both. When you're the face of your business, its brand and your personal reputation are both on the line. How you show up and the decisions you make will affect your status as an entrepreneur, so think carefully about what's important, make an oath, and stick to it.

Principle 1: Be real

Don't go into starting a business starry-eyed. Most businesses fail within the first 18 months because their owners underestimate how hard it is, how dedicated they need to be and the level of talent required. Being honest with yourself won't guarantee success, but not being so is a sure-fire way to fail.

Meet the founder: Brooke Roberts

Brooke Roberts is the co-founder and 3EO (co-CEO!) behind a wealth app many in the She's on the Money community already know and love – Sharesies. Eight years since it began, the New Zealand fintech business has over half a million investors who have collectively invested billions of dollars.

Name: Brooke Roberts

Business: Sharesies

Industry: Fintech

Product/service: Trading platform

Target audience: Everyone! Our aim is to create financial empowerment for everyone.

Secondary audience: We partner with businesses to help them manage their shareholders, shareholder communications and staff share schemes.

Unique selling point: We remove minimum investment barriers and use everyday language. We're also a certified B Corp and offer a beautiful, lovable wealth experience.

The business began: 2016

Six of us co-founded Sharesies. We were motivated to start the business because we knew that with the technology available today there's no reason that someone with $5 and someone with $5 million can't have the same money opportunities.

My favourite part of being in business is being at the forefront of creating something new, from the way we work to the money experiences we provide people. It's great to be able to innovate and provide better opportunities for more people. One downside is that, even though I'm very good at compartmentalisation, the business is always on my mind. But it's worth it for me. I love being a part of bringing Sharesies' purpose to life!

Sharesies has changed significantly over the years, but our purpose and values have remained the same. We began with offering investing on our platform and now offer a lot more. If I could change anything about the journey I would have launched into some other money products earlier.

We began with a founding team of six and now there are 160 of us! There's no way we could operate at our scale and provide such good customer experiences without a stellar team. What has worked for our company when it comes to managing staff is making our staff shareholders in the business, vesting shares over time. We offer our team at Sharesies an ESOP [employee share option plan] and help heaps of other businesses provide these to their staff, too.

We have our own legal, accounting and marketing teams, though we do reach out to experts to get specific external advice when we need it. I'm also part of a group with other founders, which I love. We meet online every Friday morning and it's so good for the soul! We connect and chat through challenges we're facing and share our wins, too.

Running a company like Sharesies really is a work–life blur. They are all in one for me. I try to make time for myself, my kids, friends and family plus work. I think about managing my energy more than my time. I'd say I'm in a good spot currently with my work–life balance. Once I decided to make exercise a priority it helped me better manage my time with family and work.

Here are my top tips for starting a business:

» Build up a support network of other founders.

» Prioritise fitness.

» Tell yourself that you've got this.

» Have fun!

Chapter Two

Igniting your business journey

Sorry, not sorry – I know I asked you a lot of tough questions in the last chapter . . . but you need know what you're getting into, am I right? If you're still here, well done! You are one step closer to entering the entrepreneurial world and starting your own small business. And although it can feel daunting at times, you're not alone. I'm here to guide you through the ins and outs of the business landscape.

We're lucky in Australia as small business gets so much amazing support from both the public and private sector – from multiple government agencies to advocacy and support groups, through to small business advisers. In this chapter we'll take a broad look at who's who in the zoo of the Australian business landscape and where your business fits. There are so many ways to run a small business these days, from bricks-and-mortar mega stores through to digital-only, one-woman shows, so let's explore the incredible power of being small and consider different types of businesses to see what might work best for you.

Entrepreneurship Down Under

It's no wonder so many people get inspired to run their own business in Australia. Like the perfect beach day our business environment is warm, inviting and full of opportunity. There are endless resources available online and in-person to help you along the way. But just like you wouldn't jump in the water without checking the currents, you shouldn't dive into business without understanding the local conditions, either. So, let's take a closer look.

As we read earlier, nearly 98 per cent of businesses in Australia are small business: 61 per cent are sole traders, 27 per cent are micro-businesses, and 9 per cent have a small team.[1] Despite their size, Aussie small businesses punch above their weight when it comes to contributing to our economy. In 2022–23, small business added nearly $590 billion – a third of its value – to Australia's total GDP (gross domestic product).[2]

The upsides

Why is Australia such a fantastic place to start a business, you ask? In my opinion, the 'good reasons' list is longer than the queue for brunch!

GOVERNMENT SUPPORT

Australia is known for its strong economy, supportive government initiatives and a community that cheers on the underdog. It's a place where innovation thrives and diversity is celebrated, supported by government grants, tax incentives and business support programs. Plus, with a robust legal system and clear regulations, you can feel safe knowing that your business baby is protected.

COMMUNITY SUPPORT AND FLEXIBILITY

Culturally, Australians love to support those who give things a go. The 'Aussie battler' is a revered part of our national identity, expressing itself through respect for the small businessperson – typically tradies and farmers – with their risk-taking and independence highly admired. Small business is often seen as the heart of the community and is supported by locals who consider it 'their own'. Communities also provide plenty of places where we can work, from free local libraries offering heaps of assistance to affordable, flexible co-working spaces dotted everywhere.

PERSONAL SUPPORT

In my experience, the Australian small business community is really wholesome. There are so many of us who want to lift each other up as we're all going through different but relatable struggles. Although I run finance-focused businesses, I have friends across all industries. I have a friend who runs a tampon business, another who's in financial advice, and others in fashion and beauty. When you start out you think it's going to be really hard to make friends but it's actually a warm, welcoming community to be involved in, which I love. Plus, because we are a small country compared to somewhere like America, you don't feel as overwhelmed or as swamped by the competition – a tiny fish in a giant ocean. Here in Australia you're a relatively reasonable-sized fish in a normal pond, and that's really good.

...and the downsides

But no-one said it would be all wine and roses. In fact, it's more like riding a roller-coaster – plenty of ups and downs!

SMALLER POPULATION

Australia has a relatively small population, which in lots of industries translates to a smaller audience or market. For example, with the *She's on the Money* podcast, our ability to generate millions of listeners is limited. If we did it overseas it could be triple the size. So when you're building a business here, unless you're going international from the start, you do have fewer potential clients or customers and the ability to scale is reduced.

TOUGH TIMES HURT

MYOB's half-yearly small business reports have tracked tough times over recent years. Its CEO Paul Robson observes that higher operating costs and lower consumer spending have been impacting small and medium-sized enterprises (SMEs) with no sign of relief on the horizon. He cites continuing inflationary pressures, the rising cost of doing business and higher interest rates on business lending.[3]

TALL POPPY SYNDROME

Another big thing in Australia is tall poppy syndrome. It's something that people warned me about at the start – a colleague used to say to me, 'Victoria, it's lonely at the top.' And I used to be like, it's not going to be lonely. I'm going to be so nice, I'm going to be so kind, I'm going to give this business my all, so it always comes back!

Sadly though, the more successful I've become, the more I've been cut down. It's as if people want you to do well but don't want you to do better than them, and the second you seem to they're not happy anymore. At the start of SOTM I was super relatable: I was coming out of debt, I hadn't purchased any property and I couldn't afford to. Since then I've changed my money story significantly. Now I own property and successful businesses and people don't like that. Since I'm no longer relatable they don't like me as much. I suppose it's something you just have to bear in mind – haters gonna hate, I guess.

Customer connections

Let's talk about the *real* power of being small in the business world. We all know how big companies often drop the ball when it comes to customer service – endless hold times, getting bounced from one department to another, and nobody really taking ownership of your issue. It's super frustrating, right?

Well, that's where the magic of small businesses comes in. When you're running a small business, you can tackle customer questions right away and with a much more personal approach. You have the power to focus on your customers' needs and provide a service that's way more responsive than what those corporate giants can offer, with their layers of red tape.

And let's talk flexibility. Big organisations are often stuck in their ways, with rigid policies that leave customers feeling unheard. If a customer isn't happy, explaining the policy doesn't help much. They're likely to walk away, feeling like just another number. But as a small business owner, you can be nimble and adjust your policies whenever it makes sense. You can listen, understand and make changes on the fly to keep your customers happy.

Personal attention? Forget about it with big companies. They send you generic form letters and make you feel like they couldn't care less if you do business with them or not. But in a small business you can provide genuine personal attention because you actually know your customers. You can show them you care by giving them the tailored service they crave.

The real advantage

The real power of being small lies in your unique ability to close the gap between you and your customer. Whether you're in consumer markets or dealing with other businesses, your timeliness, flexibility and personal touch can outshine and out-service the big guys every single time. And this means that despite the sometimes grim economic outlook, start-ups are more optimistic, viewing their operations and the broader economic environment more positively. Us Aussies are a resilient bunch, apparently. As MYOB's small business reports observe:

> While SMEs are particularly susceptible to fluctuating market conditions, with less cash available to protect against the challenges facing the business community, they are also incredibly resourceful. By the nature of their size, SMEs are in the best position to pivot with agility when conditions change.[4]

Perhaps that's why so many of us are committed to building our futures through running our own businesses. Despite all the challenges, when it's our business we are the ones in charge. We can switch things up to make hay while the sun shines and take shelter when it's wet. The fewer staff we have the more agile we can be. Our operations can scale up or down according to stock availability and spending habits.

Equally, we can reduce our own personal spending to shore up a business under duress. Look, I shudder to bring it up, but I'm sure you remember the remarkable inventiveness many small businesses showed during the Covid lockdowns – cook-at-home delivered restaurant meals, gin distilleries producing hand sanitiser and self-care salon packs for nails, skin and hair, to name but a few examples. This always-on inventiveness is what businesses need to ensure their future success, something we saw up in bright lights and fully realised during the pandemic.

BECAUSE YOU'RE IN CHARGE

If the social scientists are right (and they've done plenty of studies to prove it), being in charge of our own lives is critical to our happiness. In fact, there's even a theory for it (beyond TikTok). Self-determination theory proposes that humans need three things in order to be happy: competence, autonomy and relatedness. When we have them our internal motivation is strong and we have good mental health, and when we don't our motivation and wellbeing drop.[5] But you don't need researchers, or me, to tell you that. You already know that when you feel in control of your days – your time, your heart, your head – you just feel better. And maybe that's the best reason of all to just go for it!

BIANCA'S BUSINESS STORY

I have an accounting business aimed at women and mothers running small businesses. I started it after I was made redundant and needed flexibility to handle family responsibilities. I started as a sole trader in 2013 and restructured to a company in February 2024.

I wrote a business plan, researched local and nationwide businesses, and used my accounting knowledge. Starting my own business provided the freedom I needed. I set a goal to repay my investment and be on wages by the end of the financial year, which I achieved. It felt great! I would have left my old job sooner if I could go back in time.

As a business owner, I've learnt to be intentional with spending, use grants if available, and keep good records to claim tax deductions. I've exceeded my growth goals by consistently showing up for the business and celebrating achievements along the way.

Talk small business to me

Small businesses are the heart and soul of the Aussie economy – kind of like the barista who knows your coffee order by heart. From chic boutiques to digital dynamos, these ventures add vibrancy to our cities and towns, and create jobs like it's going out of style. And the best part? There's room for more. Whether you're into fashion, tech or something totally niche like eco-friendly glitter, there's a space for you to shine.

Small business is a vital part of our economy and plays an important role in the commercialisation of innovation, wrote the Small Business Ombudsmen's (ASBFEO) precursor in a submission to parliament, noting that it's generally small businesses that commercialise creative ideas coming from university research. It also highlighted that small businesses:

» employ around 4.5 million people (43 per cent of total private sector employment)
» generate 40 per cent of new jobs in the economy
» are more active in innovation and exporting than large businesses
» are frequently at the leading edge of innovation.[6]

Standard types of small businesses

Small businesses can be categorised under four essential types based on what they offer and the ways in which they offer it, which dictate how they're organised and how they operate. These are commonly termed:

1. retail
2. manufacturing and primary production
3. distribution
4. service.

RETAIL BUSINESSES

A retailer is what we typically might call a 'shop' or 'store' or 'seller'. They handpick a selection of goods from those who make them (manufacturers) or bulk-buy them (distributors) and resell them to their customers. The retailer's strength is their ability to curate selections and market them to specific groups of customers.

Retailers include department stores, supermarkets, discount stores, variety stores, speciality stores and convenience stores, and they range in size from national chains, like David Jones, to single-owner corner stores, such as your local independent bookseller. Within a category (such as grocery stores) each retailer has their own specific brand and customer in mind. This is what makes them stand apart from others and helps them create a unique business. Some stores are bricks and mortar, some are online only, and some sell across both channels.

MANUFACTURING AND PRIMARY PRODUCTION

A primary producer cultivates the raw materials (such as meat, wool, cotton, etc) that a manufacturer uses to makes goods. In both cases they can be large, needing vast tracks of land or big factories to produce a high volume at low cost, or boutique, like the many artisan growers and makers that are found all over Australia.

In many instances, these smaller producers will also run their own retail as it may be the only (or best) way to sell their product. Since they only grow or make small batches for a handful of niche customers, they often do better to sell to those customers directly rather than give money away to a third-party seller – think your local berry farmer, baker, cheesemaker, craft brewer or handmade jeweller.

Other producers run larger operations where they make goods in bulk and on scale. They might produce basic materials to sell on to niche manufacturers (for example, clothing 'blanks' – like a plain hoodie – that a boutique fashion brand will then customise), or they might customise the finished product in-house (such as Carman's Kitchen muesli products).

Primary producers (aka farmers) produce goods for manufacturers operating in myriad industries: building, chemicals and cleaning, biotech and pharmaceutical, food and beverage, fashion and furniture. Those who make goods by hand also sit within this category; they include builders, bakers, butchers, winemakers, tailors, jewellers and cabinet-makers.

TARA'S BUSINESS STORY

I started my business, Tage Outdoors, in December 2021. I make canvas bags and accessories for camping and four-wheel driving, targeting younger people aged 18 to 35 interested in camping, hunting, fishing and the outdoors. I used to do boat covers and canopies for cars and other vehicles, but found the stress-to-money ratio wasn't worth it, so smaller products are now my niche. Everything is made in Australia, and all by me at the moment!

I jumped from studying fashion design to making canvas products after struggling to find a job I enjoyed in my small town. I started working from the shed at home, selling online and to locals via word of mouth. In December I will be starting the fit-out of our very first shop and new factory space! I've been learning as I go and currently do everything myself, from content to contacting customers and suppliers, to making every product.

Though I'd been ticking along making an income from day one, I eventually hired a friend to run my ad accounts for Google and Facebook, which increased sales A LOT.

DISTRIBUTION BUSINESSES

A wholesale distributor buys goods in bulk from manufacturers and sells them to retailers in what's commonly called a B2B (business to business) enterprise. Businesses that sell directly to customers, on the other hand, are called B2C (business to consumer). Wholesalers do not normally sell directly to the public, though some business models are based on doing this (Costco, for example).

As a middleman, wholesalers reduce the cost of distribution for manufacturers. For retailers, they make it easier to access a wide variety of products from a single source. However, these days there are often crossovers between wholesalers and manufacturers, and even with retailers. For example, Globe is a large brand with its own fashion apparel and products, but it also represents a wide range of sub-brands such as Impala Skate, Milkbar Bikes and dot Boards, some of whom manufacture their own lines while others simply curate them.

Furthermore, drop-shipping has removed many of the barriers that traditionally kept smaller operators out of the B2B market. These days, technology platforms facilitate access to inventory and delivery in real time, so small and solo businesses are not limited by their distribution scale.

Perhaps the easiest way to think of distributors is as a directory-style service like Alibaba or Amazon. They can offer bricks-and-mortar outlets, like Bunnings, or online only. Some serve only the B2B market; others will also supply direct to the consumer.

SERVICE BUSINESSES

Unlike the preceding three categories, service businesses don't deal in products, but rather in providing services. Whereas once service businesses were typically small – because they required only a modest initial investment and depended largely on the skills of the owner (think accountant, lawyer, website designer, for example) – nowadays they can scale high, thanks to online. In today's world, the specialist skills, experience, support and equipment these businesses deliver for their customers are increasingly being powered by digital platforms and services. As such, service businesses are the perfect fit for small business ventures and represent the highest portion of the sector. The majority of small service businesses are solo or microbusinesses, operating in spaces such as:

» **transport** – car hire, taxis/ride-share, bike rentals, motor mechanics

» **compliance** – law, accounting, insurance broking, security services

» **personal care** – hairdressing, make-up artistry

» **home care** – cleaning, gardening, painting, plumbing, maintenance

» **recreation** – personal training, hostels, catering, event management

» **support services** – life coaching, childcare, financial planning, real estate.

New types of business

Beyond the four standard business types, today's world has opened up many new business channels. As things move faster, our constantly evolving technology creates new connections and unlimited opportunities for those willing to work hard and think creatively.

WHAT ABOUT ONLINE?

Some years back there was a trend to distinguish 'online' businesses as a separate category, but I think we'd all agree that today every business needs a digital presence at a minimum, and that some companies are entirely digital. In every case, the online component is now part of the business operation or process. Therefore, I grant you time dedicated to watching the quokka TikTok live stream – I mean, it's research, right? (Not to mention that these home-grown floofies are apparently the world's happiest creatures, and we all need a daily dose of sunshine!)[7]

All jokes aside, what *is* useful about thinking of 'online' as a separate function is the way in which it can inspire us to flush out a 'new' kind of business or offering. With the emergence of online, many traditional types of business evolved through using digital services, creating a type of hybrid industry: SaaS (software as a service) platforms like HubSpot spring to mind, as well as online directory-style services such as carsales.com and realestate.com. My own business She's on the Money is an example, too. Essentially an educational service, it feels 'new' because instead of operating literally 'old school' in face-to-face classrooms, I share information and training through my podcast and website.

While the most common types of emerging hybrid businesses tend to combine 'tech' with an existing industry/challenge (fintech, healthtech, greentech, anyone?), it's equally possible to combine other business types to form new models. For example, drop-shipping is a combined retail/distribution process whereby an individual can access wholesale markets, without the need for warehousing, to serve online retail customers. Such combinations are not necessarily 'new', either.

Your local butcher has been delivering a combined retail/manufacturing business since day dot – buying meats wholesale to both a) sell to retail customers and b) make their own products, like sausages.

OVER TO YOU First, determine which traditional category of small business yours fits into: retail, manufacturing, distribution or service. Now get creative with some ideas around how you might combine different processes and operations to create your own new hybrid business solution.

CREATE A HYBRID

One way to ensure profitability is to run several income streams in your business. For example, while typically a hairdresser is classified as providing a service, they will ideally also operate a retail side by selling hair products, and boost this by adding an online store. In addition, they could establish a training platform and materials – either for clients or up-and-coming hairdressers – or offer additional services, such as sharpening scissors.

With Zella Money, I was in quite a fortunate position because that was a really black-and-white, bread-and-butter business. We did accounting and financial advice initially, and then we shifted to doing mortgage broking. Both of these have pre-existing business models, so that gave me a template and I could spend ages on Google studying other people's websites and organisational structures and having a look at their LinkedIn. I'd also had the experience of working for another financial advice firm before. But SOTM was such a different business model! I didn't know anybody else who was running a media podcasting business.

Principle 2: Think big

While small businesses account for the vast majority of business types in Australia, defining them is not so easy. Traditional silos are breaking down and businesses can now encompass all sorts of operations. The only limit, really, is your imagination – and then the reality of making it happen.

Meet the founder: Angela Ceberano

After several years as Sony's national publicity manager, representing some of Australia's most beloved musicians, Angela Ceberano launched her own PR agency, Flourish, in 2010. Using her celebrity management expertise she built a thriving communications business that quickly evolved from offering media relations to becoming a full-service creative communications agency delivering public relations, social media, content creation, media training and influencer marketing.

Name: Angela Ceberano

Business: Flourish PR

Industry: Public relations and communications

Product/service: Public relations and marketing expertise

Target audience: Medium-to-large businesses – companies with a turnover of $10 million to $500 million

Secondary audience: Celebrities and leaders

Unique selling point: Expertise from working with celebrities in the music industry plus long-term media connections

The business began: 2010

I'm in the business of PR, but I feel like PR needs its own PR because everyone is so confused by what it is! It's public relations, it's communication, it's getting your message out there in a way that feels right for you and your business. We help our clients handle their communications, in both good times and bad – to help them grow as well as guide them through a crisis. We help people tell their story and communicate it in the best way possible.

In the early days, clients would come to us wanting PR and I'd look at their public presence and realise they didn't actually need PR; instead, they might need a marketing plan and then a decent website. I mean, there's no point in generating a buzz only to send people to an awful website – that would have the exact opposite of the desired effect! Often, they'd need to take four steps back. Since we didn't want to send them away, we expanded our business to offer marketing and branding, too, so we could take them through the entire journey of marketing and comms until they eventually ended up with my team in PR.

Marketing takes six to 12 months to do it right, but sometimes it can be squeezed into a month if it's urgent. We develop a library of photos, images, tone, language, branding – all of that stuff. When the client is ready, we start media training, working with them to develop their key messages. As a business or personality you need little stories up your sleeve because people remember stories more than facts. We help our clients refine their stories by helping them figure out why they're in business. We teach them what makes a good story and help them back those stories up with facts and stats for credibility. We keep refining the client's message until we reach the sweet spot where they're gaining traction and it's affecting their business in a positive way.

Since I started the business, the PR landscape has changed dramatically. Back then, social media was just emerging – people had personal accounts, but businesses weren't jumping on it yet, so there was a huge opportunity. We used to have a good six months to plan with a client, but now we'll get a phone call from someone saying, 'We're launching in two days – can you help?' So, we jump. We no longer do long-term planning, because it'll be irrelevant in three months' time – everything moves so much quicker.

On the upside, you can control the message so much better. Now that everyone does everything on their smartphone, we have access to incredible influencers (we call them 'people of influence'), and the way we communicate is very different. We use an awesome monitoring system to track public sentiment and optics so we can react to rapidly changing public opinion and respond immediately, changing our strategy to maximise positive effects. It's exciting! As a self-confessed control freak, I find it so fun.

Although I started out working with celebrities, these days we are very selective about the celebrities we take on – only those at the top of their game. And that's a strategic decision. Celebrities don't pay the bills, but they do buy us leveraging power with the media. I can offer a high-profile celebrity interview to network television, and in turn they'll support another 'less exciting' brand because of my long-term industry relationships and the trust I've developed.

It was hard work to get to this point. Not many people have worked in celebrity PR and succeeded long term. You work 24 hours a day and get paid very little – just working for the glory of it all. My work ethic helped me get to the point where I was ready to start my own PR business. I became known for my crazy schedules. I believe if you're going to do it, do it properly. So, I'd schedule fully packed publicity days with no breaks, not even for lunch. I'd prepare a picnic basket of homemade sandwiches and cookies and muffins so we didn't have to stop.

My experience is a big part of what makes our business different. When I started Flourish, there weren't many boutique agencies. I was super young – only 27. Everyone laughed at me, especially because my industry was led by a lot of powerful men. Some said, 'You're starting your own thing. That's hilarious. Good luck.' But my first client was the Backstreet Boys and New Kids on the Block tour, and my business took off from there.

In school I was diagnosed with a learning disability, so I've always had to try harder than others. I thought, *Well, if I'm going to be successful, I just have to go the extra mile to prove myself.* It's worked well for me so far. Looking back, I think it built resilience, grit. I've found I can use that to my advantage, kind of like a secret weapon. However, I also had to learn when to stop working. I burnt myself out so badly that I had to go to hospital and I was really sick for six months. At that time I hadn't yet been diagnosed with ADHD. My specialist asked me, 'Do you have a business?' And I was like, yeah, and he goes, 'It's the entrepreneur's disease. I see it all the time.'

The two best things about being in business are being able to choose the projects I work on and the people I work with. For the first couple of years, that absolutely was not the case – I had to take on anything just to be able to pay the bills, and it was bloody hard. I think for the first five years, you have to suck it up. If you want to have a long-term successful business you have to put in the hard yards unless you have awesome capital behind you and can hire 20 people from day one to help you. But that wasn't my experience. I was doing everything and wearing a hundred different hats just to try to make ends meet for those first couple of years. Now I feel like I've finally earned the right of success and can pick and choose who I work with. I have a couple of rules: 1) I don't work with arseholes and 2) I don't hire arseholes. It's taken me 15 years to work that out.

The other great thing now is the flexibility: being able to choose what I work on and when. I still spend a lot of time working on projects, but that's by choice, because I get obsessed and I love seeing the success of our clients and the impact we have.

I don't think it would be as rewarding if I was working for someone else. I started this business from nothing. The ability to employ people, train them, mentor them and then see them realise their potential has been amazing. We've had some excellent people come through as interns, and now they're account directors. Seeing staff grow and flourish is probably the most rewarding thing for me.

I'll be honest, there's a long list of negatives, too. Business is tough. I get frustrated with social media – the highlights reel can make everything look only easy and fun. I know I don't want to pick up my camera and be honest with my audience when I've just had the shittiest day in business. It's not natural for us to do that, especially in PR, but I'd like to do it more, actually, because I think it's an important message to get across.

The worst thing for me in those early years was the finance side. I had a massive tax debt because I didn't know how to manage my tax. I'm really good at it now; I hire great people to help me. Carrying the financial burden for a business lies heavy on your shoulders. If you have big bills to pay, you have tax debt, you have to pay payroll every week, it's a big responsibility. If I miss something, that's on me personally. If someone's not happy in my organisation, that's on me.

Business can also be lonely. Back when I started, I felt like all I had was my business. Later, I got married and realised, *Okay, something's got to give, I can't do 22-hour days anymore, my relationship won't survive.* I had already lost a lot of friends along the way – I felt I didn't have time to invest in them, so of course my relationships were going to turn to shit.

The responsibility I felt to make this thing work was so big I just had to focus to make sure I could get through it. I know I didn't have a good work–life balance, but I also think I wouldn't have a business today if I hadn't brought that laser focus to those early years.

I'm still learning; I haven't fully mastered the art of this business thing yet. I'm learning how to not take it so personally when something doesn't go right. I'm learning that you can't control people at the end of the day, which is really hard for a control freak!

When I look back, it's easy to say I would change so much about my business journey, but then I think, no, you have to go through your fuck-ups, it's the only way you'll learn. You have to cry, and then recover and create a process and a system so it never happens again. If I hadn't made mistakes, I wouldn't have built what I have now. You have to stuff up to be brilliant.

Chapter Three

Getting your business game plan on

Alrighty, friends! Now that we've explored the environment around us and run through the broad categories of business types, let's get the magnifying glass focused on your specific industry and see if your business idea has real potential.

In this chapter we dive into the nitty-gritty. We'll see why competitive research and market analysis are so crucial. We'll lay the foundations of your business plan – eek, things are starting to feel real! And then, just like any good party planner, we'll look at how to make it really happen by setting some realistic goals and putting dates in your calendar.

By the end of this chapter, your business dreams should be mapped out on paper – the first and most important step in making them become a reality.

Get to know your industry

Whether you do or don't have much of an idea about your industry right now, by the end of this section, you will. Market research is both the funnest (yes, this is a proper word, I swear) and importantest (also a real word, I promise!) task you'll do for your business. This is one of my favourite parts of running a business – you get to be super nosy about companies already out there, to help you find and shape the dream biz you've been searching for.

At certain points along your business trajectory – like now, before you begin, and at regular stages throughout – it's essential to take a step back and look at your business from an investor's perspective. Trust me, it is a game changer for your long-term success and survival. Stepping back from the daily grind to look at your workflow with fresh eyes can reveal potential risks and roadblocks you might not have noticed. It's like giving yourself a bird's-eye view to spot any sneaky pitfalls so you can reroute before you end up in a ditch.

So grab a cup of tea, take a deep breath, and spend some time working 'on' your business. Your future self will thank you!

Take in the big picture

In Chapter 2, we looked at the kinds of small businesses available in Australia. You probably have a good idea of where yours is going to fit based on your skills and interests. But does that make it a good idea?

Before you invest a whole heap of time and money into developing your business, it's worth spending a little time up front to determine how likely it is to succeed. What is the economy doing at large and how is that affecting your industry specifically? What are your competitors doing? How might you differentiate yourself in this space?

Conducting competitive research isn't just a box to tick off, it's a vital step in crafting a strategy that will set you up for success. So, let's break down some effective methods for gathering competitive intelligence, shall we?

REVIEW THE STATE OF THE MARKET

As with any good movie, it's best to first view things from a wide angle. You know those beautiful panoramic shots that open an epic, taking in the full scope of the mountain range ahead, lit up by a stunning sunrise? That's what you're doing here, but in the context of your business. Pull up your director's chair.

I'll assume you roughly know what industry you're in, whether it's beauty or fashion or real estate or professional services or something else. Once you've established your opening scene, it's time to review how everyone fits into place - and that means getting to know everyone who's operating in your end of town. Get personal (no, not that kind!) – just enough that you get a pretty good idea of how they do things. What works for them, and why? How do they fit into the broader scheme of things – you know, the economy and such?

Using online research and government data from centres like the Australian Bureau of Statistics (ABS) and the office of the Australian Small Business and Family Enterprise Ombudsman (ASBFEO) is a good place to start. They regularly release snapshots of the economy at large – which industries are doing well and which are in decline, based on things such as size, turnover and value.

Their graphs and data should give you a decent wide-angle view on how your industry is performing and whether now is the right time to invest in your venture. If it's on the backwards slide, while not necessarily a reason to abort mission, it is a signal to look further into what might be prompting such large-scale exits and how the current economic factors and operating environment could affect your future plans. For instance, has the government changed tax laws? Has the world stopped eating out? Or has someone invented a weight-management drug that's changing people's relationship to food? Are these likely to be long-lasting impacts or short-term fluctuations?

It's important to analyse the data from a range of angles to filter the information into something useful, like good old-fashioned mining for gold – where are the dust flakes going to sparkle? And be honest with yourself about what you find. While it always hurts to have someone pop a pin in your ideas balloon, it hurts far less than washing real time and money down the drain. So consider such research time well spent, and if you see the warning signs, run while you still can.

Know your industry

Once you've gathered your intel on how your industry is performing in the economy at large, it's time to start researching the market for your particular industry. Here, I'll run through a variety of ways you can get your nose into your competitors' business. But a couple of words of advice before you open that new browser tab:

» **Be reasonable with your market research:** Don't just compare yourself to massive established businesses. Make it a fair comparison and look around at others of a similar size and stage to you, too.
» **Look beyond your 'direct competitors':** For fresh inspiration, look outside your own industry. Lateral research and thinking has definitely played into our success here at SOTM.

ONLINE RESEARCH

The internet is your best friend when it comes to competitive research. Begin by thoroughly reviewing your competitors' websites. Pay attention to their product offerings, pricing strategies and how they position themselves in the market. How are they marketing? What new products are they launching and how are they evolving existing ones? Do some sleuthing on their team and structure: what kind of staff have they hired, and how are they attracting and retaining them? Don't stop there – monitor their social media channels to see how they engage with their audience and any promotions they run. Are they blowing up on TikTok, and if so, how are they doing it? And let's not forget customer reviews and ratings on platforms like Yelp and Google Reviews, or others more specific to your industry. These can provide a treasure trove of information about what customers love and what they don't.

CUSTOMER INSIGHTS

Want to get into the minds of customers in your target market? Conduct surveys or interviews to understand their perceptions of your competitors. You can also organise focus groups to gather detailed opinions about competitors and their products or services. This direct feedback can offer invaluable insights into what your potential customers are looking for.

PRODUCT AND SERVICE ANALYSIS

Sometimes the best way to understand your competition is to experience it firsthand. Consider mystery shopping – purchase or use your competitors' products or services to assess their quality and customer experience. Additionally, create a comparison chart of features, pricing and benefits of competitor offerings. This will help you identify gaps in the market that you can fill.

COMPETITIVE BENCHMARKING

Numbers don't lie. Compare key metrics such as pricing, market share, sales volume and growth rate. If available, analyse competitors' performance through their financial reports, or estimate it based on market data. This will give you a rational understanding of where you stand in comparison.

INDUSTRY REPORTS AND PUBLICATIONS

Stay informed by purchasing or accessing industry reports from market research firms. Trade magazines and journals are also excellent sources for keeping up with industry trends and competitor activities. Knowledge is power, after all!

NETWORKING AND INDUSTRY EVENTS

Never underestimate the value of face-to-face interactions. Attend trade shows and conferences to network, gather information and observe your competitors' presence and strategies. Joining professional associations can also provide you with exclusive insights and reports.

SEARCH ENGINE ANALYSIS

Use search engine optimisation (SEO) tools to analyse your competitors' keywords, backlinks and online visibility. Google Trends can also be a handy tool to track search trends related to competitors and industry keywords. This will help you understand how they're driving traffic and where you can improve.

COMPETITOR ADVERTISING ANALYSIS

Track your competitors' online advertising campaigns using tools such as Google Ads. Understanding their advertising strategies can help you refine your own marketing efforts.

PUBLIC FINANCIAL STATEMENTS

If your competitors are publicly traded, you're in luck! Review their annual reports, earnings calls and financial statements for insights into their operations and performance. This information can be a goldmine for understanding their strengths and weaknesses.

PATENTS AND INNOVATIONS

Keep an eye on patent databases to check for recent innovations or technology advancements by your competitors. This can give you a heads-up on what's coming down the pipeline and how you can innovate in response.

SUPPLIER AND DISTRIBUTOR INFORMATION

Understanding who your competitors' suppliers and distributors are can provide insights into their market positioning and operational strengths. This information can be particularly useful if you're looking to negotiate better terms with your own suppliers.

LEGAL AND REGULATORY INFORMATION

Finally, review any legal or regulatory filings related to your competitors. These can provide insights into their operations, challenges and even potential vulnerabilities.

I started a photo booth hire business in November 2014 after I realised there was a gap in the market while planning my wedding. I thought it could be a great side hustle for extra cash. Fast forward a decade and the business has expanded to four photo booths, audio guest books, flower walls and love signs, and we now have four staff members!

Before I set up the business, I googled photo booth hire, read other people's websites and asked friends and family questions. In the beginning I struggled with sticking to a logo/website and style, but I now have a recognisable brand.

For anyone wanting to set up a similar business, I would tell them that building professional relationships and trust is key. Be honest and transparent and respond quickly to inquiries. It's also important to research everything; don't rush, and don't take people's suggestions as gospel. Look things up for yourself and trust your gut instinct when it comes to people and staff members.

Let's get competitive

As you have been gathering data, you will have formed a comprehensive understanding of who else is operating in the market. Now you can start to pull this information together to begin developing your market position and offering.

IDENTIFY YOUR COMPETITION

First, you need to get very clear about who you're up against and how the playing field is looking. Start by listing both direct and indirect competitors within your industry or niche – you probably have most of your list from the market analysis research you've just done. By identifying both direct and indirect competitors, you can better understand the competitive landscape and develop strategies to differentiate your brand.

FOR EXAMPLE: ECO CHIC

Let's say you're looking to start a small business in the Australian fashion market that specialises in sustainable, eco-friendly clothing, called 'Eco Chic'. Here's how you might list your direct and indirect competitors (take these as general ideas only – the way the world is rapidly evolving, this list is likely to change):

Direct competitors

1. **Spell & The Gypsy Collective:** An Australian brand known for its bohemian styles and commitment to sustainability.
2. **Kowtow:** A fashion label that focuses on organic and ethically made clothing.
3. **NICO:** Another label with a strong emphasis on ethical production, specialising in sustainable underwear and basics.
4. **Outland Denim:** A fashion brand known for its sustainable and ethically produced jeans, with a focus on providing fair employment opportunities.

Indirect competitors

1. **Zara:** A global fast fashion brand that occasionally releases eco-friendly collections.
2. **H&M:** Another fast fashion giant; its 'Conscious' collection promotes sustainability.
3. **The Iconic:** An online retailer that stocks a wide range of brands, including sustainable and eco-friendly options.

4. **Kmart:** A budget-friendly retailer that offers a wide range of clothing, some of which may appeal to price-sensitive customers looking for eco-friendly options.

CONDUCT A SWOT ANALYSIS

Next, conduct a SWOT analysis – strengths, weaknesses, opportunities and threats – to get a clearer picture of what you're up against. This will help you understand where your competitors excel and where they falter, giving you valuable insights into how you can position your business. (Cheeky tip: I use SWOT all the time for just about everything, from choosing wedding venues, to buying beauty products, and of course, on my own businesses!)

FOR EXAMPLE: ECO CHIC

Continuing from the Eco Chic example, here's a high-level SWOT analysis of the first competitor, Spell & The Gypsy Collective.

Spell & The Gypsy Collective	
Strengths	**Weaknesses**
» Strong 'bohemian' brand identity	» Higher price point
» Commitment to sustainability	» Niche market focus
» Strong online and social media	» Specific aesthetic trend
Opportunities	**Threats**
» Expand product lines	» Sustainability now mainstream
» Collaborations	
» Leveraging influencer partnerships	» Boho goes out of style
	» Supply issues (cost/availability)

Following the above example, go ahead and conduct a SWOT analysis either on your business's competitors or alternatively for Eco Chic. What are those businesses doing well? What are they missing? What could go wrong for them (and therefore, possibly for you)? What opportunities are they making the most of (could you cash in on them too, or something similar)?

Find your beloved customers

Of course, there is no business without customers. So the next step is defining who you dream of selling to. Beyond friends and family, who will buy your products and champion your cause?

The way we like to figure that out is by using avatars. No, not the blue creatures running around in James Cameron's movie epics, but 'customer avatars' aka an imagined version of your ideal customer. Spend some decent time imagining exactly who they are, what they do, where they go, how they spend, how much they spend and what they like to spend on . . . It's kind of like creating your perfect imaginary-friend-in-business!

No doubt you already have a general idea of who your customers are – people who love the same things as you, which is why you're starting this business and why they're coming along for the ride. But soz, friend, general ain't gonna cut it here. For this exercise we want to get specific.

Think about demographics: age, gender, income level, education, occupation and even marital status. Are you targeting young, single professionals in Melbourne who love their brunch spots and are always on the lookout for the next big thing in tech? Busy mums in Brisbane who need quick, healthy meal solutions for their families? The more detailed you get, the better. This isn't just about knowing who they are on paper, but really understanding their lifestyle, their pain points and what makes them tick.

Let's dive deeper into psychographics – this is where you get to know your avatar's personality, values, opinions, attitudes, interests and lifestyle. Are they eco-conscious and willing to spend a little extra for sustainable products? Do they value experiences over material goods? Maybe they're fitness enthusiasts who love outdoor activities and are always on the hunt for the latest in activewear. By understanding their psychographics, you can tailor your marketing messages to resonate with their deeper motivations and desires.

Now, let's talk about where they hang out. No, not in a creepy way! I mean in a way that lets you know where to reach them. Are they scrolling through Instagram during their morning commute, or are they more likely to be found in Facebook groups sharing tips and advice? Maybe they're avid podcast listeners who love tuning in to the latest episodes on their way to work. Knowing where your avatar spends their time helps you decide where to focus your marketing efforts and meet your customers where they're at.

FOR EXAMPLE: ECO CHIC

Let's bring this to life with our running example, Eco Chic. Its customer avatar might be a 28-year-old woman named Louise, living in Sydney, who's passionate about sustainability. She follows eco-friendly influencers on Instagram, shops at farmers' markets and reads blogs about zero-waste living. She's willing to pay a premium for products that align with her values, and she loves brands that tell a compelling story about their commitment to the environment. Knowing this, Eco Chic would focus its marketing efforts on Instagram, collaborate with eco-influencers and create content that highlights the brand's sustainability practices.

Identifying your target market and customer base isn't just a one-time exercise; it's an ongoing process. As your business grows and evolves, so will your understanding of your customers. Keep gathering feedback, stay curious and be ready to pivot when needed. Your avatar is a living, breathing representation of your ideal customer, and just like real people, avatars can change over time. Stay in tune with their needs and desires and you'll be well on your way to building a loyal and engaged customer base.

PAIGE'S BUSINESS STORY

I founded a dance education business called Dance N Schools in 2020 during my university degree. I've always had a passion for sharing dance and providing new movement avenues for students.

My business is aimed at school staff and parents/guardians of students. Before I launched it, I researched potential competitors, school budgets, competitor prices and areas in which competitors were not offering. Now I keep up to date with competitors and ensure our services are modern and meet ever-changing curriculum descriptors. I also have a very structured booking process that ensures our services are personally tailored to each customer.

Establishing a new business in an established sector was challenging, but positive word of mouth has developed the brand identity. Retaining existing customers has been an essential part of my business growth, as has building professional relationships and trust. Being honest and transparent goes a long way.

Corner the market

Once you have completed your competitive analysis and identified your target market, you can then use these insights to start developing a niche position for your business. From there, you can develop a marketing strategy that supports your position and goals, enabling you to 'own' this particular corner of the market (more on this in Chapter 7). As any marketing expert will tell you, at the end of the day, consumers buy from brands they love.

What makes you different?

Having identified your customers and reviewed your competitors, you're now in a good position to identify any missed opportunities, or what people in the know like to call a 'gap in the market'. We use this to develop your USP (unique selling proposition).

FOR EXAMPLE: ECO CHIC

Brand Concept

Returning to our example, Eco Chic is a premium fashion brand dedicated to creating luxurious, eco-friendly clothing that merges high-end aesthetics with uncompromising sustainability. Our mission is to redefine the perception of sustainable fashion in Australia by offering exclusive, limited-edition collections that cater to discerning customers who value both style and sustainability.

Unique Selling Propositions (USPs)

» **Luxury and exclusivity:** Unlike competitors who focus on casual or bohemian styles, Eco Chic offers high-end, sophisticated designs that appeal to fashion-forward consumers. Each collection is meticulously crafted in limited quantities to ensure exclusivity and reduce waste.

» **Artisanal craftsmanship:** We collaborate with local artisans and creators to create unique, hand-finished pieces. This not only supports local communities but also ensures that each garment is a work of art, differentiating us from mass-produced fast fashion brands.

» **Innovative eco-friendly materials:** Our collections feature cutting-edge sustainable materials, such as recycled ocean plastics, organic bamboo silk and plant-based dyes. We are committed to staying at the forefront of sustainable fabric technology, offering our customers the best in eco-friendly luxury.

» **Transparent supply chain:** Eco Chic prides itself on complete transparency. We provide detailed information about the origin of our materials, the production process and the artisans involved. Our customers can trace the journey of their garments from raw material to finished product.

» **Customisation and personalisation:** Offering bespoke tailoring and customisation options allows our customers to create one-of-a-kind pieces that reflect their personal style. This service adds a level of exclusivity and personal connection that is unmatched by our competitors.

Create a business plan

All serious businesses need a business plan. Whether for yourself or to use when seeking funding, it helps clarify your vision and direction, guides your marketing strategy and operational plans, supports financial planning and performance benchmarking, and is a communication tool for stakeholders that ensures everyone is aligned.

You may not have some of this detail yet, so consider this your blueprint or template. As you work through the chapters in this book, you'll be able to fill out each section. Think of your business plan as your roadmap – it's going to guide you through the highs and lows, keep you on track, and help you make those big, bold moves with confidence. So roll up your sleeves, grab a notebook (or your laptop) and let's get to work.

There are several schools of thought about how best to develop and lay out a business plan. Here I'll run through the basics to get you started.

What should I include in my business plan?

A good business plan should include the following.

1. EXECUTIVE SUMMARY

This is your elevator pitch. It's a snapshot of your business, capturing the essence of what you're about. Think of it as your business's Hinge profile – it needs to be engaging, concise and compelling.

> » **Business name:** What is your business called?
> » **Location:** Where are you based?
> » **Mission statement:** Why does your business exist?
> » **Products or services:** What are you offering?
> » **Goals:** What do you hope to achieve?

2. COMPANY DESCRIPTION

Here's where you get to tell your story. It's not just about what you do, but why you do it.

» **Business structure:** Are you a sole trader, a partnership or a company?

» **Industry:** What industry are you operating in?

» **Business history:** If you're already up and running, share your journey so far.

» **Objectives:** What are your short-term and long-term goals?

3. MARKET RESEARCH

This is where all that work on identifying your target market and customer base comes into play. You need to show you've done your homework.

» **Market analysis:** What's the current state of the market?

» **Target market:** Who are your customers?

» **Competitive analysis:** Who are your competitors, and what are their strengths and weaknesses?

» **Market trends:** What are the trends in your industry?

4. ORGANISATION AND MANAGEMENT

Who's on your team? Even if it's just you right now, this section is crucial.

» **Organisational structure:** Who's in charge of what?

» **Ownership information:** Who owns the business?

» **Management team:** Who's running the show?

» **Roles and responsibilities:** What does each team member do?

5. PRODUCTS OR SERVICES

Here's where you get to geek out about what you're offering. Be detailed and passionate!

» **Description:** What are your products or services?

» **Unique selling proposition (USP):** What makes your offering unique?

» **Lifecycle:** What's the lifecycle of your product or service?

» **Research and development (R&D):** Any plans for future development?

6. MARKETING AND SALES STRATEGY

How are you going to get your amazing product or service into the hands of your customers?

» **Marketing strategy:** How will you attract and retain customers?

» **Sales strategy:** What's your sales process?

» **Pricing strategy:** How will you price your products or services?

» **Advertising and promotion:** How will you promote your business?

7. FINANCIAL PROJECTIONS

This is where you lay out the numbers. It's all about showing that your business is financially viable.

» **Revenue streams:** How will you make money?

» **Cost structure:** What are your costs?

» **Profit and loss statement:** Project your profits and losses.

» **Cash flow statement:** Show your cash inflows and outflows.

» **Break-even analysis:** When will you break even?

8. FUNDING REQUEST

If you're seeking funding, this section is crucial. Be clear and specific.

» **Funding requirements:** How much do you need?

» **Use of funds:** How will you use the funds?

» **Future funding requirements:** Any future funding needs?

There's a high chance that you can't answer all these questions right now. Don't panic! This doesn't mean your idea isn't viable; it just means you have more learning and exploring to do. I encourage you still to have a crack at jotting down even your initial ideas for each point, and then come back to your business plan every time you hit upon some new information.

FOR EXAMPLE: ECO CHIC

EXECUTIVE SUMMARY

Business name: Eco Chic

Location: Sydney, Australia

Mission statement: Eco Chic exists to redefine sustainable fashion by offering luxurious, eco-friendly clothing that merges high-end aesthetics with uncompromising sustainability.

Products or services: We offer premium, eco-friendly clothing collections, including bespoke tailoring and customisation options, crafted from innovative sustainable materials.

Goals: Our short-term goal is to establish Eco Chic as a leading name in sustainable luxury fashion within Australia. Long-term, we aim to expand our brand internationally and become a thought leader in the global sustainable fashion movement.

COMPANY DESCRIPTION

Business structure: Company (Pty Ltd)

Industry: Fashion and apparel

Business history: Eco Chic was founded in 2023 by a group of passionate environmentalists and fashion enthusiasts who saw a gap in the market for high-end, eco-friendly clothing. We have since developed a range of collections that combine luxury with sustainability, gaining a loyal customer base.

Objectives:

- » **Short-term:** Launch our first collection and establish a strong online presence.
- » **Long-term:** Expand our product line, open flagship stores in major Australian cities, and enter international markets.

MARKET RESEARCH

Market analysis: The sustainable fashion market in Australia is growing rapidly as consumers become more environmentally conscious. There is a rising demand for luxury eco-friendly clothing that combines style with sustainability.

Target market: Affluent, eco-conscious consumers aged 25 to 45 who value high-quality, unique fashion pieces and are willing to invest in sustainable luxury.

Competitive analysis:

- » **Direct competitors:** Spell & The Gypsy Collective, Kowtow, NICO, Outland Denim.
  - – **Strengths:** Established brands with loyal customer bases.
  - – **Weaknesses:** Focus on casual or specific styles, lack of high-end luxury offerings.

» **Indirect competitors:** Zara, H&M, The Iconic, Kmart.
  - **Strengths:** Wide reach and affordability.
  - **Weaknesses:** Mass-produced, occasional eco-friendly collections, lack of exclusivity and luxury.

Market trends: Increasing consumer awareness of environmental issues, growing demand for transparency in supply chains, and a rising interest in bespoke, high-end fashion.

ORGANISATION AND MANAGEMENT

Ownership information: Eco Chic is privately owned by its founders.

Organisational structure, roles and responsibilities:

» **CEO – Julie Song:** Oversees overall business strategy and operations. Responsible for strategic planning, business development, investor relations.

» **Creative Director – Jo Lane:** Leads design and product development. Responsible for design direction, product development, trend analysis.

» **Head of Marketing – Eric Johnson:** Manages marketing and promotional activities. Responsible for branding, marketing campaigns, social media.

» **Sustainability Officer – Mary Lee:** Ensures all practices and materials are eco-friendly. Responsible for sourcing sustainable materials, ensuring eco-friendly practices.

» **Operations Manager – Syd Brown:** Handles day-to-day operations and supply chain management. Responsible for logistics, supply chain management, inventory control.

PRODUCTS AND SERVICES

Description: Our products include high-end, eco-friendly clothing collections featuring dresses, suits, outerwear and accessories. We also offer bespoke tailoring and customisation services.

Unique selling proposition (USP): Luxurious, eco-friendly clothing crafted from innovative sustainable materials, with a focus on artisanal craftsmanship and exclusivity.

Lifecycle: Our products are designed to be timeless and durable, with a lifecycle that extends beyond seasonal trends. We also offer a garment recycling program.

Research and development (R&D): We continuously explore new sustainable materials and innovative production techniques to enhance our product offerings.

MARKETING AND SALES STRATEGY

Marketing strategy: Use storytelling to highlight our sustainable practices and artisanal craftsmanship. Engage with eco-influencers, host exclusive events, and leverage social media to build brand awareness.

Sales strategy: Focus on e-commerce with a seamless online shopping experience, complemented by pop-up shops and shows in high-end locations.

Pricing strategy: Premium pricing to reflect the quality, exclusivity and sustainability of our products.

Advertising and promotion: Digital marketing campaigns, influencer partnerships, eco-friendly fashion shows, and collaborations with luxury eco-friendly locations.

FINANCIAL PROJECTIONS

Revenue streams: Sales of clothing collections, bespoke tailoring services and customisation options.

Cost structure: Costs include sustainable materials, artisanal craftsmanship, marketing, operations and R&D.

Profit and loss statement: Projected profits within the first two years, with a steady increase as we expand our product line and market reach.

Cash flow statement: Positive cash flow expected within the first year due to strong initial sales and efficient cost management.

Break-even analysis: Expected to break even within 18 to 24 months.

FUNDING REQUEST

Funding requirements: Seeking $500,000 in initial funding.

Use of funds: Funds will be used for product development, marketing campaigns, establishing an e-commerce platform, and initial operational costs.

Future funding requirements: Additional funding may be required for international expansion and opening flagship stores in major cities.

Let's make a plan

Once you have your business plan in hand you're ready to take on the world, right? Hold up – before you dive headfirst into the deep end, let's talk about setting realistic goals and milestones.

Use the SOTM planning method

Having set up multiple businesses of my own, I absolutely know how challenging achieving goals can be. That's why we love setting SOTM goals and milestones – to make sure they are Specific, Optimistic, Time-bound and Measurable. This framework ensures that your goals are clear and attainable, giving you a solid plan to follow.

» **Specific:** What exactly do you want to achieve?

The more specific the goal, the better. Knowing exactly what you're aiming for and by when will help you get realistic about how to achieve it. If you can't pinpoint the details, it probably means your goal is too lofty or distant. And that's okay for the long-term, big-picture dreams you hold for your business, but it's not a goal or milestone – it's more an ideal. At this point, we're looking at setting clear targets. For example, by 1 March next year (exactly a year after I open), I will be making annual revenue of $350,000.

» **Optimistic:** What do you believe you can achieve?

Aim high, be honest. Standard goal-setting formulas include 'realistic' in their framework, but I prefer our goals to be 'optimistic'. I mean, there's no point going into this thing if you don't believe you can achieve, right? So set goals that are ambitious – a stretch, if you like – but achievable with a positive mindset.

» **Time-bound:** What deadlines need to be met to achieve your goal?

Put times to goals. In your specific goal, you will have included an overall deadline. Now, work backwards and break it down. What smaller steps could you accomplish along the way, and when will you complete them by?

» **Measurable:** How will you measure your progress?

Keep tabs on your goals. Using the example of the revenue goal above, you might establish some smaller milestones throughout the year. To make an annual revenue of $350,000 you would aim to earn roughly $30,000 per month.

How to make it happen

Getting practical with your plans and writing them down is the first step in making them become a reality. So let's look at how to plan like a pro. This will help keep you focused, motivated and moving forward without feeling like you're drowning in to-do lists.

START WITH THE BIG PICTURE

First things first, let's consider the long-term view. What's your ultimate goal? Maybe it's to become the go-to brand for affordable skincare in Australia, or perhaps it's to open a chain of fitness studios across the country. Whatever it is, write it down. This is your North Star, the thing that's going to keep you going when the going gets tough.

BREAK IT DOWN

Now that you've got your big, audacious goal, it's time to break it down into smaller, more manageable chunks. This is where milestones come in. Think of milestones as mini-goals that will help you reach your ultimate destination. They're like checkpoints on your entrepreneurial journey, giving you a moment to pause, celebrate and reassess.

For example, if your big goal is to launch an affordable skincare line, your milestones might look something like this:

1. **R&D:** Finalise product formulations.
2. **Branding:** Develop your brand identity, including logo, packaging and website.
3. **Production:** Secure suppliers and manufacturers.
4. **Marketing:** Launch your social media channels and start building a community.
5. **Sales:** Launch your online store and start selling your products.

By breaking your big goal down into these smaller steps, you make it much less overwhelming and far more achievable.

PRIORITISE AND TAKE ACTION

Once you've set your SOTM goals, it's time to prioritise them. Not all goals are created equal, and some will have a bigger impact on your business than others. Focus on the goals that will move the needle the most and tackle them first.

Create a timeline for your milestones, mapping out what you need to do each week or month to stay on track. Use tools like Trello, Asana or even a good old-fashioned planner to keep yourself organised. And don't forget to build in some buffer time – things rarely go exactly as planned, and it's better to be prepared for a few hiccups along the way. I am personally a BIG fan of checklists – the satisfaction I get from ticking something off helps keep me motivated and focuses my attention on what's next.

WORK HARD, BUT DON'T BURN OUT

Starting and running a business is hard work and it's going to take a lot of your time and energy, especially in the beginning. But here's the thing – you can't pour from an empty cup. Burnout is real and doesn't do you or your business any favours. Taking a proactive approach will help ensure you don't get to that point. Some of my favourite tips are:

» **Set boundaries:** Decide on your working hours and stick to them. It's tempting to work around the clock, but setting boundaries will help you maintain a healthy work–life balance.
» **Take breaks:** Schedule regular breaks throughout your day to rest and recharge. Even a quick walk around the block can do wonders for your productivity.

» **Delegate:** You don't have to do everything yourself. Delegate tasks to your team if you have one, or outsource where possible. Focus on what you do best and let others handle the rest.

» **Practise self-care:** Make time for activities that nourish your body and mind. Whether it's yoga, reading or spending time with loved ones, self-care is essential for your wellbeing and that of your business baby.

CELEBRATE YOUR WINS

Anyone who knows me, knows how important I think it is to celebrate along the way! Every milestone you achieve, no matter how small, is a step closer to your ultimate goal. Take a moment to acknowledge your hard work and celebrate your progress. It's these little victories that will keep you motivated and remind you why you started this journey in the first place. Many founders say they relished the wins in the early days more than the big ones that came later, so soak up every satisfying moment as your business baby develops.

Principle 3: Stay flexible

Be flexible and stay open to change. Regularly review your goals, assess your progress and adjust your plan as needed. The entrepreneurial journey is full of twists and turns, and being adaptable is key to long-term success.

Meet the founder: Michelle Hu

Michelle Hu is the CEO and founder of the stunning beauty accessory brand ÉTOILE, which has likely been all over your TikTok For You page! Michelle channelled her savvy fashion customisation skills from her childhood into a brand that demonstrates her obsession with how beauty makes her feel. The result is a marriage between the functional and the fashionable.

Name: Michelle Hu

Business: ÉTOILE

Industry: Beauty and travel accessories

Products/services: Travel bags and storage organisers

Target audience: Women aged 25 to 40

Secondary audience: Professional make-up artists and hair stylists

Unique selling point: We create solution-oriented, thoughtfully designed accessories to make your daily beauty routine more enjoyable.

The business began: 2016

For as long as I can remember, I've had the itch that inspired me to go into business. From the age of 11, I was taking my parents' old jeans and customising them to look like those distressed/studded shorts (hello, Nasty Gal era) to sell on eBay. I then spent a few years teaching myself Photoshop to create digital clothes that you could sell as a developer on the platform. If I try to connect the dots, I think the itch came from watching my parents try their hand at a bunch of different ventures, including wine exporting, restaurants and cafés.

Officially, the business was registered in December 2016 but it was operating in a very low-touch capacity (3 to 4 hours a week). I had absolutely zero intention of growing the business when I started. At the time, I was separately working on a beauty appointment booking app and I always thought that would be the thing that took off. ÉTOILE changed and grew significantly when my vision for it evolved from a passion project to something that could be a household name and in everyone's beauty routine.

In 2019 I quit my full-time job as an investment banking analyst to give ÉTOILE a proper crack. Initially, my role encompassed everything. I remember thinking I would never be able to take a day off without the business also having to pause. Since then, it's grown up a lot and I have an incredible team that helps with every vertical. We hired staff as the business grew, but because I moved to the US in 2022 and didn't want to manage staff remotely, we had to restructure the team. Excluding agencies, contractors and myself, we now have three staff: a warehouse manager, a warehouse assistant and a customer service and operations lead. We have always outsourced finance/accounting, content creation and media buying as we've not needed someone to be in-house full time. I really enjoy the flexibility to turn on/off or scale up/down these external contractors. Now, I focus my time on product development, brand strategy and marketing.

My mum has also been a part of the business since day one. She would pack orders and run to the post office while I was working full time. Having had her witness every fall, rise, struggle, growth and evolution of the business often makes it feel like I have a co-founder who I can share the mental load with. I've also been fortunate enough to meet some incredible people in business that I've formed genuine friendships with. I turn to them for advice or to bounce ideas off and often leave feeling a renewed sense of motivation.

Looking back, I wish I'd had a more robust plan going in (one that detailed market positioning and USPs and had a clearer vision). At the time, I didn't have any mentors or friends to turn to, so it felt like jumping through hoops I didn't even know existed until they were right in front of me.

The flexibility to control your own time and schedule is definitely a highlight of having your own business. But the pressure – to stay consistently motivated, inspired and keep doing more – can be exhausting! Plus, so much of my personal time is intertwined with work, and it's hard to concretely separate the two.

I've got a lot better with work–life balance over the years and (most of the time) don't let the stress of running a business get in the way of what I value most, which is spending time with friends and family . . . and a good night's sleep! However, I don't think you start a business because you're chasing after work–life balance, especially in the beginning where it takes up a lot of mindshare, time and energy. I think you're motivated by something deeper – for me, I love the process of designing and building products that I can tangibly feel, and then seeing them loved by customers across the globe.

If I could go back and start again I would:

» Spend a lot more time initially on developing an exceptional launch product.

» Define my why and who as early as possible and stay laser-focused on that while growing the business.

» *Try* not to succumb to the distraction of competitors or new, cooler and trendier brands of the moment.

» Remember that at the end of the day, this isn't heart surgery, and everything will be fine if shipments are delayed or a production run has gone sour.

» Make sure to document more of the journey along the way.

Chapter Four

Making sure your business is legal

The last chapter was all about getting you ready to get serious. Now that I've done my job of inspiring and terrifying you in equal measure, it's time to get down to business: your own small business. If you're committed to getting your biz baby up and running, the first, most important step is getting you legal. Let's walk through how to do that.

Lay the foundations

First things first, let's talk about one of the most important decisions you'll make for your business: choosing the right business structure. This is like picking the foundation for your dream home – it has to be solid, fit for purpose and able to support your big ambitions. The structure you choose will affect everything from your legal responsibilities to how you manage your finances, so let's see what's on the table.

Choose a business structure

In Australia, you've got a few main options when it comes to business structures. Each has its own set of pros and cons, so let's dive into what they are and what they mean for you. If you'd like to know more, the government's business.com.au website has pages dedicated to explaining this further.[1] The four core options are:

SOLE TRADER

A sole trader is the simplest and most common business structure. It's just you running the show, and you're legally responsible for all aspects of the business.

Pros:

» **Easy to set up:** There's minimal paperwork and start-up costs are low.
» **Full control:** You make all the decisions.
» **Simple tax reporting:** Your business income is treated as your personal income.

Cons:

» **Unlimited liability:** You're personally responsible for any debts or legal issues.
» **Limited growth potential:** It's harder to raise capital and expand.
» **Work–life balance:** It can be tough to separate personal and business life.

When to use: Perfect for freelancers, consultants or small businesses just starting out. For example, if you're a graphic designer working from home, a sole trader structure keeps things simple and straightforward.

When not to use: If you're planning to scale quickly or take on significant debt, the unlimited liability can be risky.

PARTNERSHIP

A partnership involves two or more people running a business together. There are general partnerships and limited partnerships, with varying degrees of liability for the partners.

Pros:

» **Shared responsibility:** You're not in it alone; partners share the workload and decision-making.

» **Combined resources:** Pooling resources can make it easier to start and grow the business.

» **Simple structure:** Relatively easy to set up and manage.

Cons:

» **Joint liability:** Partners are personally liable for the business's debts.

» **Potential conflicts:** Disagreements can arise, and resolving them can be tricky.

» **Shared profits:** Profits are split between partners.

When to use: Ideal for businesses with multiple founders or family businesses. For instance, if you and a friend are starting a café, a partnership allows you to share the responsibilities and rewards.

When not to use: If you prefer full control or if there's a high risk of disputes, a partnership might not be the best fit.

COMPANY

A company is a separate legal entity from its owners (shareholders). It can be a private company (Pty Ltd) or a public company (Ltd).

Pros:

>> **Limited liability:** Shareholders are not personally liable for the company's debts.

>> **Easier to raise capital:** Companies can issue shares to raise funds.

>> **Perpetual existence:** The company continues even if ownership changes.

Cons:

>> **Complex and costly:** You'll be up for more paperwork, more regulatory requirements and higher set-up costs.

>> **Fiduciary duties:** If directors breach their duties, they may be held personally liable for the company's debt.

>> **Less control:** Decisions may need to be approved by a board of directors.

When to use: Suitable for businesses planning to grow significantly or seeking external investment. For example, if you're launching a tech start-up with plans to scale and attract investors, a company structure provides the necessary framework.

When not to use: If you're a solo entrepreneur with no immediate plans for significant growth, the complexity and costs might outweigh the benefits.

TRUST

A trust is an arrangement where a trustee holds property or assets for the benefit of others (beneficiaries). There are different types of trusts, including discretionary and unit trusts.

Pros:

- » **Asset protection:** Trusts can protect assets from creditors.
- » **Tax benefits:** There's potential for tax savings through income distribution to beneficiaries.
- » **Flexibility:** Trusts can be tailored to suit specific needs and goals.

Cons:

- » **Complexity:** Setting up and managing a trust requires legal and financial expertise.
- » **Costs:** There are higher set-up and ongoing management costs.
- » **Limited control:** The trustee has legal control over the assets, which can be restrictive.

When to use: Often used for estate planning or holding family assets. If you're a family running a property investment business, a trust can provide tax benefits and asset protection.

When not to use: For small, straightforward businesses, the complexity and costs may not be justified.

OTHER OPTIONS

There are some other types of business structure that are less common but may suit your needs. They include:

» **Co-operatives:** A co-op is a legally incorporated entity that serves its members by providing goods and services, operating under principles like democracy and non-discrimination. Members share costs, have an equal say and are governed by state and territory laws.

» **Indigenous corporations:** Indigenous business owners can register as an Indigenous corporation through the Office of the Registrar of Indigenous Corporations (ORIC) to access additional benefits and support initiatives like education, housing, land security, legal assistance, infrastructure development, and promoting First Nations art and culture.

» **Joint ventures:** A joint venture is a collaboration between two or more entities for a specific project or purpose like R&D, creating a new product, providing a new service, or expanding markets. Participants share profits, losses and costs but the venture remains separate from their other business interests.

How to choose?

Sometimes it can be hard to choose which structure to run your business under. If you're unsure, it might be worth consulting with an expert. As a guide, here are some examples of the right fit for different operations:

» **Freelance photographer:** Starting out as a sole trader makes sense. It's easy to set up, and you maintain full control over your work and finances.

» **Family-owned bakery:** A partnership allows you and your family members to share responsibilities and combine resources. Just make sure you have a partnership agreement in place to avoid conflicts.

» **Tech start-up:** If you're planning to seek venture capital and scale rapidly, setting up a company provides the structure needed for growth and investment.

» **Property investment:** A family trust can offer tax benefits and protect your assets, making it a smart choice for managing property investments.

Ask the experts

This is one area where I'd really encourage you to seek independent expert advice. The future plans you have for your business will make a big impact on which structure you decide to run with, and if you don't set it up right in the first place, it could end up costing you a lot of money down the road. Making the right choice now can ensure that you, your family and your personal assets are protected. Here's where to go and who to talk to for expert advice:

» **Accountants:** can help you understand the tax implications and financial aspects of each structure.

» **Lawyers:** can guide you through the legal requirements and help with setting up more complex structures like companies and trusts.

» **Business advisers:** can offer advice to help you make informed decisions. You might seek paid independent advice tailored to your needs or seek free general advice through services like Business Australia and local business chambers.

I decided to go out on my own and start an occupational therapy business after not getting sufficient professional development and resources in a senior role. I offer services for paediatric clients and some adults in the NDIS [National Disability Insurance Scheme] space.

When I started out, I got tips from a finance officer friend, joined a Facebook group for solo private practice allied health, and had a strong reputation from working in the area. My first goal was to have enough money to set up a clinic space, which I achieved in six months. I hit $200,000 in sales last financial year.

I work in a remote area, which increases revenue. Other occupational therapists in the area are colleagues, not competition. There isn't much competition in my industry when working remotely, but keeping up with training and professional development is important.

The business has been running for two years and I wish I had given myself a budget for business expenses and retained an accountant earlier. I learnt how to change from a sole trader to a company, how to bill properly and how to budget for taking leave.

I use my personal name in my business name. Although it may limit expansion, it's great as many clients want to be with the brand. In the future, I'm not looking to expand; I just want to keep doing what I'm doing but have more holidays to reduce my risk of burnout.

Let's make it official

Once you've decided on your structure it's time to make things official. Before you start trading, you need to register your business name and business number – either an ABN (Australian Business Number) or ACN

(Australian Company Number) depending on the structure you chose. Registering your business name and acquiring an ABN are not just bureaucratic hoops to jump through, they are critical steps. It's like getting your business's birth certificate and it's essential for making everything legit and above board.

Name your business

Your business name is the name under which your business operates. It's your brand's identity and becomes how your customers will know and recognise you. In other words, it's kinda (very) important. Not only does it have to sound right, but it also has to reflect you and your business, stand out from the crowd but not alienate people, be memorable but not cringe, and roll off the tongue – bonus points if it works for optimising your Google search results.

What's more, it has to be available. Not just the name itself, but the social media handle(s) and website URL – because your digital presence is the equivalent of setting up your shopfront online. It's no good calling yourself Blue Hats and then finding ten other Blue Hats websites online and on Instagram and TikTok. While being so direct might be good for targeting search results, people will confuse you with your competitors if there are others operating under the same banner.

I WANNA MAKE US EXCLUSIVE

It's important to know that registering a business name doesn't give you exclusive rights to it. While there are protections in place that mean you can't register a business name that is identical or too similar to the registered name of another Australian business or company, this does not stop someone who has registered the name as a trademark from using it. What's more, you may be in breach if they've trademarked it – and the last thing you want is to get sued. As I always say, do your research before you get burnt.

First, if you've got a business name in mind, look it up on the various registration sites available: the ABN lookup, the trademark register and the domain name register. Does it exist? If it does, who owns it? Is it in a similar industry? Is it going to cause you issues in the future?

I have a friend who recently started a business and she didn't do that, and now she's looking at completely changing the name of the community she's built. It grew organically and she hadn't expected it to take off; now that it has, someone's come to her and said, we actually own that business – what are you doing? She's like, oh my gosh, I didn't think about this at all! And now she's having to rebrand and that's a massive struggle when you have a pre-existing audience.

ADDITIONAL CONSIDERATIONS

I would also say that even if you don't plan on going international, if you can afford to, purchase the international domains. When I established my business, I only bought 'shesonthemoney.com.au'; I didn't purchase '.com'. Ultimately that shot me in the foot because we had a copycat company pop up in the UK and that wasn't fun. Thankfully, it doesn't exist anymore (it's rebranded), but I ended up spending a lot of money purchasing that domain from them because, ultimately, I'd like to grow She's on the Money to be an international business and, especially for people in the US, they prefer to support '.com' businesses.

How to choose?

But how to choose? First, go back to the previous chapter – look around, do your market research and customer research. You likely have a feel for what's happening out there, but if not, make a point of finding out. If you're in the early phase of an industry or idea, you may be fortunate enough to nab a name that states exactly what you do, thereby securing SEO wins and memory-grabbing attention.

FOR EXAMPLE: MOBILE SKIPS

Take Mobile Skips, for example. While it may not sound like the most sexy of businesses, it was very deliberately targeted by local entrepreneur Jacob Spencer, who'd been trained up through working at Boost Juice with Janine Allis. Jacob saw an opportunity to fill a gap in the market and bought an underperforming business called Mobile Skips. In 2023 it turned over $8 million, thanks to the efficient franchise system and unique skip bin design he developed. Among the many strategies he deployed, he focused on a highly effective SEO strategy, supported by the decision to stick with the simple and direct name: Mobile Skips. Not only does the name clearly identify what the business does, it also highlights its competitive advantage and the business culture that drives it – mobile, flexible and agile. Simplicity is key to everything Jacob stands for and is the cornerstone of his business success.[2]

Register your business name

Ready to make it official? Here's how to register your business name in Australia:

1. **Choose your name:** Make sure it's unique and reflects your brand. You can check if the name is available using the Australian Securities and Investments Commission (ASIC) website.

2. **Create an ASIC Connect account:** Go to the ASIC website and create an account. This is where you'll manage your business name registration.

3. **Register your name:** Once your account is set up, follow the prompts to register your business name. You'll need to provide details like your proposed business name, your ABN (more on this next) and your contact information.

4. **Pay the fee:** There's a small fee to register your business name – at the time of writing it was $37 for one year or $87 for three years.

5. **Receive confirmation:** Once registered, you'll receive a confirmation email from ASIC and your business name will be officially registered.

Obtain an ABN/ACN

An ABN (Australian Business Number) is an eleven-digit number that uniquely identifies your business to the government and the community. If you are running a business or supply goods and services to other businesses, you'll need an ABN. In addition, if you have a company structure, you'll also need an ACN (Australian Company Number). Acquiring an ABN is free and quite straightforward. As well as being a legal requirement, ABNs are useful to:

» **Facilitate business transactions:** Many suppliers and customers will require you to have an ABN, and many larger companies will withhold 47 per cent of your payment if you don't include an ABN on your invoice.

» **Enable you to register for GST and claim GST credits:** If your business has a turnover of $75,000 or more, you must register for

GST. If you're registered for GST, you can claim credits for the GST you pay on purchases.

» **Simplify tax and business reporting:** Use your ABN to register for GST if necessary and to file your tax returns. It simplifies the process and ensures you're meeting all legal requirements.

» **Enable access to grants and opportunities:** Your ABN allows you to access various government services and grants that can support your business growth.

RUN THE CHECKLIST

The Australian Government requires you to complete a series of registrations in order to legally operate a business in Australia. When setting up an ABN it uses a list of indicators to determine whether your activity amounts to a business. While not all of these must apply for you to be eligible, it is expected that your business will demonstrate several of the following features:

» an intention to engage in commercial activity
» an intention to make a profit from the activity
» activity is of a recurrent or regular nature
» activity is carried on in a similar manner to that of other businesses in the same or similar trades
» activity is systematic, organised and carried on in a businesslike manner and records are kept
» activity is of a reasonable size and scale
» a business plan exists
» the entity has relevant knowledge or skill.[3]

HOW TO ACQUIRE AN ABN

To obtain an ABN, you simply go to the ABR (Australian Business Register) website and complete the online application. It's free and usually takes about 15 minutes. You'll need details like your tax file number (TFN), business structure and contact information to complete the form and should receive your ABN back within 28 days.

Protect yourself!

Now that you're registered, it's time to look at protecting your business value. In Chapter 8 we'll discuss operational protections such as insurances and risk mitigation, but here we're looking at how you might protect that special something that makes your business unique – otherwise known as IP (intellectual property). Intellectual property refers to creations of the mind, such as inventions (recipes, products and systems), literary and artistic works, and designs, symbols, names and images used for commerce. It is the secret sauce (literally, in some cases) that makes your business sing.

Protecting it ensures you have exclusive rights to use, produce and profit from your creations. Whether its your brand name or logo, a unique product design, an innovative system, or even that catchy jingle you created, protecting your IP is essential for safeguarding your business's assets and competitive edge.

IS IT REALLY WORTH IT?

If you have aspirations of scale, then I think it's worth investing in protections up-front as defending them can be really expensive. Even then, there's no guarantees.

At the start of my business journey, I thought if I purchased the trademark no-one could ever touch me, but unfortunately that's not the whole story. As I touched on earlier with regard to registering a business name, although this has some protections, they're not impenetrable. Knowing which IP protections to take up can get quite complicated, not to mention costly. It's not always necessary or even useful to buy up every IP option available.

As with most complicated things, if your business relies on a specific unique element as its point of difference, then it's worth speaking with an expert – an IP lawyer or patent attorney is a good place to start.

Types of intellectual property rights

There are several types of IP rights, each offering different levels of protection. Let's break them down in easy-to-understand terms.

TRADEMARKS

A trademark is a sign, symbol, word or phrase that distinguishes your goods or services from those of others – in other words, your brand's identity. Setting up a trademark is perfect for businesses with a unique brand name, logo or slogan. For example, if you're launching a new clothing line, a trademark protects your brand identity and ensures no-one else can use your name or logo. However, if your brand name is generic or descriptive, it may not qualify for trademark protection.

If you find a trademark similar to yours that already exists, it may be possible for both trademarks to coexist if the goods and services they relate to are different. For example, DOVE soap and DOVE chocolate. Although both trademarks are for the same word, soap and chocolate are considered to be different goods with a different purpose and sold through different trade channels.

Pros:

>> **Brand protection:** A trademark prevents others from using your brand name or logo.

>> **Market recognition:** It helps customers identify and trust your products.

>> **Legal recourse:** As the owner of the trademark, you have legal grounds to take action against infringement.

Cons:

>> **Cost:** Registering a trademark can be expensive.

>> **Maintenance:** A trademark requires ongoing renewal and enforcement.

PATENTS

A patent protects new inventions or discoveries, granting the inventor exclusive rights to use, make and sell the invention for a certain period (usually 20 years). It is legally enforceable and protects any device, substance, method or process that is new, inventive and useful. It does not protect artistic creations, mathematical models, plans, schemes or mental processes. A standard patent provides long-term protection and control from the day you lodge your application.[4]

Patents are ideal for businesses with unique, innovative products or technologies. For example, if you've developed a groundbreaking medical device, a patent protects your invention and allows you to capitalise on it. However, if your invention is likely to become obsolete quickly, the lengthy patent process may not be worth it.

Pros:

>> **Exclusive rights:** A patent prevents others from making, using or selling your invention.

>> **Competitive advantage:** It gives you a monopoly on your invention.

>> **Potential for licensing:** You can license your patent to others for a fee.

Cons:

>> **Complexity:** The application process is lengthy and complicated.

>> **Cost:** The costs for application, maintenance and enforcement are high.

>> **Public disclosure:** You must publicly disclose details of your invention.

COPYRIGHT

Copyright protects original works of authorship, including literary, artistic, musical and dramatic works. It gives the creator exclusive rights to reproduce, distribute and display the work and means others can't use it without the creator's agreement. For example, if you're a photographer, copyright ensures that your photos can't be used without your permission.

In Australia we're well protected by copyright laws, which means it's not usually necessary to independently register copyright. Nonetheless, it's usually worth adding a copyright statement to your website and unique creative content to protect you globally.

It's equally important as a business operator to ensure you don't infringe others' copyright – for instance, reposting another person's imagery or words for commercial gain without their agreement is a breach of Australian copyright laws. The right to 'fair dealing' allows material to be used without permission for research/study, criticism/ review, parody/satire or reporting news.[5] However if you will be profiting from the exercise, you should seek permission before you proceed. In all cases, it's best practice to credit the creator and link to their work. For more information, visit the Australian Copyright Council's website.

Pros:
- » **Automatic protection:** Copyright protection is automatic upon creation.
- » **Broad coverage:** A wide range of creative works are protected.
- » **Duration:** Protection lasts for the creator's lifetime plus 70 years.

Cons:
- » **Limited scope:** Copyright only protects the expression of ideas, not the ideas themselves.
- » **Enforcement:** It can be challenging and costly to enforce.

DESIGNS

A design right protects the visual appearance of a new and distinctive product, such as its shape, configuration, pattern or ornamentation. It gives you exclusive rights to use, license and sell the design for a maximum of ten years, preventing others from using it without your permission.

These are ideal for businesses with unique product designs. For example, if you've created a stylish new furniture line, design rights protect the distinctive look of your products. If your product's value lies in its functionality rather than its appearance, you would instead go for a patent.

Pros:

>> **Aesthetic protection:** The unique look of your product is safe-guarded.

>> **Market differentiation:** A design right helps distinguish your products from those of competitors.

>> **Exclusive rights:** Others are prevented from copying your design.

Cons:

>> **Limited protection:** Design rights only cover visual appearance, not functionality.

>> **Cost:** Registration can be expensive.

>> **Maintenance:** The right requires renewal to maintain protection.

ADDITIONAL PROTECTIONS

In addition, there are two further industry-specific IP protections available, for 'computer-generated circuits' and for 'plant breeds', which can be registered with IP Australia. Furthermore, you may protect your business IP through trade secrets. A trade secret is confidential information – think a formula, process or customer list – that provides a business with a competitive edge. Let's say you have a secret recipe for a popular food product. You'll want to keep it as a trade secret to protect your competitive advantage.

With trade secrets, no registration is required as protection is based on trust and secrecy. Employee and supplier contracts often contain clauses that aim to specify this but keeping people accountable can be difficult and costly to enforce. The advantage of relying on trade secrets to protect your IP is that they cost nothing and cover a wide range of confidential business information, and as long as the information remains secret, it's protected. Nonetheless, if the information is critical to your business advantage and there's any chance of others independently discovering or reverse-engineering it, you may want to consider registering your protections using the formal mechanisms above.

What to use when

Not everything in your business needs formal IP protection. Sometimes, the sheer complexity of attempting to mimic your process can protect it – the amount of time a competitor would need to do so offers its own in-built safety net (eat my dust, suckers!). There are times when it's worth paying for some muscle men in the form of legal protection and times when it's not. For instance:

» **Tech start-up:** You've developed a unique software application. A patent protects your innovation, while a trademark ensures your brand name and logo are safeguarded.

» **Fashion brand:** You've designed a distinctive clothing line. Trademarks protect your brand name and logo, while design rights protect the unique look of your products.

» **Author:** You've written a novel. Copyright automatically protects your literary work, ensuring no-one can reproduce or distribute it without your permission.

» **Food business:** You have a secret recipe for a bestselling sauce. Keeping it as a trade secret ensures your competitive edge remains protected.

I have a dog-walking and training business. As part of my services, I offer dog walking, behaviour and obedience-based consultations, walk-and-trains, and pet-sitting/check-in services and I'm looking to expand into an online retail store. I've been running the business for eight months.

I've found the transition from full-time work to having my own business incredibly hard. I've realised how essential it is to have a business emergency fund, savings and expense accounts. Looking back, I should have kept a part-time job and been more realistic with my business spending.

Before starting the business I looked up legal requirements like getting an ABN, but that was the extent of my research. Due to the unregulated and high-risk nature of the industry, I quickly learnt the importance of legal protection and proper documentation.

Australian business laws and regulations

Okay, let's revisit our *Legally Blonde* era and look a little closer at the law side of your new biz venture. If Reese Witherspoon can make torts look glamorous (and I'm not talking chocolate cake here), then I know you can, too. Besides, I know you're a boss babe or you wouldn't be reading this book in the first place, which means there's definitely a part of you that likes rules. So think of this section as your business's rulebook – knowing the guidelines inside out ensures you play the game right and gives you the best chance of being the winner, winner, chicken dinner.

One of the best things Australia has going for it is its robust legal framework. Though it can occasionally feel a little restrictive on the personal front, in business and consumer terms it really does provide us with a lot of protections. Our laws ensure fair trading, protect consumers and keep competition fair, creating a level playing field for businesses. Here's a rundown of the most important laws and regulations you need to know.

Comply with these

Sure, business regulations can feel like the less exciting parts of business – but keeping on the right side of the law is a must. Staying compliant isn't just about avoiding penalties; it's about building a trustworthy, sustainable and successful business. It will protect you now and into the future, so all the hard work you've put into building your business can bear fruit. The various business laws and regulations Australian businesses need to adhere to include:

AUSTRALIAN CONSUMER LAW (ACL)

You best believe that I, Ms Victoria Devine, will fight for every last cent I'm owed, especially when it comes to clawing back my rights from dodgy operators. And I hope through my *She's on the Money* rants over the years that I've inspired you to do that, too! We all hate being ripped off, especially when we work so hard for our coin. So, if you're going to go into business, don't become one of the dark ones. Treat your customers as you would like to be treated – or even better. Be the queen you were born to be. People will remember you for it and you'll feel good inside, too.

One of the most important laws in place to protect us is the Australian Consumer Law. Designed to protect consumers and ensure fair trading across Australia, covering areas like product safety, consumer rights and misleading advertising, it is made enforceable by penalties and compensation. It covers both large and small businesses, formal and informal contracts and all retail sales channels, including online, phone, over-the-counter and door-to-door.[6]

Consumer law applies to all Australian businesses that sell goods or services, including businesses that are overseas. Whether you work with customers or businesses, provide services or sell goods, you must know how ACL affects your business. For example, if you run a retail store, you must comply with the law by providing accurate product descriptions and honouring consumer guarantees. There's no opting out of ACL – it's mandatory for all businesses dealing with consumers.

Some examples of how you must comply with the ACL include:

» If your customer asks for an itemised bill, you must provide it free of charge.

» If you sell goods or services worth more than $75 (excluding GST), you must give your customer a receipt.

» Your receipts must include information identifying: you (the supplier), your ABN and/or ACN (if any), what was supplied, the date of supply and the price.

» If the goods or services do not meet a consumer guarantee (for example, where goods are not of acceptable quality), your customer has the right to ask for a refund, replacement or repair where:

- the goods or services are under $100,000

- the goods are over $100,000 and normally bought for personal or household use

- the goods are business vehicles or trailers mainly used to transport goods.

» If there is a problem with your goods or service and you could have reasonably foreseen the problem, your customer has the right to ask you for compensation for damage or loss.

» You cannot have a store policy and/or signs in store that seek to override consumer guarantee rights (for example, 'no refunds' or 'no refunds on sale items'). This is unlawful.

PRIVACY ACT

The Australian *Privacy Act 1988* regulates how businesses handle personal information, ensuring it's collected, used and stored responsibly. It's designed to protect your customers' privacy and builds trust in your business, and it applies if your business collects personal information. For example, if you run an online store, you must comply with the Privacy Act by securing customer data and providing a clear privacy policy.

In recent years, managing people's privacy has become increasingly important and regulated. If you operate globally, you may also have to comply with international data laws such as Europe's General Data Protection Regulation (GDPR). Regardless of size, any Australian business may need to comply if it has an establishment in the European Union (EU), offers goods and services in the EU or monitors the behaviour of individuals in the EU.

The GDPR and the Australian Privacy Act share many common requirements, including those to:

» implement a privacy-by-design approach to compliance
» be able to demonstrate compliance with privacy principles and obligations
» adopt transparent information handling practices.

However, there are also some notable differences in the GDPR, including certain rights of individuals (such as the 'right to be forgotten') that do not have an equivalent right under the Privacy Act.[7] For example, you may run an Australian fashion company based in Melbourne, Victoria, selling internationally. If you track and analyse EU visitors to your company's website or store their personal data for shipping purposes, then you may be subject to the provisions of the GDPR as well as our local Privacy Act.[8]

FAIR WORK ACT

The *Fair Work Act 2009* governs employment relationships in Australia, including minimum wages, working conditions and employee rights. It's designed to ensure you provide fair and lawful working conditions, which in turn helps attract and retain good employees. The Act applies to all businesses with employees. Say you own a café – you must comply with the Fair Work Act by paying staff the correct wages and providing appropriate working conditions. If you're a sole trader with no employees, the Fair Work Act won't apply to you.

The Fair Work Act and its related Fair Work system are managed by the Fair Work Ombudsman, whose website is chock-full of details about all aspects of your responsibilities as an employer and the rights of your employees. It covers such things as:

» **Pay and wages:** Pay guides for all levels of worker, including apprentices, trainees and juniors, and covering casual, part-time and full-time employees.

» **Leave:** Paid sick and carer's leave, parental leave and long service leave.

» **Employment conditions:** A list of industry awards and the National Employment Standards conditions, public holidays and breaks.

» **Managing workplace issues:** Common problems, how to fix them and where to go for help.

» **Ending employment:** Notice periods, redundancy, final pay and entitlements, and unfair dismissal.

While I love Fair Work for my employees, the terriblest (add to dictionary, please) thing about it is that it exists *only* to protect employees. If you're one of the vast majority of Aussie small business owners who are sole traders, sadly none of these protections are in place for you. That means you must take extra care to provide them for yourself. It's super easy to pour your heart and soul into your business and not schedule any time off, but you must or you will burn out eventually – and then what's going to happen to your biz baby? Perhaps reading through these workplace awards and conditions could help you create a set of goals outlining protections you can put in place for yourself.

WORKPLACE HEALTH AND SAFETY LAWS

Workplace health and safety (WHS), otherwise called occupational health and safety (OH&S) laws, ensure safe working conditions for employees and cover areas like risk management, employee training and incident reporting.[9] Not only can WHS compliance reduce injury and illness and lessen the costs of injury and workers compensation, but it can also have the added bonus of boosting morale and productivity. I mean, who doesn't love seeing Lucy from Accounts herding everyone down the back stairs while wearing her Fireman Sam helmet. Personally, I'll always take a coffee break, too, especially if it's mandated.

Health and safety laws apply to all businesses, and not just to your workers but to your customers, visitors and suppliers, too. These laws even apply to remote workers, so yes, you are responsible for ensuring that your staff's work-from-home environment is safe, and that your WHS policies and procedures include those working remotely. You may have to update your policies to account for this.

With all your employees, both at home and in the office, think about:

>> how staff can report incidents or injuries
>> how to set up safe working environments
>> providing access to equipment
>> providing information to support mental health and wellbeing.

You must put health and safety practices in place as soon as you start your business. It can cost money and time to implement WHS practices and install safety equipment, but not taking action can result in prosecution, fines and loss of your skilled staff. Workers compensation laws also require you to have a workers compensation insurance policy for your employees (there's more about insurance in Chapter 8).

OVER TO YOU Consider what supports and protections you can put in place to keep your employees safe at work — whether from home or in the office. What aspects of HR do you need to formalise as policies?

CORPORATIONS ACT

The *Corporations Act* 2001 governs the formation and operation of companies in Australia, including directors' duties, financial reporting and corporate governance. This means your company will operate legally and transparently, which is crucial for attracting investors and maintaining credibility. The Corporations Act only applies if you're running a company. For instance, if you've incorporated your tech start-up, you must comply with the Act by keeping accurate financial records and holding annual general meetings (AGMs). If you're a sole trader or partnership, the Act won't apply to you.

When we talk about determining which business structure is right for you, noting that it may cost more to manage structures that deliver stronger personal protections, it's these kinds of reporting requirements that we're talking about. Often it becomes easier to engage professional services – such as a tax accountant and/or legal adviser – to assist with preparing and submitting such reports, too, which is a further cost to consider.

TAXATION LAWS

Australia's taxation laws cover various taxes that businesses must pay, including income tax, GST and pay-as-you-go (PAYG) withholding. The ATO is very active in Australia so it's important that you stay on top of your requirements and keep good records. You want to ensure you meet your tax obligations and avoid penalties.

Unfortunately, there's no getting around it – tax applies to all businesses, regardless of size or structure. If you're a solopreneur, you must comply with taxation laws by lodging your tax returns and paying GST if you exceed the threshold. However, as we always say, paying tax is a good problem to have – you only have to pay it if your business is making a profit, and if your business ends up running at a loss over the year, you can carry your tax losses forward against profits in the following year.

Near the end of each financial year, we always run a few special *She's on the Money* podcast episodes highlighting how to get prepared and make the most of tax time. For instance, if you know you need to upgrade your laptop, June can be a good time to buy a new one. Often retailers offer EOFY (end of financial year) specials, and the large expense may help bring your earnings down to a lower tax threshold. So tune in to our podcast specials each year for more hot tips based on what the ATO has announced that they are targeting and for any opportunities we've spotted for you!

ENVIRONMENTAL LAWS

Environmental laws regulate how businesses impact the environment, covering areas like waste management, pollution control and resource conservation. These laws ensure your business operates sustainably and responsibly, which can enhance your reputation and attract eco-conscious customers.

Environmental regulations affecting small businesses in Australia stem from both state and federal levels. These laws might relate to waste management, emissions, water use and hazardous materials handling. The *Environment Protection and Biodiversity Conservation Act 1999* (EPBC Act) is the primary environmental law of the Commonwealth of Australia; it's designed to protect our wildlife and natural environments.

To run your company legally, you must research and comply with all applicable regulations. At the time of writing, amendments are being made to the EPBC Act, including formalising a new set of National Environmental Standards,[10] so it's important to keep on top of any changes. Ensuring sustainable practices, obtaining necessary permits and conducting regular environmental impact assessments are vital.

The key to effective environmental management is planning and setting priorities. In addition to meeting legal requirements, many businesses also make efforts to minimise their operation's ecological footprint regardless of their size or industry. This is great – but don't overexaggerate! The consumer watchdog, the Australian Competition and Consumer Commission (ACCC), is keeping an eye out for green-washing – where a business uses a claim or omits key information that makes a product or service seem better or less harmful for the environment than it really is. To stay on its good side, the ACCC advises that:

>> environment and sustainability claims must be truthful and accurate

>> you should have reasonable grounds for making representation about future events

>> businesses have responsibilities under the Australian Consumer Law (ACL) not to make false or misleading claims

>> a business needs to consider the claims it makes. It also needs to consider the information that's left out and the visual elements, colours and logos used.[11]

So, by all means, please do your part to help save our beautiful planet, but don't lie about it. If you do, you're not just hurting yourself but everyone else and the innocent koalas, too. So. Just. Don't.

Principle 4: Lay strong foundations

Spend time laying solid foundations and ensuring your business is set up to operate legally. How you structure your business could have significant impacts down the track, so take the time to think through both your immediate and long-term objectives. It won't guarantee a straight line, but it will help you get there.

Meet the founder: Jasmine Dowling

Jasmine Dowling has built a business from creating stunning online content and has developed a successful creative career that includes work for some of Australia's biggest and brightest fashion and beauty brands. Her visually enticing content is testament to her skills as an artist and business owner.

Name: Jasmine Dowling

Business: Studio Jasmine

Industry: Creative

Product/service: I deliver still life and in-motion creative campaigns for clients predominantly in the beauty space. I also work as an artist/illustrator and design for brands across the beauty, fashion and lifestyle industries, sell my own prints, and collaborate on products such as phone cases. Lastly, I do a mixture of the above as a content creator and I partner with brands.

Target audience: Brands within the beauty/fashion space

Secondary audience: People between 25 to 35 interested in all things beauty, fashion, lifestyle and creativity

Unique selling point: Creating high-quality and visually stunning content

The business began: 2013

Starting my business happened organically. In 2013 I was sharing my personal design work on social media while doing a Bachelor of Design, and had interest from my very small audience to sell my work and freelance on small projects. I thought, *Why not? It will be a great way to get more experience before I graduate and move into an agency role.* However, by the time I graduated I was booking work consistently enough to sustain myself full time. I had always worked well independently and am very self-motivated, so being self-employed suited me.

My services have evolved a lot. I started mainly working as a graphic designer/illustrator, working with brands on campaign typography and selling artworks. Early on I faced a lot of legal issues around copyright infringement and fighting large corporations. Going through that changed how I viewed the work at the time and I started leaning more into other creative avenues I loved, like photography and, later, creative direction and videography.

My business has a management team that helps run the communication and contract side of my social media partnerships. This is an area I had very little experience in and having the team means I'm able to spend more time creating and less time on emails, which is always my goal. When I bring external people into my business, it should help me spend less time doing the tasks I don't enjoy and more time focusing on the tasks I do.

I learnt to outsource the financial side of the business when I needed to. I started working with an accountant the first year I was working for myself full time. After my first BAS [business activity statement] arrived, I realised I had no idea what I was doing and I needed a professional! Even though I knew I could understand the cash flow of my business quite well, I can be quite anxious about money, so I wanted to know that area of my business was in good hands. It meant I could sleep well at night if I was ever audited.

The best thing about working for myself is the creative freedom and flexibility it allows me. I'm at the point now that I can choose what work

I take on and what isn't the right fit. The ability to choose projects that I find creatively fulfilling is the main reason why I have chosen to keep working for myself. Secondly, there's the flexibility. Even though I would say my hours are much more than the usual nine to five, I know if I ever need to book in a doctor's appointment or take a month off, I can. No-one is there to tell me no; I just need to deal with the financial consequences.

Then there's the other side of the coin: the reality of working for yourself is that everything comes down to you. Your to-do list is never-ending. When things are bad, the only person to blame is yourself and the only person to get you out of it is yourself. You experience any wins alone, too.

Pursuing legal actions against large corporations for infringing my copyright has been another big challenge. Looking back, I don't know if I'd do the same again, and I hate admitting that. As much as I think it's very important to stand up for creative rights and for your work, I don't think it achieved what I hoped it would. It unfortunately doesn't change how large corporations treat creative work, and 'copies' or 'dupes' have only become more common. It didn't teach anyone not to steal from artists. Even though all cases went in my favour, early on in my career I felt it took a lot of time (six to 12 months for each case, with some overlapping) and money, and it took a toll on me mentally in relation to my work.

But all things considered, I wouldn't complain about my business journey to date. My work–life balance has never got to the point where I'm missing out on big life moments, so I don't have any memorable regrets there. I definitely push myself quite hard when it comes to my work, but I think I've been rewarded with opportunities because of that. (I don't know if it's delusional to think those two things are related.)

As for a lot of business owners, for me the line between work and personal is blurry. Working as a creative person, it's hard to say that I will only be creative between the hours of X and X, which means work inevitably bleeds into all hours of the day. Since social media is a part of my business, that also bleeds into hours well beyond the traditional nine to five.

I have recently taken email off my phone (unless I'm travelling for work) to stop those late-night or weekend 'let me see if they've replied' habits, but I could definitely be better at sticking to a healthy work–life balance. As I've become older, I've realised that I've developed the habit of putting my work before myself to meet self-imposed expectations. I definitely need to put in some better boundaries and non-negotiables for myself to regain some of that balance.

I would tell any aspiring business owner to celebrate the wins, because it all happens so fast, even if you're currently stressed about the next thing. Secondly, set some boundaries between yourself and your work so you get into the habit early. It's much harder to put them in place later.

Chapter Five

Financing your small business

This chapter is all about setting up your business for financial success. It might be hard to fathom, since I'm a trained financial adviser, but getting the financials right for my first business really caught me out. Before starting out, I thought the financial part would be the easy bit for me and the complicated parts would be setting up business things like ABNs (as we discussed in Chapter 4). But turns out that those were the easy bits and the parts I thought I had totally under control – budget and cash flow – really threw me for a sixer.

Although I'm all about financial forecasts and budgets, I soon realised that trying to predict what things were going to cost in a business I'd never run before was a lot harder than it sounds. I mean, you can do six million beautiful projections and it makes sense on paper, right? Based on a typical financial advice business, I thought I had my projections down. A standard practice covers its costs in thirds: one third of the income for business overheads, the second third for salary, and the final third for profitability. So I had this really clean structure, but in reality that's not how it worked. Our rent took up different amounts of the business and our overheads were a bit different to other people's, and it really came down to trying to budget and work out the unique operations of my business – which, it turned out, couldn't be based on anyone else's.

It was a good lesson for me: the things I thought would be easy were hard, and the things I thought would be hard were easier than I expected. Consider me your fairy godmother here, because I truly wish someone had sat me down and been like, actually, although the spreadsheets are going to be easy to put together, the reality is going to be harder. Never be afraid to ask questions or to engage support, and always keep learning.

Cash flow and budgeting

No matter whether you start it as a passion project or you're gunning for world domination, the ultimate goal of your business is to be profitable. And one of the most crucial aspects of running a profitable business is managing cash flow and budgeting. Think of cash flow as the lifeblood of your business – it keeps everything running smoothly. Without proper management, even the most promising business can run into trouble.

Managing cash flow means keeping track of the money coming into and going out of your business. Budgeting involves planning your finances to ensure you have enough funds to cover your expenses and invest in growth.

Getting started

From the start, managing cash flow and budgeting is essential. Whether that's a simple spreadsheet or you have a full Xero set-up, will depend on what works for you. But you can calculate all of it before spending a dollar. You can work out what your initial investment cost is going to be to set up the business. You can google what your ABN registration is going to cost. You can google what trademarking would cost. You can call up lawyers and make inquiries about how much things might cost to set up. If you need any licences, you can look that up; if you need any industry memberships, you can look that up too. If you're establishing a product-based business, there's nothing stopping you from reaching out to a supplier and understanding the costs of quotes, your minimum order quantities, what shipping might cost, and what insurance for that shipping might cost.

Now, put all that into a spreadsheet so you can assess your business idea critically, with all the costs up-front. In business there are a lot of, I won't say 'hidden costs', but costs that you didn't think about to begin with. So while there are many things you can do to protect yourself in the immediate term, there are always going to be things that pop up later that are specific to your industry. You're never going to capture everything in your initial forecasts, but nonetheless it's crucial to try to enter as much information and do as much pre-planning as you can. Dive as deep as you can and ask as many questions as possible before you get started, to help uncover things like software licences and professional accreditation and WorkCover insurance. These are all really important to budget for.

I absolutely advocate for having an emergency fund, too, like you would for your own personal expenses. While it may not seem feasible at the outset, as soon as you start earning income, make sure you're setting some back-up funds aside, especially in the first year – the number of community and founder business stories where people have been caught out with a huge first-year tax bill is incredibly high! Prioritising an emergency fund means you've got something to fall back on if your projections are slightly off – which they will inevitably be to begin with, until you get into a bit of a flow. So many businesses were caught out because of Covid – some with unexpected growth, others with unplanned declines. Knowing you have back-up funds can really help you sleep at night during those tough times.

The three key financial statements

SOTM community members will be very familiar with my fangirling about good cash flow and budgeting systems. To manage cash flow and budgeting effectively in business, you need to understand and use three key financial statements:

1. INCOME STATEMENT (P&L)

Also known as the profit and loss (P&L) statement, the income statement shows your business's revenues and expenses over a specific period, resulting in a net profit or loss. Your P&L statement helps you understand your business's profitability and identify areas where you can cut costs or increase revenue. As such, you should track it regularly to monitor your financial performance. Let's say you run a retail store – reviewing your income statement monthly can help you identify trends and make adjustments to boost profitability.

2. BALANCE SHEET

The balance sheet provides a snapshot of your business's financial position at a specific point in time, showing your assets, liabilities and equity. You should review it periodically to assess your business's financial health. For instance, if you're a tech start-up looking to attract investors, a strong balance sheet can demonstrate your business's value and stability. Beyond just your day-to-day cash flow, your balance sheet helps you understand your business's net worth and financial stability, which is crucial for making investment decisions and securing loans.

3. CASH FLOW STATEMENT

Your cash flow statement tracks the flow of cash in and out of your business over a specific period, divided into operating, investing and financing activities. You should be reviewing this regularly to manage your cash flow effectively. It helps you understand your liquidity and ensures you have enough cash to cover your expenses and investments. Take a café, for example. Reviewing the business's cash flow statement weekly can help the owner make sure they have enough cash to cover payroll and inventory purchases.

WHEN TO USE WHICH STATEMENT

1. **Early stage start-up:** You've just launched an online store. Focus on your income statement to track sales and expenses, and use the cash flow statement to ensure you have enough cash to cover marketing and inventory costs.

2. **Growing business:** Your tech start-up is scaling rapidly. Use the balance sheet to demonstrate your financial stability to potential investors, and the cash flow statement to manage your liquidity as you expand.

3. **Established business:** You run a successful café. Regularly review all three statements to ensure profitability, financial health and sufficient cash flow to cover ongoing expenses and invest in new opportunities.

Getting help

From Excel spreadsheets to online accounting systems, there are plenty of tools available to help you manage your cash flow and budgeting. In Australia, some popular options are:

1. **Xero:** Cloud-based accounting software that helps you manage your finances and generate financial statements.

2. **MYOB:** Popular accounting software that offers comprehensive financial management tools.

3. **QuickBooks:** Easy-to-use accounting software ideal for small businesses.

4. **Wave:** Free accounting software that's great for start-ups and small businesses.

5. **Cash flow forecasting tools:** Tools like Float and Fathom that can help you predict and manage your cash flow.

Once your business becomes a little more complex, it's worth considering engaging an external professional, such as a bookkeeper or an accountant, to help manage your finances and ensure you meet your legal obligations. This is often the first hire business founders make. While it's always important to keep a close eye on the performance of your business and regularly review your numbers, having someone managing the data entry (bookkeeper) and reviewing your finances (accountant) can save you time and deliver peace of mind.

OVER TO YOU

How can you streamline the financial aspects of managing your business — either through using software or outsourcing to professionals? Can you establish some routine practices to make your finance processes more efficient?

Know your obligations

As with all great things, running a business comes with its fair share of responsibilities. Here we'll dive into the nitty-gritty of accounting and tax obligations – crucial elements that can make or break your business dreams. Don't worry, though – we'll break it down in a way that's easy to understand and easy to put into action!

Accounting obligations are the responsibilities you have to keep accurate financial records for your business. They include tracking income, expenses, assets and liabilities. Think of them as the financial diary of your business. Tax obligations refer to the requirements set by the Australian Taxation Office (ATO) to report and pay taxes on your business income. They include goods and services tax (GST), pay-as-you-go (PAYG) withholding, and other relevant taxes.

Key obligations

1. **ABN registration:** Every business needs an Australian Business Number (ABN). It's your business's unique identifier. See Chapter 4 for more information.
2. **GST registration:** If your business has a turnover of $75,000 or more, you must register for GST.
3. **Record keeping:** Keep all financial records for at least five years. This includes receipts, invoices and bank statements.
4. **BAS lodgement:** If registered for GST, you need to lodge business activity statements (BAS) regularly.
5. **Income tax returns:** Lodge your business's income tax return annually.
6. **Superannuation:** If you have employees, you must pay super contributions.

7. **PAYG withholding:** Withhold tax from employee wages and report it to the ATO.

Find support

There's a lot to manage in terms of your business accounts and tax. Often these jobs are the first you might outsource as a business operator. Even though I formally qualified as a financial adviser, hiring a business accountant was one of my top priorities once my business could afford it.

ACCOUNTANT

An accountant can help you set up your financial systems, advise on tax matters and ensure compliance. They can provide personalised advice, expertise in tax laws and peace of mind. Of course, they come at a cost – albeit tax deductible – which may be expensive in the early stages.

SELF-EDUCATION

The alternative to outsourcing is educating yourself, and if your accounts aren't too complicated, the ATO's website might have all the information you need.[1] You can attend online or in-person workshops on small business tax and accounting, many of which are run for free or subsidised by local councils or support services. While they are inexpensive and can be great networking opportunities, they may also be time-consuming and may not cover your specific needs.

TOOLS

There are a bunch of tools to help you meet your accounting and tax obligations. They include:

» **Accounting software:** Tools like Xero, MYOB and QuickBooks can automate many accounting tasks. Using this type of software can help save time and reduce errors. It's designed to be easy to use but generally comes with monthly subscription fees and a steep learning curve.

» **ATO online services:** The ATO provides free online tools to help manage your tax obligations. They are directly linked to the ATO but are limited to tax-related tasks and are not a full accounting solution.

» **Expense-tracking apps:** Apps like Expensify and Receipt Bank help you track expenses on the go. They can be super convenient as they integrate with accounting software, but some may incur additional costs and may require manual input.

WHAT'S THE WORST THAT COULD HAPPEN?

Several issues could arise if you fail to meet your accounting and tax obligations, including:

» **Penalties and fines:** Failing to lodge BAS or pay taxes on time can result in hefty fines.

» **Cash flow issues:** Poor financial management can lead to cash flow problems, making it hard to pay bills and employees.

» **Legal trouble:** Not complying with tax laws can result in legal action from the ATO.

» **Business closure:** In extreme cases, poor financial management can lead to business failure.

Small business funding options

Starting a business is super exciting, but let's face it – you need money to make your dreams a reality. Whether you're launching a tech start-up, opening a cosy café or starting a fashion line, securing the right funding is crucial.

In my first business, I didn't seek funding to begin with for a number of reasons. One, I didn't know where to get it. I didn't know how to research it, what to look into; I probably thought it was just about going to the bank and asking for a loan. Now, my thoughts on funding are that you need to do what's right for you – it might be right for some people but not for others. I don't want to bring in an investor who gets to own part of my business as it grows and scales, but for you, that might work really well.

Let's have a look at the various funding options available and how to choose the best one for your business.

Bootstrapping

Bootstrapping is not just the cool kids' way of saying you're funding yourself using your own money. It's a little more than that. The full definition, for business, is: not relying on external sources to build and grow. So, as well as the coin, it implies that you're relying on your own smarts and sheer hard work. In other words, bootstrapping means only using existing resources, such as personal savings, personal computing equipment and garage space, to start and grow a company – as opposed to bringing in investors to provide capital, or taking on debt to fund a business's expansion. It's about stretching what you've got – whatever that is – to get the job done.

This type of funding is ideal for businesses just starting out if they have low start-up costs. For example, if you're starting a freelance graphic design business, personal savings might be enough to cover initial expenses like software and marketing. Bootstrapping shows you're committed and reduces the need for external funding. It can reduce the stress of starting out, as the only person you need to pay is yourself. There's no additional pressure (yet!) to repay loans or turn a profit, so you can put all your energy into developing your business.

Australia has a history of successful entrepreneurs who bootstrapped and created global companies. Tech giant Atlassian, now capitalised at US$45 million, famously bootstrapped for eight years, although founder Scott Farquhar later told the *Australian Financial Review* that he wouldn't recommend it in today's market, suggesting that in an industry like theirs now, you'd need more capital.[2]

Bootstrapping can also be a challenge if you start lean but need to scale or grow quickly. If your business requires significant capital, relying solely on personal savings can be risky – although arguably safer than using your home as collateral for a business loan, which is equally popular among small business start-ups.

Friends, family (and fools)

Borrowing money from family or friends is what venture capitalists (people who raise money to invest in new ventures or start-ups) call 'pre-seed funding' or, colloquially, F&F or FFF capital raising (friends, family and fools).

For some of us, these loans might be the only option when traditional funding sources aren't available. And hey, there's absolutely nothing wrong with kickstarting your business with a little help from those who know you best. They're likely to be a lot more flexible than banks or investors. But let's be real, diving into financial waters with loved ones requires some serious precautions. So, let's explore how you can ensure Sunday lunch doesn't turn into an awkward investor update.

F&F funding can be suitable for businesses with moderate funding needs; for instance, if you're opening a local gym, family and friends might help cover the costs of equipment and initial stock. However, mixing personal relationships with business can be tricky. While there are technically no lengthy forms or due diligence to go through, and you'll generally get low or no interest rates and flexible payment terms, I'd nonetheless recommend formalising the agreement and terms, for both your sakes. At the end of the day, these are your personal relationships and you don't want to ruin them if your business goes south.

Writing up the terms can help save misunderstandings. That way, there are no assumptions. Even if the lending party (thanks, Mum!) is gifting the funds to you, it's worth approaching the exercise as if you're engaging them as an investor or creditor. Agree on what they expect in return for their investment and, equally, on what input you're prepared to take on from them.

Friends and family will likely have opinions on your business. Sometimes their advice will be gold, and other times not so much. Be clear about whether this is a loan to be repaid or if they're getting a share in your business. If it's a loan, draw up a repayment schedule. If it's a gift, put it in writing that it's not repayable. Make sure they understand they can't get their money back quickly if a family emergency comes up.

Think about getting a lawyer and/or accountant involved to ensure the terms are fair and everything is covered, including interest and tax and what penalties there may be for late or non-payment. Loans in business are more than financial obligations; they can lead to legal consequences. Always keep a formal record of any agreement – WhatsApp messages won't cut it. Make sure you document:

1. the amount of the loan
2. the interest rate (if zero, clearly state it's interest-free)
3. the loan period, including start and final payment dates
4. specific repayment terms – regular amounts or a lump sum
5. any provided security and potential top-ups
6. penalties for late or non-payment
7. if it's an investment, specify the number of shares and the investor's involvement in business decisions, as well as if they'll be liable for business debts or lawsuits.

Crowdfunding

An option gaining popularity is crowdfunding – that is, raising small amounts of money from a large number of people, typically via an online platform. This is generally used at the early stages of a new venture. Along with generating funds, it validates your business idea and builds a community of supporters.

Crowdfunding can be great for consumer products or creative projects. For instance, if you're launching a new gadget, crowdfunding can generate funds and buzz simultaneously. However, if your business idea doesn't resonate with the public, crowdfunding may not be successful and, like anything, setting it up takes time away from working on your business. So, before you spend time setting up a crowdfunding initiative, think through whether it's likely to succeed, or if your efforts might be put to better use elsewhere.

Bank loans

A bank loan is still the most common way that Australian small businesses fund their operations. As with any formal lending arrangement, such loans come with repayment terms, including interest.

The nice thing about bank funding is that it's fairly straightforward, with no messy obligations to friends and family. Financial lenders provide substantial capital with structured repayment plans – ideal for established businesses with a solid business plan and credit history. For example, if you're expanding your retail store, a bank loan can help finance renovations and additional inventory. However, if you're just starting out, if your business is high-risk or if you have poor credit, securing a bank loan can be challenging.

HELP! HOW DO I SECURE A BANK LOAN?

Even if you're not a numbers gal, having a basic grasp of your finances is crucial. A cash flow statement is your BFF here – it shows you the money coming in and going out. Think current income, net profit, expenses and future projections.

Craft your business plan

Lenders want to see the big picture, and that means your business plan needs to shine. If you don't have one yet, it's time to get cracking – see Chapter 3 for how to do it. Your business plan should outline your financial situation and business goals, giving lenders confidence in your vision.

Know your financial boundaries

Understanding your financial limits is key. Ask yourself:

1. Do I want the money up-front or as needed?
2. What's the maximum repayment I can handle?
3. Do I meet the bank's lending requirements?
4. Do I have assets for collateral?
5. Who could guarantee my loan if needed?

Pick the perfect loan type

Once you know what you need, it's time to find the right loan. Look at costs, interest payments and any hidden fees. Each loan type has different tax and GST implications, so chat with a business adviser or accountant. Don't just settle for the first option – shop around for the best deal.

Get your docs in order

Before you meet with lenders, make sure you've got your paperwork sorted. You'll need:

1. proof of ID
2. your business plan
3. financial reports from the last three years (if available)
4. financial forecasts
5. ratio calculations
6. personal financial info.

Vet your lender

Do your homework on who you're dealing with. Check out registered companies on professional registers and avoid any dodgy operators. Get a copy of your credit report to see where you stand.

Seek expert advice

Not feeling confident about answering financial questions? No worries! Practice makes perfect, or, better yet, bring along a business adviser or accountant to back you up.

Nail that loan application

When you're ready to apply, double-check all the details. If an offer seems too good to be true, dig deeper. Look out for hidden fees and changing interest rates, and make sure it's from a reputable provider. If you get turned down, don't stress. Ask for feedback, make improvements and try again.

Trade credit

Trade credit is an arrangement where suppliers allow you to buy now and pay later. If you can secure credit from your suppliers, it will improve cash flow as it allows you to stock up without immediate payment.

Such terms are ideal for retail or manufacturing businesses. For instance, if you're running a clothing store, trade credit can help you stock up on inventory for the new season. However, if you have poor credit or a new business relationship, securing trade credit can be difficult. On the flip side, if you're in the business of supply or manufacture, you might consider offering trading terms as a way to entice new customers or retain existing ones. While it will cost you money (as in these cases you are the moneylender and will be carrying these obligations on your books), many consider such practices a form of sales/marketing incentive and cost it through accordingly.

No matter how you manage to secure funding for your business, having access to capital can help propel your business to new heights, so choose wisely and explore all your options.

OVER TO YOU } When was the last time you reviewed your cashflow statement? Does it suit your plans for future growth? If not, where might you secure additional funding or investment? Which lending options sound like the right fit for you?

Investors and venture capital

This type of funding doesn't apply to all types of small business. Typically, angel investors and venture capitalists are looking to invest in high-growth start-up ventures (HGVs) – think tech start-ups primarily, in Australia at least. Some will go so far as to say that HGVs are not actually small businesses – at least, not in the traditional sense. So how do they differ?

WHAT'S THE DIFFERENCE BETWEEN A SMALL BUSINESS AND A HIGH-GROWTH VENTURE?

First things first, a start-up isn't just any small business. A start-up is all about high growth and scalability. It's designed to grow fast and replicate its success over and over. On the other hand, a small business often aims to sustain a certain lifestyle and income level without the primary focus being scaling up.

High-growth start-ups are companies that have the potential for rapid and significant growth, typically in the form of revenue or customer base. They often have a unique product or service offering, a disruptive technology, or a new approach to an existing problem.

FUNDING DIFFERENCES

One major difference between small businesses and high-growth start-ups is how they get their funding. Start-ups often go through several funding stages, starting with friends and family, then angel investors and finally venture capital firms. Small businesses usually don't attract that kind of investor. They rely more on friends and family, bank loans, and grants. Why? Because angels and VCs look for scalable businesses with high ROI potential, which small businesses often can't promise.

SEED FUNDING FOR HIGH-GROWTH VENTURES

Seed funding can offer significant capital and strategic support to scale rapidly. It's typically used to fund high-growth ventures and generally comes from three primary sources:

1. **Angel investors:** Wealthy individuals who provide capital in exchange for equity in your business. Typically suitable for early-stage start-ups with high growth potential. For instance, if you've developed a unique app, an angel investor can provide the capital and guidance to scale your business.

2. **Venture capital:** Investment funds that manage pooled capital from investors to invest in high-growth start-ups. Ideal for high-growth start-ups needing substantial investment – for example, if you're a biotech company with a groundbreaking product.

3. **Business incubators and accelerators:** Typically work with cohorts, creating a powerful community vibe. Unlike venture capital funds, which cherry-pick start-ups one by one, accelerators bring together a whole squad of innovators, enabling them to compare, learn and grow alongside others in their field.

Generally these types of investors are prepared to take on more investment risk than traditional investors. Realising there are fewer guarantees, they speculate that across their portfolio there will be at least a few high-performance results making the risk worthwhile. Since they have an appetite for and specialise in high-growth ventures, beyond funding they can also offer valuable mentorship and industry connections.

To balance the risks, all three types generally invest in return for equity in your company. Venture capitalists, in particular, expect high returns and significant control. If you prefer to retain full control, this might not be the best option for you.

Securing funding

When you're looking for investment funding, in certain phases of the economy it can feel like the world is raining money; other times it's nowhere to be found. Just like any market, the availability of funding can have its highs and lows and understanding these cycles can help you time your fundraising efforts more effectively.

Also, as we've just outlined, different types of funding are best suited for different operations. Seed funding, for example, is generally reserved for start-ups in high-growth ventures – typically the tech sector. As such, this funding option is unlikely to be available to many of the small businesses that the SOTM community is interested in running.

FLUSH TIMES FOR FUNDING

» **Economic boom:** During periods of economic growth, more capital is flowing through the market. Investors and banks have more disposable income and confidence in the market's stability.

» **High market confidence:** When the stock market is performing well, investors feel optimistic. This positive sentiment spills over, making it easier to attract investment and secure funding.

» **Technological advancements:** Breakthroughs in technology can create a buzz that attracts investors – think about the dot-com boom or the rise of social media platforms. When new tech trends emerge, investors flock to be part of the next big wave.

» **Government incentives:** Sometimes, government policies and incentives can spur investment. Tax breaks, grants and favourable regulations can make it more attractive for investors and banks to put more money on the table.

LEAN TIMES FOR FUNDING

» **Economic downturn:** During a recession or economic slow-down, investors and lenders become risk-averse. They prefer to hold onto their capital or invest in safer, more stable opportunities.

» **Market volatility:** When the stock market is unpredictable, investors' confidence wanes. This uncertainty makes them less likely to invest.

» **Industry saturation:** If a particular industry becomes oversaturated, lending might slow. For example, if there are too many similar start-ups in one sector, or a business plan doesn't have a strong competitive edge, it becomes harder to stand out and secure funding.

» **Regulatory changes:** New regulations or changes in government policy can create uncertainty. Lenders might hold off on funding until they have a clearer understanding of how these changes will impact the market.

TIMING YOUR FUNDRAISING EFFORTS

Understanding these cycles is crucial for timing your fundraising efforts. If you're launching during a flush period, you might find it easier to secure funding and attract investors. But if you're starting out during a lean period, you might need to get creative with your funding strategies – think bootstrapping or seeking alternative sources of capital.

My business is in health care. We provide speech pathology, OT and AHA services for neurodivergent and neurotypical people needing help with their communication and swallowing. We do remote, fly-in fly-out telehealth and face-to-face work with people all over Australia.

The motivation for me to start my own business in this area was to give holistic support to individuals and their families – if they have a problem anywhere along the line, they can come to me!

Before launching, I researched profitability and different scenarios with my accountant, looking into different software and what resources, mentoring and support I needed, and bouncing around ideas as to what the business would look like.

I've learnt four important lessons about the financial side of having a business: 1) do a budget with your accountant; 2) be realistic in your budget (don't kid yourself); 3) have an emergency plan; and 4) get insurances. In addition, all feedback is good feedback. Fly-in fly-out work was a big goal of mine and it was great to get to that point, but it's also important to realise what it takes to stay there.

Apply for grants and government support

Let's talk in a bit more detail about something that can give your business a real boost: grants and government support. These are fantastic resources that can provide the financial backing and additional support you need to get your business off the ground or take it to the next level. Think of them as a helping hand from the government, designed to support innovation, growth and sustainability in the business community.

In 2016 the Australian Government launched the 'Inquiry into innovation and creativity: workforce for the new economy', which was tasked with investigating the necessary supports to embolden a start-up culture in Australia.[3] In 2017 the inquiry published 38 recommendations. Now, while these weren't directly translated into actions (a formal response was only delivered in May 2024, saying all recommendations had been noted), the government is nonetheless committed to positioning Australia as a robust economy for small businesses and start-ups. As such, it provides grants and support across a variety of industries at different stages.

As with most things led by government, these grants and supports change regularly, so there is no way I could give you a static, comprehensive list here. I recommend jumping online to find out more at the time you'd like to access them.

Government grants

At the time of writing, the Australian Government's business website listed 623 grants and programs that could provide you with non-repayable government funds to support your business.[4] What's more, these often come with additional support and resources.

The business.gov.au grants directory offers a quick Q&A to help direct your search, and you can filter by location, industry, business structure, support type, objectives and business stage. In the search results today, on the first page alone, there were grants for EV chargers in workplaces, harm reduction in Victorian workplaces, conservation and heritage protection in WA, and support for women in male-dominated industries – to name a few. So, before you look anywhere else for some financial support, I'd look here first. If you secure a grant, it's kind of like winning the small-business-funding Lotto.

However, grants don't come without some effort. They can be highly competitive and time-consuming to apply for, which means they're often not a quick funding solution. Generally you have to put together a grant application, which means gathering details and writing a report. These days your trusty friend ChatGPT could lend a hand there. So why not give it a go – after all, there's little to lose and potentially a lot to gain!

Broadly speaking, government grants and support fall into the following categories.

OVER TO YOU Have you taken a look at the government's grants directory yet? If not, I urge you to grab a cuppa and spend some time scrolling through it. These grants cover a surprising range of activities and operations, so you may well find one suitable for your business. If not now, maybe in future. Set a calendar reminder to check in every few months.

START-UP GRANTS

These offer financial support specifically aimed at helping new businesses get started and contribute to providing the initial capital needed to launch your business, covering costs like equipment, marketing and initial stock. They are ideal for businesses in their early stages – for example, if you're launching a tech start-up, a start-up grant can help you cover the costs of developing your first product. If your business is already established and generating revenue, you may not qualify for a start-up grant.

INNOVATION AND R&D GRANTS

These grants are aimed at businesses involved in research and development, to encourage innovation. They support the development of new products, services or processes, helping you stay competitive and innovative. Such grants are perfect for businesses in tech, biotech or any industry focused on innovation – for instance, if you're developing a new medical device, an R&D grant can fund your research and prototype development. Of course, if your business isn't involved in R&D or innovation, these grants won't be relevant.

EXPORT MARKET DEVELOPMENT GRANTS (EMDG)

These are designed to help businesses expand into international markets by reimbursing export promotion expenses. They can make or break your export venture, helping to reduce the financial risk of entering new markets so you can grow your business globally. Businesses looking to export their products or services will find these grants ideal. For example, if you're a fashion brand wanting to break into the US market, an EMDG can cover costs like marketing and travel. Naturally, if your business is solely focused on the domestic market, such grants won't be applicable.

SUSTAINABILITY AND ENVIRONMENTAL GRANTS

These grants are aimed at businesses that are implementing sustainable practices or developing eco-friendly products. They encourage environmentally responsible business practices and innovation in sustainability. If you're developing a line of biodegradable packaging, these grants might fund your research and production. Given the work required to apply for grants, be sure that your business has a sustainability focus before you focus your energies here.

TRAINING AND SKILLS DEVELOPMENT GRANTS

These apply to a range of industries and are designed to fund training and skills development for you and your employees. One of the greatest gifts of self-employment is that you're on a path of continual learning, and as a great boss you'll provide these opportunities for your staff, too. These grants can help support the cost of building the skills and capabilities of your team, which will ultimately improve your productivity and competitiveness, and are great for any businesses looking to upskill their workforce. For example, if you run a digital marketing agency, a training grant can fund advanced courses for your team.

BUSINESS GROWTH AND EXPANSION GRANTS

These grants are aimed at helping businesses scale and expand their operations, providing the capital needed for expansion such as opening new locations, increasing production capacity or entering new markets. They are perfect for established businesses ready to grow. If you're a successful beauty store looking to open a second location, for example, an expansion grant can help cover those costs. If your business is still in the start-up phase, you may not qualify for these grants.

INDIGENOUS BUSINESS GRANTS

Specifically aimed at supporting Indigenous entrepreneurs and businesses, these grants provide financial support and resources to help Indigenous businesses at any stage thrive and grow. For example, if you're an Indigenous artist wanting to open a gallery, these grants can help fund your venture. If your business isn't Indigenous-owned, you won't qualify for these grants.

REGIONAL BUSINESS GRANTS

If your business operates in a regional or rural area, there may well be a grant for you. These grants are designed to encourage economic development and job creation in regional communities and are perfect for businesses located outside major cities. For example, if you're starting a winery in a regional area, they can help with infrastructure and marketing costs. They may also make it affordable to relocate your business to a regional area. If there's no real reason why your business needs to operate in the city and you've always dreamt of living regionally, this could be your chance.

APRIL'S BUSINESS STORY

I design video games to support real-world mental health issues and therapies – for example, CBT [cognitive behavioural therapy] for anxiety. I decided to go into business because I wanted to gain control of my life and be able to work around my family. I love the flexibility and thrive on the pressure of running a business. I always want more, and my business allows me to grow as an entrepreneur and constantly learn and evolve. It's been running for 18 months.

After having an idea for a game, I engaged in mentoring and consultation with others to understand more about the process in what was a completely new industry to me. While I'm yet to release my first game, I've reached other business goals, including submitting grant applications and attending international conventions. Ticking that off was a fantastic and enlightening experience.

In my industry it's important to have strong communication with staff/developers. Setting goals, holding each other accountable to deadlines and being supportive helps everyone to do their best. In hindsight, I would take my time choosing staff and be fussier with selecting employees. Having the wrong employees can be so damaging to the brand and success of a business. Everyone needs to share the same passion.

Starting my business has meant being able to fulfil my dreams and goals in ways that wouldn't have been possible if I hadn't taken the plunge and made it happen. I have learnt many new skills and thrive under the pressure of having the responsibility.

I recommend to always save for a rainy day and invest back into the business. It's easy to get caught up in paying yourself well, but there's no profit until expenses and growth have been considered.

Principle 5: Make coin

Money makes the business world go round! Whether you bootstrap or seek funding, eventually your business must become profitable, otherwise, by definition (given that a business's goal is to make money), you've failed. Make turning a profit a priority, otherwise: hobby, yes; business, no.

Meet the founder: Zara Seidler

Zara Seidler is the co-founder of Gen Z–focused news brand The Daily Aus (TDA). Since it launched, TDA has amassed more than half a million followers on Instagram and 200,000 newsletter subscribers.

Name: Zara Seidler

Business: The Daily Aus

Industry: Media

Product/service: News in the form of written, podcast and video content

Target audience: Australians aged 18 to 35

Secondary audience: Anyone who cares about the world around them!

Unique selling point: We meet people where they are at rather than expecting them to come to the news.

The business began: 2021

I'd absolutely never planned to go into business – TDA started as a hobby and I expected it to stay that way. And it did for a while . . . but then that all changed when our audience spiked exponentially during the Covid pandemic and we ended up raising a round of capital that allowed me and my co-founder, Sam Koslowski, to quit our jobs and pursue TDA full time. The business officially began in February 2021.

It's not lost on me how much of a privilege it is to get to do something I love each day. That and building a team of like-minded people around me are the two best things about starting TDA. We now have an office full of incredible young journalists who are passionate about building the company and going on that journey with us. It's no longer a singular vision but one that is shared by some of the smartest and most ambitious people I've ever come across.

We employ more than 15 full-time staff. We decided to do this because we had ambitions to build the next big Australian media company and knew we couldn't do it alone. It's the best decision we ever made!

I'm by no means an expert when it comes to managing people and I'm learning along the way, but I think compassion is the best thing you can bring to leadership. You need to have lots of different tools in your kit, including strength, empathy, loyalty and decisiveness. It's about knowing what to use and when to use it.

In terms of other help and support, in addition to our staff we use bookkeepers (because I'm useless with numbers), but that's it. I've discovered that other female founders are incredibly gracious with their time and willing to help. The relationships I've built with other founders have been unexpected and deeply validating – I've learnt that we're all facing the same challenges.

I'm the first to admit we've made many mistakes along the way, but equally we've learnt a lot. I've never built a business before, and I truly think the only way to learn is by doing it. An investor of ours once said the balance of a start-up is 'building a plane and flying it at the same time'. I feel that every day!

There's no off switch, but I feel like I'm in a stage of life that allows me to throw myself into my work fully. The line between my personal time and work is a bit blurred, because reading the news and listening to news podcasts is what I enjoy doing in my spare time. Because of that,

I have no work–life balance. However, I signed up for this and I'm bloody proud of what we've achieved.

The best piece of advice I've received is not to be reckless in either direction. It's something I think about often. Running a business is about walking the line between being conservative (with capital) and pushing yourself to break barriers and be innovative. Not being too stuck in your position means you're able to build a nimble, agile and exciting business.

Chapter Six

Setting up solid business operations

When you're establishing a business, how you set it up – from selecting your business premises (whether they are physical or digital, need to accommodate staff or just yourself) to installing the right tools, systems and processes, and hiring your team – can have a make-or-break effect on the success of your operations.

In this chapter I'll guide you through finding the perfect location and creating an inspiring workspace that boosts productivity. We'll dive into sourcing reliable suppliers and mastering inventory management so that your products are always in stock, without overflows. We'll also cover establishing clear operational processes and procedures to keep your business running smoothly and efficiently. And we'll explore leveraging technology, from customer relationship management systems to accounting software, to streamline your operations and ensure your business is both modern and secure.

Setting up your workspace

Having covered off much of your behind-the-scenes operations in the previous chapters, it's now time to concentrate on your physical space and daily operations. Your business location and workspace set-up can significantly impact the way you operate, your customers' experience and your overall success. Whether you're opening a chic café, setting up a boutique or launching a tech start-up, the right location and workspace set-up are crucial. Let's take a look at how you can create a brilliant space for your business.

The costs of running a business lease for premises may be one of your largest recurring outgoings, not to mention the initial cost of setting up the place and any ongoing maintenance that's not covered by your lease agreement. Whether you're setting up a shopfront or an office or managing employees who work from home, these are the things to consider:

» **Visibility and accessibility:** A prime location makes it easier for customers to find and visit your business.

» **Operational efficiency:** A well-designed workspace boosts productivity and employee satisfaction.

» **Legal compliance:** Meeting legal requirements ensures you avoid fines and operate safely.

» **Health and safety:** A safe and healthy environment protects you, your staff and your customers.

What to look for in a business location

If you're setting up physical premises, such as a shopfront or a warehouse operation, you should consider the following aspects.

FOOT TRAFFIC AND VISIBILITY

What I mean by this is the number of people passing by your location and how easily they can see your business. High foot traffic and good visibility can drive more customers to your business and are especially important for retail stores and hospitality ventures. For example, if you're opening a boutique, a high-traffic area like a shopping district can attract more customers.

Interestingly, though you may think that being the only type of your business in your area will give you a competitive advantage, often the reality is the opposite. When customers identify a location with a certain type of business – for example, this is the suburb for furniture shopping – they'll often make a beeline for it, planning to spend a day scouring the stores. Like attracts like, as they say. On the other hand, if your business is, say, a consulting firm or an e-commerce store that relies more on appointments or online sales than face-to-face interactions, foot traffic may be less critical.

ACCESSIBILITY AND PARKING

It's important to consider how easy it is for customers and employees to reach your location, including parking availability. Naturally, having convenient access and parking will enhance the customer experience and make it easier for your employees to get to work. If your business doesn't require your customers to carry away heavy items, your walkability factor may be more important than parking. However, if they are generally collecting bulk goods, then providing easy access and additional support, such as large trolleys, will add value. For some businesses, like cosmetic surgeries, protecting customers' privacy is critical.

PROXIMITY TO SUPPLIERS AND PARTNERS

Something first-time business owners may not take into consideration is the distance between their premises and those of key suppliers or partners. This is especially important for businesses with physical products. For example, if you're running a bakery, being close to your suppliers can ensure fresh ingredients and timely deliveries, and can reduce shipping costs and improve supply chain efficiency.

Alternatively, your business may rely on digital products or services. In such cases, physical proximity to suppliers may not be as relevant, but ensuring smooth connectivity across your different operating platforms will be. In these cases it's worth establishing what systems your key suppliers use and identifying how you can connect with them as seamlessly as possible. Many online sales platforms provide application programming interfaces (APIs) that can easily connect your ordering, inventory and billing systems.

ZONING AND PERMITS

Local government regulations dictate how properties in certain areas can be used. Some areas may be zoned 'residential only', which means you can't legally run a commercial operation from premises there. So it's critical to check zoning laws before signing a lease. You might want to open a gym or be planning to cook at scale – if so, make sure the location you're looking at is zoned for commercial use and meets any specific requirements for your type of operation. The last thing you want after spending all your time and money setting up your business is for it to be fined or forced to shut down! As always, preparation meets planning.

COST AND LEASE TERMS

A lease is a contract, so it's super important to examine the financial aspects of your location, including rent, utilities and lease conditions. Commercial lease terms are generally longer than residential (anywhere from two to five years), so it's important you know you can afford the location and understand your obligations.

Run best- and worst-case scenarios to test whether the location fits your budget and business plan. Do you feel confident you can meet your ongoing rent repayments through the ups and downs of the market? If not, analyse whether your business really needs a full-time public-facing space. If you're a service provider, could you instead offer at-home visits, or rent a co-working space for two days a month and schedule all your face-to-face client meetings there?

One of the greatest challenges of running a business is meeting your regular outgoings, regardless of how well you or the economy is going. Before you commit to a regular fee, consider other ways in which you might meet your business needs without the commitment of such ongoing costs.

Key considerations for setting up your workspace

Once you've decided where you're going to run your business from, the next step is setting it up so it becomes a place where you can do your best work. Here's what you'll want to consider.

LAYOUT AND DESIGN

A well-designed layout boosts productivity and creates a pleasant environment, so it's important to consider the physical arrangement of your workspace, including furniture, equipment and flow. The idea is to optimise your workspace for safety, efficiency and convenience. For example, if you're setting up a team office environment, you'll want to have a layout that promotes both collaboration and productivity. As such, you'll need spaces where the team can come together and spaces where people can work quietly and independently.

Commercial kitchens are the ideal example of this. They have workstations for specific tasks, where everything needed for that task is at hand. Commonly used resources, like the cool room, are centrally located for convenience, while specific tools remain near individual cooks' workbenches, aiming to minimise crossing into each other's workspace during service.

HEALTH AND SAFETY

It's important to identify and put in place any measures needed for a safe and healthy environment for employees and customers. This not only protects everyone's wellbeing, but also ensures compliance with legal requirements and insurance cover. There's no time when this isn't crucial – health and safety are always a priority! You should always be on the lookout to prevent accidents and negative health issues. For instance, if you're opening a restaurant, you need to make sure it has proper ventilation, sanitation and emergency exits.

TECHNOLOGY AND EQUIPMENT

Apart from setting up your space for safety and best practice, furnishing your business with the right tools and technology means it will run efficiently and smoothly, and also be more productive. For example, if you're starting a tech company, invest in high-quality computers and software and set multiple automatic backups of your work to the cloud. As a hairdresser, buy the best-quality scissors, hairdryers and heat machines you can afford. Investing in quality tools may seem expensive, but their performance will reflect how your customers experience your business, and will ultimately determine your success.

COMFORT AND ERGONOMICS

Creating a comfortable and ergonomic workspace will support employee wellbeing and enhance employee satisfaction and productivity, so always aim to create a pleasant work environment. If you're setting up an office, invest in ergonomic chairs and adjustable desks. Even if it's just you in your own home office, consider how many hours you spend there and how the space makes you feel. What can you do to enhance your space – better light, noise-cancelling headphones, fresh flowers? Sometimes little things can make all the difference.

BRANDING AND AESTHETICS

Following on from the previous points, consider that your workspace is an extension of and physical experience of your brand. What visual elements can you deploy that reflect your brand and create an appealing environment? How can you reinforce your brand identity and create a positive impression? A cohesive brand image is crucial, so always ensure your workspace aligns with your brand. For example, if you're opening a boutique, design the space to reflect your brand's style and appeal to your target customers.

Getting help

Finding the right location and setting up your workspace can be challenging, but you don't have to do it alone. Here's where to go and who to talk to for expert advice:

» **Real estate agents:** Can help you find the perfect location and negotiate lease terms.

» **Interior designers:** Can create a functional and aesthetically pleasing workspace.

» **Health and safety consultants:** Make sure that your workspace meets legal requirements and promotes wellbeing.

» **IT specialists:** Can set up your technology and equipment for optimal performance.

» **Business advisers:** Through services like Business Australia and local chambers of commerce, can provide free or low-cost advice on location and workspace set-up.

However, nothing can beat physically experiencing a site and its operations for yourself. Visit your intended location at several different times of the day and week, noting how busy and how quiet it gets. Check out the kinds of clientele and other people who frequent the area. List any nearby support services that your business may use, and equally, how far away others are – especially critical ones or those you might need to rely on in an emergency. For instance, if you're a café and you run out of milk, where is the closest place to buy emergency stock?

Finally, once you've decided on a location, make sure you negotiate the lease terms like a boss. Never accept the original offer – remember, this is business and there's always a deal to be had.

I have a business in the beauty industry offering brow and lash services. It began on the Sunshine Coast and we had a clear vision from the start, with cohesive branding. We evolved as opportunities came up, staying open to new ideas and adapting naturally.

We have relocated our NSW store to a larger, more prominent location, which has significantly increased our number of new clients and our revenue. The future for us is continued growth, with two more stores and developing product ranges in the pipeline.

Along the way I've learnt that customer service is crucial and small things can have a big impact. I would tell past me not to try to please others but, rather, to make choices that are best for me and my business.

Operational processes and procedures

Let's dive into one of the most foundational aspects of running a successful business: establishing operational processes and procedures. Think of these as the playbook for how your business will run day-to-day. They ensure everything operates smoothly, efficiently and consistently. We're going to break it down and get you on the path to operational excellence.

Operational processes and procedures are the backbone of your business. They outline how tasks should be performed, who's responsible and what standards need to be met. Here's why they're essential:

» **Consistency:** Guarantees that tasks are performed the same way every time, maintaining quality and reliability.

» **Efficiency:** Streamlines operations, saving time and resources.

» **Compliance:** Helps you meet legal and regulatory requirements, avoiding fines and penalties.

» **Training:** Provides a clear guide for training new employees, reducing onboarding time.

» **Risk management:** Identifies potential risks and establishes protocols to mitigate those risks.

Where you can afford to, set your processes up as if you were a big business, even if you're just starting out, because that will help you scale if you plan to scale. And if you're not planning to scale, it will help you to be as efficient as possible.

Be aware, though, that you can't just 'set and forget' your processes. Tech changes so rapidly now that I change my systems every year. In my mortgage-broking business, which I set up myself back in the early days and was so proud of, I've realised it's no use saying, 'Well, that's how we've always done things.' Now it's 'Oh, that's really not working for us now, there's a new system that could do that in half the time' or 'That's not worth doing anymore – we need to change it.'

Pricing changes, too. Take your email. Have you looked at your email system since you've increased your number of subscribers? Have you gone back to basics and worked out whether you're still using the right email management software? This is something that's got away from me in the past. Ultimately it cost a lot to find the right, new one, but the change was worth it in terms of efficiency and price.

The idea of establishing processes is to make your business run as smoothly and efficiently as possible – so set them up like that in the first place, then review them regularly to ensure they're still delivering.

Establishing operational processes and procedures

Okay, gang, are you ready to make your business run like a well-oiled machine? Far from this section being like a boring 'how-to' manual, you'll find that sorting out your operational processes and procedures is a magic key to unlocking your future success. Some business ideas are built purely on this secret sauce, and it's the difference between them and their competitors!

How can you find the magic key for yourself and turn your dreams into actionable steps that mean everything runs smoothly and efficiently? Goals, documentation, roles, quality control, compliance and safety are the answer – so let's look at them in more detail now.

DEFINE CLEAR OBJECTIVES

As you now know, I love a good SOTM goal: Specific, Optimistic, Time-bound and Measurable (see Chapter 3). Setting objectives for how best to run your business is no different. What do you think will make your business stand out from its competitors? How can you deliver magical service or super-efficiency to wow your customers? Online fashion retailer The Iconic did just that when it promised three-hour delivery to metro customers – unheard of at the time, it blew its competition out of the water.

Clear objectives guide the development of effective processes and ensure everyone understands the desired outcomes. For example, if you're running a marketing agency, one of your objectives might be to streamline client onboarding to improve customer satisfaction and reduce turnaround time.

Once you've decided your main objective – sometimes called an OKM (one key metric) – you can move heaven and earth to make it happen. Clarity is queen.

DOCUMENT PROCEDURES

Writing down the steps involved in each process helps to create a clear and accessible guide for you and everyone else in your business to follow. Documentation means that everyone knows how to perform tasks correctly and consistently. Not only will this create efficiencies in your operations (since you're not continually reinventing the wheel), but it will also make sure your customers receive a consistent experience. If you're operating a café, documenting the procedure for making coffee guarantees that every cup meets your quality standards. Think about how McDonald's manages to deliver a similar experience the world over. Much more than just the pickles on a Big Mac (though they're definitely a part of it), their operational procedures are their secret sauce.

ASSIGN RESPONSIBILITIES

Clearly defining who is responsible for each task or process guarantees it will get done, ensures accountability and helps avoid confusion. For example, if you're running a retail store, assigning specific tasks like inventory management to designated employees leads to efficiency and accountability.

IMPLEMENT QUALITY CONTROL

Establish checks and measures to make sure processes are performed correctly and meet quality standards. It may seem a little yawn, but looking at quality control helps maintain high standards and identifies areas for improvement. For instance, if you're manufacturing products, implementing quality-control checks at each stage of production means the final products will meet your standards.

ENSURE LEGAL AND REGULATORY COMPLIANCE

I know I can sound like a boring big sister at times, but it is super important to make sure your processes comply with relevant laws and regulations to help you avoid legal issues, fines and penalties. For example, if you're running a healthcare clinic, you want your patients to be safe, which means you need to comply with health regulations.

PRIORITISE HEALTH AND SAFETY

Establishing procedures will mean a safe and healthy environment for your employees and customers. Not only will you be looking after everyone's wellbeing, but you'll be complying with health and safety laws. For instance, if you're operating a construction business, implementing safety protocols and training is essential to prevent accidents and injuries.

REGULARLY REVIEW AND UPDATE

Although the basic idea of documenting processes is to define them once and do them continuously, it's also important to review them every so often. Laws may change, employees may leave or new technology may change the goalposts. Regular reviews will ensure your processes remain effective and have been adapted to changes in your business or industry. For example, if you're running a tech start-up, regularly updating your processes to incorporate new technologies will help keep you competitive.

OVER TO YOU

Write a list of at least five critical procedures in your business and all the steps required to implement them safely, efficiently and effectively. It's important to consider your legal and safety requirements, but also ways in which you can streamline systems and processes.

Need a good SOP?

No, that's not a typo and I'm not talking about having a good cry –
although I'd highly recommend that, too, at times along your biz journey!
No, a SOP is a standard operating procedure: a set of clear, step-by-step
instructions to guide your team through routine operations. And yes, you
definitely need a few good SOPs.

SOPs are all about boosting efficiency, ensuring quality output and
creating consistent performances across the board. Plus, they help cut
down on miscommunication and make sure you're always in line with
industry regulations. In short, SOPs are your secret weapon for running a
smooth, successful business.

It's easy to say you don't have time to document things, especially if
it's just you and a handful of staff, but the sooner you write things down,
the better. Without a good SOP, things can go wrong, such as:

>> **Inconsistent quality:** Without documented procedures, product
   or service quality can vary, leading to customer dissatisfaction.

>> **Inefficiency:** Lack of clear processes can result in wasted time
   and resources.

>> **Compliance issues:** Without proper procedures, you risk
   non-compliance with legal and regulatory requirements, leading
   to fines or shutdowns.

>> **Safety hazards:** Poor health and safety procedures can result in
   accidents and injuries.

>> **Employee confusion:** Without clear responsibilities, employees
   may be unsure of their tasks, leading to errors and inefficiencies.

SOP EXAMPLE:

Business type: E-commerce store

Objective: Streamline order fulfilment to improve delivery times and customer satisfaction.

Documented procedure:

1. **Order received:** Order is automatically logged into the system.
2. **Inventory check:** System checks stock availability.
3. **Order picking:** Staff picks items from the warehouse.
4. **Quality check:** Items are checked for defects.
5. **Packaging:** Items are securely packed.
6. **Shipping:** Order is shipped with tracking information.
7. **Customer notification:** Customer is notified of shipment with tracking details.
8. **Follow-up:** Follow-up email to ensure customer satisfaction.

Assigned responsibilities:

1. **Order picking:** Warehouse staff
2. **Quality check:** Quality control team
3. **Packaging:** Packaging team
4. **Shipping:** Logistics team
5. **Customer notification:** Customer service team
6. **Follow-up:** Customer service team

Quality control: Regular audits of the fulfilment process to identify and address any issues.

Compliance: Ensuring packaging and shipping comply with industry standards and regulations.

Health and safety: Implementing safe handling and packing procedures to protect staff.

For each of the procedures you identified earlier, expand upon the steps you outlined, being clear and specific, to create a detailed standard operating procedure that everyone in your team (including you when you're feeling tired and forgetful) can follow.

Help, I need somebody!

There are plenty of tools available to help you establish and manage your operational processes and procedures. But in reality, the most important thing is that you've sat down and written it out. A basic list works just as well as fancy charts.

Remember, a well-structured playbook is key to running a successful business. With the right tools and support, you can be sure of smooth operations, happy customers and a thriving business. You've got this!

My business provides human resources advice, expert knowledge and resources to small business owners and people leaders to create better employee experiences, including fostering a workplace culture that employees want to be a part of, with best practices and compliant employment conditions, and to build stronger relationships between employers and employees. I have been in business since 2011 and have maintained a fairly consistent business over the years in terms of services and resources, but have recently introduced more technology and social media accounts.

I decided to go into business to share my HR expertise and knowledge to bridge the gap between employers and employees. A friend was opening up an accounting business and suggested I start my own business so we could work together. I had lots of friends in business so I started with them and then accepted referrals.

HR doesn't have to be tricky, but you need to know where to start to suit the needs of your business. There are lots of other businesses who do what I do, but we all do it differently. I try to remain relevant to my clients by understanding their businesses and their needs while producing content. I've recently connected with some individuals who I use for beta testing, too.

I've learnt plenty of good lessons along the way. It's important to understand the expectations of your clients, as everyone is different. This includes turnaround times, communication methods and level of support to review work. In addition, I've learnt to set clear goals and stick to them, not to spend money I don't have, and to surround myself with the right connections. Building and growing a business takes time. Run your own race and don't compare it with someone else's journey!

Maximise efficiencies

Let's talk about something that can take your business from good to great: efficient systems and technology solutions. Think of these as the extra-special garnish that can streamline your operations, boost productivity and give you a competitive edge. Once you document your processes, you can enhance them by leveraging the right tools and systems to make your business run smoother and smarter.

It may seem like a lot of extra effort, but there are plenty of resources available to help you out, from software to people. Many times, small business owners get overwhelmed but say they can't afford to hire someone, and that's where the conversation ends. But being able to identify the problem is really important to begin with. You might be feeling overwhelmed with admin and think you need an admin assistant, but then you realise it's actually just one very specific part of admin that is overwhelming you. It's taking you 20 hours a month because you're just not that efficient at it, and you could outsource it for three hours a month to someone who can do it more efficiently.

So if you're planning on outsourcing, what are you outsourcing? Could you outsource it using a platform like Airtasker or Fiverr? Could you hire a freelancer for one day a month to take that pressure off you? Could you find some AI that helps you do it? Could you automate it? It might take you three days to set that process up, but then you'll never have to do it again.

Plan your resourcing

While resourcing requires some thought and planning up-front, it truly can save you time and money in the long run. So what's the best way to go about it? First, identify your needs, then choose the right tools and ensure seamless integration. Security is key, as is protecting your data. Training your team is crucial for effective use, and regularly reviewing and updating your tech will keep you ahead. Let's look at these in a little more detail.

IDENTIFY YOUR NEEDS

First, assess what areas of your business could benefit from technology and system improvements. Understanding your needs will help you select the most appropriate solutions that will provide the biggest impact. For example, if you're running an online store, you might identify a need for better inventory management systems.

When I started Zella, I wasn't aware of the many things you can implement to manage things for you – including CRM systems. A system I could automate and organise to send out birthday messages to my clients? How good!

Look at your business operations and ask yourself whether you're doing things in the most efficient way. There's always more than one way!

CHOOSE THE RIGHT TOOLS AND INTEGRATE THEM

Next, select the technology and systems that will best meet your business needs. The right tools can significantly improve efficiency and productivity and help grow your business – particularly if they've been especially designed to service your industry – while the wrong ones can be a waste of time and money. It's always going to be a matter of balancing your budget with your needs. Don't get taken in by fancy marketing – consider if you really will spend the time to learn and use a particular tool. If not, don't bother with it.

Equally important is to make sure your new systems and technology integrate seamlessly with your existing processes and tools. This will prevent data silos and lead to smooth operations across different parts of your business. Overlooking this step may mean you end up with less efficient workflows in the long run. For example, if you're running a marketing agency, integrating your project management tool with your time-tracking and billing software means a seamless workflow and you'll avoid having to manually input data to generate anything useful.

PRIORITISE SECURITY

Critically, in this day and age, it's important to implement measures to protect your systems and data from cyber threats. Security is essential to protect sensitive information and maintain customer trust. I've released whole podcast episodes on this, and I strongly encourage you to take time to review your practices and make sure you're cyber safe. Sadly, a recent survey of more than 2000 small business owners and employees showed that while female business owners are less likely to be scammed than their male counterparts, they're not as confident as men when it comes to their general cybersecurity knowledge.[1]

Follow these basic steps to keep things secure:

1. **Passwords/passphrases:** Never reuse them! Create complex, unique passwords for every site and app you use. Yes, it can be frustrating, but they're easy to keep on top of if you use a secure digital vault to store them. Some of these will allow you to grant access to shared passwords across your team, so look into what you need and implement a system that allows you to regularly update your passwords.

2. **Multifactor authentication (MFA):** Use it to add a second layer of security to your logins and transactions. This usually requires downloading an MFA app to your mobile device to confirm your identity before a request is processed.

3. **Gateway protection:** If you're selling products or services, ensure that your transaction gateway is protected from fraudulent scammers – BIN (bank identification number) attacks and the like.

As well as providing peace of mind, having strong security systems in place is generally required for business insurance (Chapter 8). Without it, any compensation claim in the case of an attack or theft may be denied. Just as you must have locks on your physical doors and windows, cybersecurity is vital for your business.

TRAIN YOUR TEAM

Provide training so that your team can effectively use new systems and technology. Allowing them time to come up to speed will ensure they can fully leverage the new tools, maximising their benefits. If you're implementing a new CRM system, for instance, training your sales team in how to use it effectively is essential. In the early days, run regular sessions where everyone is using it together, so they can share and learn from each other. Don't forget to provide this training to new employees, too, when they come on board.

REGULARLY REVIEW AND UPDATE

For better or worse, technology is constantly evolving. As such, it's important to continuously evaluate and update your systems and technology so they remain effective and relevant. Taking time out of working 'in' your business to think strategically about how you could improve practice and process will allow you to stay ahead of the competition. This should include regular reviews of your technology, systems and processes to make sure your tools are keeping up with your business needs and technological advancements. For instance, if you're running a tech start-up, regularly reviewing your software tools will ensure you're using the most efficient and up-to-date solutions.

Source suppliers and manage inventory

Not every business will need to consider suppliers and inventory to the same extent, especially if you're a sole trading digital designer, for example. Nonetheless, every business needs supplies, so in this final section of the chapter, let's consider best practice for sourcing suppliers and managing inventory. Whether you're opening a boutique, running a café or launching a fashion empire, having reliable suppliers and an efficient inventory system is key to smooth operations and happy customers.

In fact, understanding your supply chain is crucial to delivering great customer service. A lot of people think customer service is just about being nice, when in fact it's about delivering a certain level of communication. If customers don't get that, they'll be asking you questions about when something was supposed to happen, or panicking about when their package will be shipping. Clear, consistent communication is the best thing in customer service, and it's often left by the wayside. The more you communicate, the more they're going to understand; and the more they understand, the more forgiving they'll be when things go wrong.

If you know the expected delivery times from your supplier, you can set the right expectations with your customer from the get-go. Let's say they order a custom pot from you. If you receive the order and thank them for it, no worries, end of story, they might expect to receive it next week so they can gift it to Aunty May. But a custom-designed pot might take three months to manufacture and deliver. If you let your customer know that from the outset, they'll be okay with the process. You need to outline on your website that the process is custom and takes this long. Once they've ordered, provide tracking updates throughout the process – for instance, you can expect me to have made it by this date and fired it on this date and shipped it on that date, and shipping usually takes seven days.

If you set clear expectations, your customers will come on board and you can use each update as a way to engage and increase connection with them – make them part of the journey and build their excitement. Not setting clear expectations about delivery is where most small businesses get into trouble. Good customer relationships are less about being kind and sending fluffy emails and more about that base level of how you have set your customer's expectations. For the most part, this comes back to your systems and processes. And if you rely on third-party suppliers, they become a critical part of your success.

Things to think about when sourcing suppliers

It can take time to find a great supplier, and it's important you don't just sign up with the first operator you come across. In the beginning it's worth trialling a few options to test for cost, timing and reliability. Ask for samples and trial runs before you pay any large sums or sign any long-term contracts. And don't be afraid to retest down the track – while initially your supplier may offer you favourable terms to win your business, they'll look to claw back profits later. It's up to you to keep them honest. Let's run through a few things you'll want to consider.

QUALITY AND RELIABILITY

Engaging high-quality, reliable suppliers means you can offer the best to your customers and avoid disruptions in your supply chain. Maintaining the consistency and dependability of the raw products or materials you use in your business will in turn give your customers a positive experience they can rely on. For example, if you're running a café, sourcing high-quality coffee beans from a reliable supplier will be crucial to maintaining your product standards. If you're creating a fashion brand, ensuring your clothing manufacturer delivers quality products will be key to your business success.

COST AND PAYMENT TERMS

Managing costs and having favourable payment terms can improve your cash flow and profitability. The price of the products or materials and the payment conditions agreed upon can generally be negotiated, so don't be afraid to push for terms that suit you. For instance, if you're opening a retail store, negotiating good prices and payment terms with your suppliers can help you manage your budget effectively.

Trade credit (see Chapter 5) can be incredibly useful, especially when starting out, so look around for someone who can offer this if you think it will benefit your cash flow. That said, such offerings may come with invisible costs – are you paying a higher price per unit for the credit terms? If you don't need credit, then the higher price point will erode your profitability. It pays, literally, to consider everything individually first, and then again with the bigger picture in mind.

LEAD TIME AND DELIVERY

Lead time is the time it takes for suppliers to deliver products or materials after an order is placed. Short lead times and reliable delivery schedules help you maintain optimal inventory levels and meet customer demand. However, a longer lead time may allow you to offer much more competitive pricing. The type of business you run can affect what a customer is willing to tolerate – for instance, most furniture stores come with a lead time of several months, whereas fashion buyers want to wear what's seasonal. Lead times and delivery times are a key brand promise, so determine what's important to your customers and then create a business process and supplier relationships that can support it.

CONTRACTS AND AGREEMENTS

Once you have found a supplier you're happy with, you'll want to agree terms. Signed contracts document the terms and conditions of the supplier relationship and protect your business by clearly defining expectations, responsibilities, and remedies for breaches. For instance, if you're sourcing raw materials for a manufacturing business, having a contract ensures both parties understand their obligations and reduces the risk of disputes.

Before you lock yourself into a contract, shop around to get the best deal and make sure you're happy with the quality and service provided. The last thing you want is to be locked into a contract with a supplier who is not delivering value. I experienced this in my early days when I engaged a marketing firm to run my online ad spend. In hindsight, I would have been much better off learning how to do this myself. Unfortunately I was locked into a six-month contact with them and saw no uplift from the money I spent. Twenty-twenty hindsight is a marvellous thing!

SUSTAINABILITY AND ETHICS

It's important to consider the environmental and ethical practices of your suppliers as ultimately they can affect your brand's reputation. If you position your business as a sustainable enterprise but then source supplies from companies that don't, you'll undermine your reputation. For example, if you're launching a fashion line, sourcing materials from ethical suppliers can appeal to environmentally conscious customers and differentiate your brand, but there's no point delivering eco-friendly threads if you ship them out in unrecyclable plastic. Sometimes, though, cost is a factor. The most important thing is to think it through and stand by your values and principles. Don't just pay them lip-service – try to consider all the ways in which you can bring your value propositions (USPs) to life in your everyday business operations.

How to manage inventory

Next up, let's talk about the backbone of your business: inventory management. Simply put, inventory is all the goods and materials you hold in stock to sell to your customers. It's the lifeblood of your business, whether you're running a boutique, a café or an online store.

Managing your inventory well is essential because it directly impacts your cash flow, customer satisfaction and overall efficiency. Too much inventory ties up your cash and space, while too little can mean missed sales and unhappy customers. Striking the right balance ensures you're always ready to meet demand without overcommitting resources. So, let's dive into mastering inventory management to keep your business thriving and your customers coming back for more!

INVENTORY LEVELS AND REORDERING

This is the super-important process of maintaining optimal stock levels and knowing when to reorder products or materials. Doing this well will ensure you have enough stock to meet demand without overstocking, which ties up capital. For example, if you're running a bookstore, keeping track of inventory levels and reordering popular titles means you'll be able to meet customer demand without having to store excess stock.

STORAGE AND ORGANISATION

The way you store and organise your inventory to ensure easy access and efficient use of space can be a game changer. Proper storage and organisation improves efficiency, reduces waste and prevents stock damage or loss. For instance, if you're operating a warehouse, efficient storage and organisation systems can streamline order fulfilment and reduce errors.

INVENTORY TRACKING AND SYSTEMS

There are various tools and methods you can use to track inventory levels, movements and sales. Accurate tracking helps you make informed decisions, reduces stock discrepancies and improves overall efficiency. For example, if you're managing a retail store, using an inventory management system can help you track sales, manage stock levels and reorder products when you need them.

HEALTH AND SAFETY

Making sure you've implemented procedures for the safe storage and handling of inventory to protect employees and customers is essential. It prevents accidents, injuries and adverse health issues, ensuring a safe working environment. For instance, if you're running a food business, following health and safety guidelines for storing perishable goods is crucial to prevent contamination and ensure customer safety.

LEGAL REQUIREMENTS

Certain industries, including food and medical, have strict rules around the ways in which you manage your inventory. It's crucial to comply with any laws and regulations, such as labelling, storage and record keeping, to make sure your business operates legally and avoids fines or penalties. For example, if you're selling pharmaceuticals, adhering to legal requirements for storage and record keeping is essential to comply with regulations and ensure customer safety.

Principle 6: Be in flow

Your business should run like a well-oiled machine. Implementing the right systems and processes may be your competitive advantage – so how can you turn 'boring' business practice into the sparkle that makes your business magical?

Meet the founder: Rachael Wilde

Rachael Wilde is the co-founder of the well-known social media brand tbh skincare, which has been hailed as a game changer for people with acne-prone skin. It's proven so popular that the brand says one of its acne spot treatments is snapped up every four minutes! In April 2023, Rachael co-founded York St Brands and tbh skincare merged with fellow beauty brand BOOST LAB.

Name: Rachael Wilde

Business: tbh skincare

Industry: Skincare

Product/service: Skincare

Target audience: Australian women aged 18 to 34 who have struggled with acne but found little success with conventional treatments

Secondary audience: Mums of teenagers who are looking for new solutions to help manage their teens' breakouts

Unique selling point: Advanced patented technology that provides a meaningful solution for acne

The business began: 2020

I'd always had a passion for business strategy and I had a background in marketing, but I'd never imagined myself running a company. Then I happened upon the technology that became the heart of tbh's hero product, and it all just seemed to fall into place.

We had a strong start, hitting $1 million in sales within the first 18 months with just my co-founder (my mum) and me juggling every role. Mum managed the operations and finances – she's a real powerhouse when it comes to numbers – and I handled everything else, from marketing to customer service, branding, packaging design and social media.

Scaling up was challenging as we had limited cash resources. After running the business from our homes for two years, we moved into our first office in a co-working space in Alexandria, Sydney at the end of 2021. It was a modest set-up with racking for stock and a few desks. Having an actual office, surrounded by other start-ups, was a huge boost and the creative haven we'd been missing. We expanded our product range from the original three to six by the end of 2022, which boosted our margins and prepared us for retail expansion.

From August 2022 to August 2023 the business transformed dramatically. Firstly, we had a viral TikTok that sent our sales skyrocketing overnight, delivering us a different kind of problem (though much welcomed) – we literally kept running out of stock. At the same time, as a result of capital-raising efforts, we ended up merging with another skincare brand, BOOST LAB, and co-founding a new parent company, York St Brands, to manage them both.

Both brands still operate independently in the market, but behind the scenes we're all employed by York St Brands and everyone works across both consumer brands. At the time of the merger, we united the original founder-led teams to create a team of eight staff, which we doubled to 15 within six months. As of August 2024, we have 27 people employed in the business and the brands are generating over $20 million in annual revenue.

It's been a whirlwind of change and growth and my role has changed dramatically, especially over the last 12 months. With the creation of York St Brands, I became the chief marketing officer. In a short time that meant I moved from being a hands-on founder wearing many hats, to managing just one part-time team member and being deeply involved in every aspect of daily operations, to now leading a team of 15 people in marketing alone and overseeing two consumer brands.

This transition has meant moving away from the day-to-day tasks and focusing more on high-level strategy, which has given me more time for the things I'm truly good at (and that I love). However, it also means I've had to let go of some control. My main focus now is on people management and supporting the team's success, rather than doing the hands-on work. I do sometimes miss being on the tools, but the growth I've experienced through leadership is invaluable, and being able to manage such a talented and inspiring team is a dream come true.

We decided to expand our team when the business was mature and stable enough to ensure we could provide reliable incomes – taking on the responsibility for others' livelihoods is not something to be taken lightly. By that point, we recognised that building our internal capabilities was crucial for long-term growth. With the new structure of the merged entity, we were able to create an efficient marketing engine that serves both brands, sharing resources in a way that made a lot of sense for us. Given our specific situation, I'd say it was a great decision.

Managing staff effectively has been a journey for me, and it's taken a lot of personal growth. Over the past year I've worked closely with an executive coach who's been invaluable in honing my people management skills. To become the leader I aspired to be, I had to first understand my own values and how they aligned with the team's values, and the kind of culture I wanted to foster. I now have a solid framework that helps me gauge team behaviours and outcomes, and the team has really embraced these values, shaping our culture every day.

I've also focused on developing deep listening skills, which can be quite challenging. It's about listening to truly understand rather than just to respond. It sounds simple, but it's a skill that people rarely use. My coach introduced a helpful concept to me: as a leader, you should spend most of your time asking 'why' and 'how' questions. While there are times to 'tell how' or 'tell why', it's generally more effective to guide your team by asking questions and helping them find their own solutions. This approach has helped my team to become more autonomous and confident problem-solvers who rely less on me and more on their own thinking.

In the early days we outsourced most functions, which I think was a smart choice for a small business. It's lower risk, especially if you avoid long-term contracts, and allows you to get expertise without the overhead of hiring full-time staff. My advice when choosing agencies is to get recommendations from other business owners in your field. There are some less reliable options out there, and you want to avoid costly mistakes during those critical early stages.

From the very beginning we've worked with accountants, who have been crucial in advising on and setting up our corporate structure as well as assisting in the management of things like BAS. Early on, we also brought on a PR agency, which turned out to be a fantastic move, especially in our industry. Securing strong media coverage helped us build credibility when we were still a new name. However, for our e-commerce media buying (Meta, TikTok and Google Ads) we have a slightly different approach whereby we subscribe to a service that provides the platform and teaches us the skills we need to do this ourselves.

The best part of being in business for myself is watching an idea that started out as just a spark become a reality. It's incredibly thrilling to see a vision come to life from the initial concept all the way to execution. Even though it involves a lot of hard work and moments of, *Oh my gosh, what am I doing?*, the excitement of bringing something to fruition never gets old. Having that autonomy and creative freedom is something unique to being in business for yourself.

On the flip side, you literally cannot pass your problems on to anyone else! I've gained a whole new appreciation for the days when you can simply clock off at 5 pm and leave work behind. When you're running your own business, there's no clocking out – work follows you everywhere. It follows you home, it follows you on holidays, it's a 24/7 commitment that doesn't switch off. While it has stretched me in ways I never expected, the rapid growth and learning curve have been the most challenging and rewarding aspects of this journey.

What's been most unexpected about running a business is how the growth and evolution of the company has made me less certain of myself over time. It's funny to think that when I was 23, pitching for the licensing rights to our patented technology with my co-founder, I was brimming with confidence. Now, even with the business thriving in many ways, I find myself feeling less sure. They say that the more you learn, the more you realise there's still so much to know, and I've found this to be absolutely true. Over the past four years I've gained a deeper awareness of the challenges and potential pitfalls, which has made me wiser and a better leader. However, this increased awareness has also shifted my confidence, my appetite for risk, and sometimes even my creative spark.

The business is pretty all-consuming in terms of the time it takes up, so there's little time when it is not requiring my attention in some form.

But if I had to quantify the hours I'm typically 'working', I would say it's about 50 hours in a regular week. That's why you have to love it. If your heart isn't in it, you won't be able to justify the amount of work it takes.

I wouldn't say my work–life balance is perfect, but as the common saying goes, if you love what you do, it never really feels like work. For me, it's about recognising when I've been in a high-stress zone for too long and I need to slow down. I have to remind myself it's a marathon, not a sprint, especially now that I'm leading a team. I need to be able to support them for the long haul, so I've had to get better at scheduling downtime.

There have definitely been sacrifices over the past four years, but I've still managed to make time for other important aspects of my life, especially my loved ones. Losing yourself entirely in your business can be risky. For me, staying connected to who I am outside of work – whether as a partner, sister, daughter or friend – has been crucial. Maintaining these relationships has kept me grounded. In the end, nothing is worth sacrificing the important people in your life for – you need to find a way to keep that as priority number one.

Looking back, I wouldn't change much because every decision and challenge has brought us to where we are today, and I've learnt so much along the way. If there's one thing I'd consider doing differently next time, it would be securing investment capital from the start. The personal financial pressure we faced in the first three years was intense. There were times when it felt like we were on the brink of collapse, and we had to do whatever it took to keep things going. Fortunately, things worked out well in the end. If you have the ability to secure investment capital from the start, then that is something I would recommend.

If I could go back and give advice to my past self, it would be this: focus on the journey, not just the destination! I know it sounds clichéd, but it's true. There have been many moments over the past four years when I hit major milestones that I'd only dreamt of at the start, only to realise that reaching them didn't quite feel as I'd imagined. What I've learnt is that the joy doesn't come from the success itself, it's the joy in the process that creates the success. I would tell myself to prioritise enjoying the journey and having fun along the way. That way, when you do reach your goals, they mean so much more and you'll cherish the small moments throughout the journey rather than just the milestones.

Chapter Seven

Building your brand and nailing sales

Finally! We've covered so many logistical (and important) things to set up in your business, but now we come to the fun bit. This is where we turn your passion into a brand that stands out and attracts your dream customers. This chapter is all about branding, marketing and sales strategies for building your small business.

In Chapter 1 you found your purpose, in Chapter 3 you reviewed your industry and competitors, unearthed your customer avatar and defined a niche for your business in the market, in Chapter 4 we discussed the importance of business names and your unique special sauce (IP) and in Chapter 6 we set up business systems and processes to help you deliver the ultimate experience for your customers. These are all critical to laying the foundations of a strong brand identity – without them in place you're in danger of spruiking hot air. But because we spent time setting them up right, in this chapter we focus on the fun part of bringing the experience alive for your customer.

Build a strong brand identity

One of the most exciting and impactful aspects of starting your own business is building a strong brand identity. Your brand is so much more than just a logo or a catchy slogan – it's the essence of your business, the story you tell, and how your customers perceive you. It's also about the promises you deliver, which will help to build emotional resonance with your customers.

Emotional connection is perhaps more important than anything, as it's what makes your customers stay and buy from you beyond tactical pricing strategies. When they have so many options to choose from, why would they choose your business over someone else's? It's the way you connect with them and the way you make them feel, that almost-intangible thing known as 'brand essence'. As such, your brand identity and understanding your brand DNA are really important. Who are you? Why are you here? What do you do? How do we make these things an integral part of your story?

And, it's not something you can just set and forget. It's important to keep monitoring and evolving your brand. The market changes, and so should you. At SOTM, we update our website annually. Not just what it looks like (although as our community knows we did a complete brand overhaul in 2024) but also the experience – driven by the tech and back-end integrations – so our SOTM community gets the value they expect from us.

Your brand not only needs to be strong, but also adaptable and enduring! A strong brand generates:

» **Recognition:** A strong brand makes your business instantly recognisable, helping you stand out in a crowded market.

» **Trust and loyalty:** Consistent branding builds trust and fosters customer loyalty, encouraging repeat business.

» **Value perception:** A well-defined brand can command higher prices by conveying quality and value.

» **Emotional connection:** A powerful brand identity creates an emotional connection with your customers, making them more likely to choose you over competitors.

I'm very much a believer in not being everything to everyone because then you dilute your value. As we talked about in Chapter 3, She's on the Money has a very clear customer avatar – a specific demographic we speak to – when we create our content. I believe this generates bigger, louder advocates for our brand than if we diluted it and tried to be a news platform that just shares generic finance content. Having a clear brand increases our value – we've found our community and our people.

How to build a strong brand

Building on the strong foundations you've created for your business – its purpose, USP, niche position and target customer – it's now time to create a brand. A brand is much more than a logo. It includes the rest of your visual identity (colours, typography, illustration and photography styles) as well as how you communicate, both on paper and in person, and how customers engage with you, both physically and online.

BRAND STRATEGISTS/AGENTS

A brand strategist or brand agency will put you through a bunch of exercises to make you really think about your brand DNA – who you are, what you stand for, your purpose and how you want to show up in the world. That way, you'll develop an unshakable confidence in who your business is so you can stand firm, knowing you're staying true to your core beliefs. For those who prefer to do this themselves, HubSpot's brand strategy templates are a great place to start.

A strategist or agency can also help you develop a suite of brand visual and communication guidelines to ensure you and your team are delivering a consistent identity when getting the word out on social media and other marketing platforms. This is where developing your storytelling becomes important. People – aka customers – remember and engage with stories, so embed your messages to create sharable content.

UNIQUE VISUAL IDENTITY

A unique visual identity makes your brand memorable and instantly recognisable. It incorporates your logo, colour palette, typography and imagery. Being consistent with these in everything you produce – from your shopfront, to online ads, to uniforms, to product packaging – will help cement your customer relationships, as people will feel confident and assured by the consistency and professionalism that the visuals convey. To keep yourself on track, create a visual style guide and a library of images.

CONSISTENT VOICE AND TONE

As well as your visual appeal, developing a consistent voice and tone builds trust and makes your brand feel cohesive and reliable when you communicate with your audience across all channels. For instance, if you're running a fitness studio, a motivating and energetic tone can resonate with your audience and reinforce your brand's personality.

Developing a written style guide that includes directives on tone, style, spelling, grammar and punctuation, can help you stay consistent.

TELL YOUR STORY

Sharing the story behind your brand, including your journey, challenges and successes, will help build rapport and an emotional connection with your audience. Sharing your highs and lows creates a personal bond with your customers and humanises your brand. Ultimately, people will buy for the emotional connection they have with your brand more often than they'll buy on price. They relate to how you make them feel, and building these human bonds is a powerful way to create an unbreakable connection. For example, if you're launching a fashion line, sharing your inspiration and the story behind your designs can engage your audience and help build a loyal following.

Keep it fresh

Once you've established your brand identity, you'll want to make it flourish. To stay relevant, you need to ensure it remains aligned with your audience's needs and market trends. This means regularly assessing your brand's performance and making adjustments by regularly updating your branding to reflect new innovations and market shifts. It's an ongoing effort. If you want to grow, you have to evolve, and even though the ride can be hard work and even a little terrifying at times, it's definitely worth it!

For example, at She's on the Money, in late 2023, we engaged a branding company to completely overhaul our look. After several years of being in business, we knew we needed to go through a branding update, so we did a lot of market research. We talked to our community about what they thought She's on the Money was and how it made them feel. Inherently we wanted them to feel the same and be validated about it, but we also felt it was time to step away from the more juvenile branding that we'd started the business with.

Nonetheless, it was a big change. When we launched it we got a lot of backlash because some people didn't like the colours we'd chosen – some thought they were too aggressive, while others said they didn't feel like that's 'who Victoria is'. What that told us was that they didn't know who we had become. And honestly that upset us a bit, because we'd tried so hard and worked a lot on bringing a new style forward. In reality, I was the one driving the change. I was the one who picked it, I was the one working hand in hand with the designer, and to me, the old branding was who I wasn't anymore and the brand refresh reflected who I'd become.

I love that our community was so passionate in their response – it showed just how invested they are and how much they care about our brand. They're so committed to it that they don't like change. Some just couldn't see the bigger vision I had for where we want to take the business.

Having said all that, eventually people do get familiar with you – even the 'new' you. That's why we did a big rebrand all at one time instead of doing it gradually. We set a hard and fast launch date of absolutely everything. And while this may have got some people offside initially, they've come around now and our community has grown because of it. Ultimately, that's what we wanted to achieve. We wanted to get more international listeners and have a bigger voice, and we've created that.

You won't always need to completely overhaul your brand to this extent, but you will need to regularly create materials, so here are some ways to maintain brand engagement.

DELIVER ON YOUR BRAND PROMISE

The most important thing is to continue to deliver on your brand promise so you can build trust and reinforce your brand's credibility. This amounts to ensuring that your products, services and customer experience align with the promises you make in your branding. For instance, if you're running an online store that promises fast shipping, consistently meeting delivery times will be crucial to maintaining customer trust.

CONTENT CREATION TOOLS

Tools like Canva and Adobe Creative Cloud offer user-friendly design tools for creating logos, social media graphics and marketing materials. My best tip is to create a suite of base templates which you can re-use to a) keep your look and style consistent and b) save you time. If you have, say, four templates – one that's word-heavy, one that's image-dominant, one that's numbers-based and one that's a cute combo, you'll have four 'looks' you can consistently roll out with minimal effort. This is key, because as you'll read next, posting regularly is critical to building audience engagement.

SOCIAL MEDIA

Use social media to get your story out there, making sure you're consistently on brand and on message, and your posts appear at regular times. Online platforms like Hootsuite and Buffer can help you maintain a consistent brand presence across social media platforms. The more consistent you are, the more people will get to know you. There's more on this later in this chapter!

GEORGE'S BUSINESS STORY

Inspired by my dad and my friends, I pursued photography as a hobby and then a business. I specialise in editorial wedding photography and my services are aimed at couples with elegant, modern taste.

I studied marketing at university, learnt on the fly and created a brand strategy. One of my early struggles was trying to be like everyone else instead of making my work unique. Seven years in and my work now has a distinct editorial style and my clientele has changed drastically. I hired a business coach, learnt how to market and price myself, and exceeded my goals. Recently I booked out a two-month Europe season for 2025, which is very exciting.

In my line of work, it's important to be prompt in replies, communicate necessary information and go above and beyond for clients.

Looking forward, I want to dive deeper into mentorship, do fewer weddings at a higher price point, and refine my offerings.

Develop your marketing strategy

Once you have completed the foundational work of positioning (Chapter 3), and created a strong brand framework, it's time to let people know all about your biz. First, by developing a marketing strategy and then by implementing an effective plan.

Without a clear plan, your marketing efforts may be scattered and ineffective. Poorly planned marketing can result in wasted time and money, and inconsistent marketing messages can confuse customers and undermine trust. Failing to target the right audience or use the right channels can result in missed opportunities for engagement and sales. Without clear goals and metrics, it's difficult to assess the effectiveness of your marketing efforts.

That's why one of the most crucial aspects of running a successful business is developing an effective marketing strategy. This becomes your roadmap to reaching your target audience, building your brand and driving sales – it's all about making sure your message gets to the right people at the right time.

FOR EXAMPLE: ECO CHIC

Marketing strategy

Continuing on from Chapter 3, our example business, Eco Chic, aims to carve out a niche in the Australian fashion market by offering high-end, eco-friendly clothing that combines luxury with sustainability. By focusing on artisanal craftsmanship, innovative materials, and a transparent supply chain, we will differentiate ourselves from both direct and indirect competitors, appealing to a discerning clientele who demand the best in sustainable fashion.

> » **Target audience:** Affluent, eco-conscious consumers aged 25 to 45 who value high-quality, unique fashion pieces and are willing to invest in sustainable luxury.

> » **Customer avatar:** 28-year-old Louise, passionate about sustainability, educates herself through Instagram and blogs, shops at farmers' markets and follows zero-waste principles. She spends carefully and is willing to pay a premium for products that align with her values.

> » **Brand storytelling:** Leverage storytelling to highlight the journey of each piece, from sustainable sourcing to artisanal craftsmanship. Use social media, blog posts and video content to showcase

the stories of the artisans and the sustainable practices behind our collections.

» **Collaborations and partnerships:** Partner with local artists, designers and eco-influencers to co-create limited-edition collections and expand our reach. Collaborate with high-end eco-friendly hotels and resorts to offer exclusive pop-up shops and trunk shows.

» **Sustainability events:** Host exclusive events, such as sustainable fashion shows, eco-friendly workshops and panel discussions on sustainability in fashion. These events will position Eco Chic as a thought leader in the sustainable fashion movement.

» **Premium packaging:** Use eco-friendly, luxurious packaging made from recycled materials. Offer a garment recycling program where customers can return old Eco Chic pieces in exchange for store credit, promoting a circular fashion economy.

» **Online presence and e-commerce:** Develop a sophisticated e-commerce platform with virtual styling consultations and a seamless shopping experience. Utilise targeted online advertising to reach eco-conscious consumers and drive traffic to our website.

OVER TO YOU

Using the above example from Eco Chic as a template, write out a marketing strategy for your business. You completed a lot of the groundwork for this in Chapter 3, by identifying your industry niche, ideal customer and USPs. Use this knowledge to build out your marketing strategy.

Putting your plan into action

Once you have outlined your overarching marketing strategy, it's time to get practical. How will you put these ideas into practice? Let's get specific.

Not every business will focus on social media, but there's a good bet that most will. In today's digital age, having a strong online presence is non-negotiable. It's all about connecting with your audience, building your brand and driving sales through the power of the internet. It's not just doing silly little dances on TikTok, it's social validation.

Historically, people would get on the train or bus and read the newspaper, so companies allocated a lot of their marketing spend to placing ads in newspapers – that was how to get in front of potential customers. But now the power's been put back into the hands of small business owners. While you don't have to pay for traditional ads, it's important to find new ways of reaching your demographic.

SET YOUR BUDGET

Setting a budget ensures you can execute your marketing plan without overspending. Allowing for this cost in your cash flow means you should be able to fund any activities you want to undertake. For instance, if you're running a small boutique, you might set a budget for online ads, influencer partnerships and promotional events. If you're engaging external agencies, setting a budget is especially important.

CHOOSE YOUR MARKETING CHANNELS

Selecting the platforms and methods you'll use to reach your target audience is a critical element of your marketing plan. Different channels reach different audiences, so choosing the right ones makes sure your message gets to the right people. There's no point, for instance, running Facebook ads if your audience only hangs out on TikTok.

If you're anything like me, you get excited and want to jump online immediately to share anything cute – and we're all about spreading the love here at SOTM. But let's face it, there's only so much time a biz gal has at her disposal so, as with anything, it's worth developing a bit of a plan before you start posting on a whim.

It's important to select the social media platforms and digital marketing channels that will best reach your target audience. Different platforms reach different audiences, so choose the right ones to ensure your message gets to the right people. For example, if you're targeting millennial women, Instagram and Pinterest might be effective platforms.

At SOTM we spend a lot of time thinking about this, and you should, too. Here's a very brief summary of the pros and cons of each platform, but these things are constantly changing, so please do your own research when it comes time to market your business!

Facebook

» **Pros:** Large user base, versatile ad formats, detailed targeting options.
» **Cons:** Organic reach is declining, can be more expensive for ads.

Instagram

» **Pros:** Highly visual, strong engagement, popular among millennials.
» **Cons:** Requires high-quality visuals, can be time-consuming to maintain.

X/Twitter

» **Pros:** Real-time engagement, great for customer service, trending topics.

» **Cons:** Fast-paced, content life span is short, can be noisy.

LinkedIn

» **Pros:** Professional network, B2B (business-to-business) marketing, high-quality leads.

» **Cons:** Less effective for B2C (business-to-customer), can be more formal.

Pinterest

» **Pros:** Highly visual, great for discovery, strong referral traffic.

» **Cons:** Requires high-quality visuals, niche audience.

TikTok

» **Pros:** High engagement, popular among Gen Z, viral potential.

» **Cons:** Requires creative video content, trends change quickly.

OVER TO YOU

Make a list of all the media platforms you like to spend time on and which catch your attention – from social media to the more traditional. Where do you like to engage with the things that interest you?

Now, do this same exercise but from your customer avatar's point of view – where do they like to hang out, both digitally and physically?

Finally, note where these two lists overlap. This crossover defines your most natural fit of the media channels and, as such, is where you should invest your time and budget, as this will feel the most natural to you while meeting your customers where they are at.

CREATE A CONTENT CALENDAR

A content calendar will lead to consistent and timely execution of your marketing strategies and can help with planning your marketing activities and content. For example, if you're managing an e-commerce store, planning your social media posts, email campaigns and promotions in advance keeps your marketing efforts organised. Planning is the key to consistency, and you already know that consistency is queen when it comes to marketing on social media!

CREATE ENGAGING CONTENT

Engaging content drives likes, shares, comments and, ultimately, conversions. Let's face it, if you're going to put time into creating and posting content, you want to make sure it captures your audience's attention and encourages interaction. For example, if you're managing a bar, you could post mouth-watering photos of your cocktails and fun, behind-the-scenes videos.

BE CONSISTENT

Posting consistently builds trust and keeps your audience engaged. Maintaining a consistent posting schedule and brand voice across all platforms is key and can help develop an emotional connection with your customers. During Covid lockdowns, Aussie fashion brand Girls with Gems did this really well, posting a daily 'Same, Same but Different Size' feature that grew a rapid following on TikTok and saw them become a breakout brand in the highly contested fashion market.[1]

MEASURE AND ADJUST

Measuring results helps you understand what is and isn't working so you can refine your strategies. It involves tracking the performance of your marketing activities and making adjustments as needed. Regularly analysing your website traffic, conversion rates and social media engagement will help you optimise your marketing efforts.

ADAPT AND EVOLVE

The media landscape is constantly changing, so staying adaptable will ensure your marketing efforts remain effective. As such, it's important to keep adjusting your strategies based on performance data and market trends. For instance, if you're managing a beauty brand, staying updated on the latest social media trends and adjusting your content accordingly keeps your brand relevant. Adaptability is another key to long-term success.

Meet the founder:
Marty Fox

Marty's company, WHITEFOX Real Estate, is not your average suit-and-tie business. As a point of difference, it taps into social media and video content, pushing to constantly evolve. Marty's approach is an example of consistent growth, hard work and keeping clients front of mind. In less than a decade, he has built WHITEFOX from one office to 12, located in cities across Australia and New Zealand, including Melbourne, Perth, Adelaide, Brisbane, Gold Coast, Queenstown, Wanaka and Auckland. Industry expectations have never held them back!

Name: Marty Fox

Business: WHITEFOX Real Estate

Industry: Real estate

Product/service: We are specialists in 'the art of the deal' for luxury properties across Australia and New Zealand.

Target audience: People looking to buy or sell property, particularly digital natives and anyone interested in beautiful properties marketed in fresh ways. We welcome a diverse clientele.

Secondary audience: Anyone looking for an exceptional selling experience and who puts a premium on how their property is marketed.

Unique selling point: Replacing 'traditional' approaches with a distinct voice that's 'bold, polished and matter-of-fact', we showcase property through the latest technology, social and marketing trends.

The business began: 2016

As soon as I left uni, I realised that sometimes, to get things done, you need to do them yourself. I've used this philosophy in every job I've ever had and it's helped me get to where I am today. Both my parents were fighters and I inherited their sense of drive. For me, the best way to get things done is to be in control of my own destiny. So, if I see something being done inefficiently or in a way I perceive to be illogical or wrong, I want to find a way to do it better.

When it came to starting WHITEFOX, after working for many years in the real estate industry, I began to notice that everyone did the same things in the same boring, traditional style. I felt there had to be another way. Why did we all have to wear a suit and tie? Why did we need to speak a certain way? Why did we have to advertise in the newspaper and not talk in our videos? I had so many questions, and their answers led me to realise there was another way to go about it. And so WHITEFOX was born.

Industry expectations have never aligned with WHITEFOX. Our vision has always been to be the pinnacle of property marketing world-wide. We were the original disruptor of the real estate industry through tone of voice, visual identity, fashion, social media and a constant push to evolve video content and marketing avenues. WHITEFOX clients have spent $0 on traditional print media since inception, proving our digital strategy has worked. We strive to ensure every transaction and experience is memorable for our clients, and have always seen ourselves as the industry influencer.

We were different from the outset: saying 'no' to suits and 'yes' to quality, narrated property videos, a digital-first marketing strategy, standout black-and-white photography, bespoke touches along every step of the selling journey – the list goes on. We do things differently and challenge the industry, and eventually our ways started being adopted by our competitors. They say imitation is the greatest form of flattery, so I guess we are constantly being flattered!

I never change suppliers if we have a good relationship – that's something I live by. I've been using the same photographer for 14 years and he's like family to me. Our signage company has been with us since day one, and if not for Agent Admin (who look after our accounts and services), this business would not have succeeded. The best idea is to establish relationships with trusted suppliers and if they deliver on their promises, never break up!

When I started WHITEFOX, I was the lead lister and seller in the company. That lasted until I stepped out of that role three years ago and into the role of CEO, because I got sick and had to step away from the business for a while. While I still oversee a lot of what goes on from the selling point of view, my main focus now is on growth and recruitment. That's seen us go from three offices to 12 in only a couple of years, with even bigger plans on the horizon.

One of the hardest things about running your own business is the inherent risk. It's hard when you're taking it all on. Financially, decisions affecting the business also affect me, and that can be a challenge. Rather than relying on external support, we use internal teams to drive the day-to-day running of the business. We encourage our staff to keep upskilling and have used external suppliers to help them level up when it comes to their sales skills.

Managing staff can be hard, but they're the cornerstone of good business. I focus on creating a good culture. Be a good person and your staff will be good to you. That doesn't mean don't be firm and don't provide feedback, because without that there's no growth. But cuddle when you need to cuddle and be stern when you need to be stern. It's also important to build good people managers in the team. The way we structure our business means our staff have leaders they can confide in. We offer multiple layers of support, including our head office, which has personnel who excel in dealing with people.

All of my personal time goes into running the business. I'm lucky to have such a supportive wife and family, but WHITEFOX is our life. Fortunately, I can spend time with my kids while also being able to put everything I have into my business – I guess that's one of the benefits of the industry I'm in and running my own business.

It's tough at times, but the satisfaction I get from it outweighs everything else. I have some of the most amazing work partners and colleagues who have put their faith, energy and effort into my vision for WHITEFOX, and for that I'm truly grateful. If I didn't put all of my time into making sure this business is a success, I'd be doing them a disservice.

It's not always easy to maintain a healthy work–life balance, though. I've had my ups and downs with it all, and my health has taken some significant hits from the pressure and stress. In 2021 I suffered severe pericarditis after a bout of Covid and had to step away from the business, but in some ways, if that hadn't happened we may not have ended up on the trajectory we are on. I'm an incredibly driven individual, so I can be my own worst enemy by eating the wrong things or training too hard when I've been told to rest (I have a hernia right now that is evidence of that).

Nevertheless, I wouldn't change anything – it's all worth it. What you learn in the troughs is what helps you reach the peaks. Having the bravery to challenge the traditional nature of the real estate industry has not only brought me success but a sense of achievement that there really is more than one way to get things done. And I'm incredibly proud of that.

Sell, sell, sell!

Whereas marketing is about raising awareness of your brand, your sales strategy is your game plan for generating revenue, reaching your sales targets and growing your business. This is where the rubber hits the road, as the results will speak for themselves. Quite literally, money talks and each sale is a win.

Creating a sales strategy involves defining your sales goals, identifying your target market and outlining the steps you'll take to achieve your sales objectives. Previously you've identified your offer and audience and developed ways to communicate to them. Now, how do you get them to buy?

CHOOSE YOUR SALES CHANNELS

These will differ from those in your marketing strategy. Your sales channels may include partnering with other retailers, listing on directories or running market stalls. Many e-commerce platforms offer widgets to help you add tactical promotions, such as volume discounts, to your online store and checkout cart. Experiment with these to see what works.

Depending on your business model, your sales channels will include in-person or online. Even if you are predominantly one or the other, it might be interesting to see how you might use the alternative to generate sales.

In-person sales

Whether at your storefront, a local market or a networking event, in-person sales give you the chance to engage directly, answer questions on the spot, and build trust with your audience. It's about making every interaction count and turning potential customers into loyal fans.

Online sales

Running online sales for a small business involves leveraging digital platforms to reach and engage a broad audience, ultimately driving sales and growth. This means setting up an intuitive and user-friendly e-commerce website, utilising social media channels, and employing digital marketing strategies like SEO, email campaigns and online ads to attract and convert customers. Online sales allow you to operate beyond the constraints of a physical location, offering convenience for both you and your customers. They're about creating a seamless online shopping experience, from browsing to checkout, and providing excellent customer service that builds trust and loyalty in the digital space.

SET YOUR PRICING STRATEGY

A well-thought-out pricing strategy will make sure you remain competitive while maximising your profit margins. Determine the pricing of your products or services based on market research and cost analysis, and set prices that reflect the quality of your offerings and the local market conditions.

TRAIN YOUR SALES TEAM

Building a dream team who not only hit targets but also thrives in a supportive and empowering environment is critical to your success. It starts with hiring the right people who align with your company's values and culture, and continues with developing training programs that deliver.

1. **Define your sales process:** Create a roadmap outlining the steps and stages of your sales process from lead generation to closing the sale. For example, if you're running an online boutique,

your sales process might include stages like product discovery, customer engagement and checkout.

2. **Develop a training program:** Create a structured program to train your sales team on the features and benefits of your products, sales techniques and customer base, which also includes training on how to effectively meet customer needs and handle challenges.

3. **Set targets:** Set targets and provide support to reach them. Communicating your expectations for performance, behaviour and goals provides direction and accountability.

4. **Foster a positive culture:** Create a supportive and positive work environment that encourages collaboration and motivation, which is critical for your business success. A positive culture boosts morale, reduces turnover and enhances team performance, and a happy team is a high-performing team!

OVER TO YOU

Using the steps above, write down some ideas for training your sales team. List what you want them to achieve, and what tools and training you might provide to help them get there. If you don't have a team and it's just you running sales, you can still define your process and set targets!

MONITOR AND ADJUST

As with any plan, your sales strategy needs to adapt to evolving trends. While you should develop an overarching strategy that will guide your tactical campaigns, it may change over time depending on customer response and feedback. A valuable part of your sales process could (dare I say, *should*) be sending follow-up communications post-sale. Some businesses use these to gather feedback; others may simply send their thanks, with suggestions for similar products based on the previous purchase.

Again, many e-commerce systems build such functionality into their platforms, so play around to see what works best for you.

My business sells home and personal fragrances, offering a range of products to suit a range of preferences and aesthetics. We are still learning our audience, but we know that 85 per cent of our customers are female. We try to be unique by offering a personal experience and handmaking a lot of our products to order, and we also offer customisations.

The business has been running for seven years. We began at a market offering a small range of candles but hardly sold a single thing. There are heaps of things we could have done differently, but basically, I just didn't have the knowledge at the time.

The number one thing we learnt is, it's all about social media. We should have been regularly engaging online with potential customers, but neither I nor my business partner is so inclined – our skills are more operational. We've had to change our mindset to 'just do it' – resigning ourselves to putting out content we're not completely satisfied with. We've learnt to accept that we'll get better over time. We also got a bit excited and bought many things that we wanted to sell but just didn't work with the brand – for example, teas.

We haven't yet brought on external help because one of us values external help and the other wants to do everything independently. We'll do it when we have a good cash flow set up. I spend a lot of time looking at content on YouTube and Instagram and listening to podcasts. The Learn with Shopify YouTube channel has some great content. I've also learnt to be very careful about influencers' courses and their paid content because, honestly, many of them are still learning themselves!

If I could start all over again, I would tell myself to put blinders on, ignore the shiny cool things and focus! Otherwise, you spread yourself too thin and none of your time is spent valuably.

Community is queen

To my mind, community in business involves two things:

1. **Your customer community:** The folks who love your brand and biz and are your ultimate champions.

2. **Your business community:** Colleagues at the same stage and growth as you, not necessarily in the same industry, but who can lift you up and support your goals, and vice versa. Basically, it's all about creating and nurturing connections with people who can help your business grow, one way or another.

CUSTOMER COMMUNITY

Here's another angle on understanding your target customer. I often talk about the importance of building community before building your product, because if you build a product and hope that the masses love it without taking on their feedback, you could be very wrong – and that's a massive risk. But if you build a community and get their feedback along the way; firstly, that's much cheaper to do because social media and community-building can be free if you invest the time and energy, and secondly, you're more likely to be successful in that space! So if your business idea is something that lends itself to having a community around it – even a small one – consider developing that group of people as you go, to bring you real-time feedback.

BUSINESS COMMUNITY

Networking with colleagues can lead to new business opportunities, partnerships and collaborations that can help increase your visibility and credibility. They can generate their own kind of upwards spiral, leading to referrals and recommendations. I would count collaborations in this category.

Personally, I tend to network outside my own industry as finance is male-dominated and I'm specifically looking for ways to do things differently. Networking with other women in business across different industries allows me to learn from others' experiences and gain insights into trends and practices that are working elsewhere that I may be able to bring into finance to change things up.

Let's connect

I'm sure you know the saying, 'It's not what you know, but who you know'. Believe me, this is true of the business world! Let's look at how you might turn casual encounters into powerful partnerships that drive success.

There's a way to weave any type of business into social media – you just have to sit down and make a strategy for it. A lot of the time people think you have to get on social media for your small business and sell, sell, sell, but that's not the case. It's more about presence and being around, sharing your experience and connecting with a community. That's certainly what has built She's on the Money. People want to feel that the brands they engage with are interested in them in return – that's what creates strong advocacy from your community, which helps grow your business. Unless your entire business model is based on social media sales channels, it's less about making an income stream from social media and more about giving your community social validation. It's free marketing. You're getting to people in the places where they're hanging out. My top tips for creating connections are:

BE GENUINE AND AUTHENTIC

Build relationships based on honesty and authenticity. That means that if you're attending a networking event, be yourself and show genuine interest in others. Genuine connections are more likely to lead to meaningful and long-lasting relationships.

LISTEN MORE THAN YOU TALK

Listening helps you build rapport and shows that you value others' input. Instead of talking about yourself, focus on understanding others' needs and perspectives – you'll learn much more this way. For example, if you're meeting a potential business partner, listening to their needs and challenges can help you find ways to collaborate.

FOLLOW UP

Always stay in touch with your connections after that initial meeting. Following up helps you maintain and strengthen relationships over time. If you've met someone at a networking event, send a follow-up email or LinkedIn message to keep the conversation going.

OFFER VALUE

Offering value – providing support, advice or resources to your connections – helps you build mutually beneficial relationships. For example, if you're part of a business networking group, sharing useful information or connecting others with resources can build goodwill.

BE CONSISTENT

Consistency helps you stay top-of-mind and build deeper connections over time. There are many ways to do this, so find one that works for you and ties in naturally with your personality and interests. For instance, if you're part of a local business association, attending meetings and events regularly will keep you engaged with the community.

LEVERAGE TECHNOLOGY

A key theme in this book is using technology to your advantage. Here, using digital tools and platforms to network and build relationships can help expand your reach and make it easier to stay connected. Using LinkedIn to connect with industry professionals or joining an online business community can enhance your networking efforts.

OVER TO YOU The key to creating connections is authenticity. Using my suggestions as inspiration, come up with your own cheat sheet for connecting that suits your style, personality, skills and approach.

Customer service is customer success

Great customer service can set your business apart, build a loyal customer base and drive long-term success. It means providing a positive and memorable experience for your customers at every touchpoint.

That said, I probably have a slightly different mindset around customer service than some others, as I do NOT believe that the customer is always right. In fact, I've been known to get into little fights if I think our business needs protecting. There's a difference between offering good customer service and bending to the will of every customer who comes along.

I mean, inherently, one plus one equals two. If your customer's like, 'But I should get three', well, sorry, but that's not how it works. And to be honest, that's not the type of customer I want in my community. We're a community of women who build each other up and support each other.

If we accept one ratbag, then we're setting ourselves up to accept more people like that in the future. See, if we bend to Karen and make her feel really good, she's going to introduce Sharon, and Sharon's going to expect what Karen got, which keeps pushing us in the wrong direction, and then we end up too far from what our initial offering was and how we want to run our business.

So, something I've always tried to do is have my team's back. If customers come to us with a concern, then of course we have those conversations and absolutely kill them with kindness and give them every opportunity to do the right thing. But raise your voice and you're out. I'm not having my team be treated poorly. That's not the culture I'm fostering. It's more important to me that my team knows I have their back – and because of that, their confidence has grown. They've learnt more about their own abilities and trusted themselves more, and that has then added to the community we've built of strong, independent women, inside and out.

When it comes to bringing my customers into that community and vibe, you can bet your bottom dollar that I'll bend over backwards to make it happen, and so will my team. I think that's the underlying foundation of customer service – it's really about customer success. Our approach is that we want to see everyone succeed – our business and our customers. Training my team is about bringing them on board with that as a concept and then empowering them to deliver it.

Now that we've covered your sales team's culture, let's look at how you can empower them to make your customers feel great.

UNDERSTAND YOUR CUSTOMERS

Understanding your customers helps you tailor your service to meet their expectations. It helps you gain insights into their needs, preferences and pain points. For example, if you're running a beauty salon, knowing your customers' preferred treatments and products will enhance their experience.

PERSONALISE THE EXPERIENCE

Personalisation creates a memorable and positive experience for customers. Tailor your interactions to make customers feel valued and appreciated.

BE RESPONSIVE

Respond promptly and effectively to customer inquiries and issues. Prompt responses show customers that you value their input, time and concerns and are committed to resolving their issues. Make it your aim to address negative feedback and complaints as quickly as possible, ideally within 24 hours. The same goes for general inquiries and positive feedback or compliments!

LISTEN AND ACT ON FEEDBACK

Feedback provides valuable insights into what's working and what needs improvement, so you should always be actively seeking and using customer feedback to improve your service. As such, it's important to create an environment where customers feel comfortable sharing their thoughts and concerns. For example, if you're managing a café, you might put a suggestion box near the door or a feedback form on your website.

1. **Listen actively:** As you know, I don't wholly agree with the saying, 'The customer is always right'. But where it is valuable, is in the way that it encourages you to pay close attention to what your customers are saying and show empathy. Active listening helps you understand the customer's perspective and demonstrates that you care. For example, if you're managing a fitness studio,

actively listening to customer concerns about class schedules or facilities can help you address their needs.

2. **Acknowledge and apologise:** Recognise the customer's issue and offer a sincere apology. This will show them that you take their concerns seriously and are committed to making things right.

3. **Resolve the issue:** Beyond lip-service, it's important to take action to address and resolve customers' concerns. Effective resolution demonstrates your commitment to their satisfaction and can turn a negative experience into a positive one.

4. **Follow up:** You can build extra credit by checking in with customers after resolving their issue. Follow-up shows customers that you value their feedback and are committed to their satisfaction.

5. **Learn and improve:** Use negative feedback and complaints to identify areas for improvement and make necessary changes. Continuous improvement based on feedback helps you enhance your offerings.

CASSANDRA'S BUSINESS STORY

I started a non-surgical cosmetics clinic two-and-a-half years ago, offering injectables, IPL [intense pulsed light] therapy and skin treatments. I was driven to start the business because of my love for beauty and my desire for freedom in both my personal life and career.

Our services are timeless and not trend-driven; they focus on making people look and feel their best. My target audience is women aged over 35. We're in a tough industry with Therapeutic Goods Administration [TGA] requirements and ever-changing regulations, but we conform and keep going.

My business brand identity is very important – we focus on how we come across on social media and how we make people feel in the clinic. Customer service is key – people always remember how you made them feel. Be genuine and personable yet professional.

I was naive when I started and knew nothing, but I figured out things along the way. One great lesson I can share is to always put more money away than you think for tax, unexpected costs and savings. My advice is to get a business coach and keep your books clean. Every cent that comes into my account has a purpose, and we allocate money down to the dollar every week.

GO THE EXTRA MILE

This creates memorable experiences that build customer loyalty. Exceed your customers' expectations by providing additional value or service. This is what business guru Geoff Ramm calls 'celebrity service'. He asks companies to identify what would happen if a celebrity became a client. Let's say this happens in your business. How will you reply to an email from the celebrity – is it the usual cut-and-paste, or do you add a bit more character or personalisation? Do you take a little more time?[2] This is the gap in your customer service levels you probably didn't realise existed. For instance, if you're managing a retail store, offering personalised shopping assistance or surprise discounts can delight your customers. Such acts are often termed 'surprise and delight' or 'reward and recognition'.

GET TECHNO

Using digital tools and platforms can enhance customer service. Many client booking systems, for example, can be set up to automatically send reminders and even to offer discounts at regular intervals. Much of the hard work has been taken out, so you just need to get creative. For instance, you might use a CRM system to track customer interactions and preferences to enhance your service.

CRISIS POINTS

Sometimes the complaints are BIIIG. In terms of crisis management, it's crucial that businesses own their mistakes in the public eye. The problem may have been created by you, or you may have given the wrong response to a bad situation. In all instances, once you see a negative backlash rising, it's important to address it head on. These days, with social media always on, you can't afford to stick your head in the sand and ignore a problem. You have to own it. When mistakes happen, it can be a really great opportunity to ask yourself how and why the issue occurred. What did it look like? What would be the best way of fixing it?

Initially, you might feel you need to justify your behaviour because you want your community to continue to see you as smart and capable: 'I didn't mean it – we be cool?' Of course you didn't mean it, but that's not constructive in that moment. Many people think that 'taking responsibility' means justifying their behaviour – but that's not what your community is looking for. They want you to take ownership, and they want to know you're going to make a positive change because of the mistake you've made. You need to think about your community and how they're feeling, not about yourself. So taking 'you' out of the picture is really important in these situations.

If your apology has anything in it about how you feel, it's not an apology – it's a justification. We humans are very good at justifying our behaviour. But remove your feelings from the equation and let your customers know they're being heard. When you mess up, that's the best way to set an example of who you are as a business and as a community and show how you behave when things go wrong. Everyone's always happy when it's sunshine and roses, but if you can prove yourself in trying times, that's when you'll win advocates for life.

Principle 7: Love your brand

Your brand is the heart of your business. Be clear and consistent with your values, purpose and passion across every touchstone of your business, from marketing, to sales, to community building. The emotional connection your customer has with your business is why they buy.

Meet the founder:
Jess Hatzis

Jess Hatzis is a co-founder of one of Australia's most recognisable skincare brands, frank body, and until recently was its long-serving chief marketing officer. Its success was, in part, propelled by her first business: creative branding agency Willow & Blake, which operates to this day. In turn, she credits the agency's success with the in-house knowledge she brought to running a consumer brand like frank body.

Name: Jess Hatzis

Businesses: frank body; Willow & Blake

Industries: Skincare; branding

Products/services: Body-care products for frank body; branding services for Willow & Blake

Target audiences: For frank body, women in their twenties and thirties; for Willow & Blake, medium-sized businesses, consumer brands and start-ups

Secondary audiences: For frank body, women in their forties looking for anti-ageing products; for Willow & Blake, other businesses that are value-aligned with what Willow & Blake can offer

Unique selling points: At frank body, we create high-performance skincare with a sensory experience; at Willow & Blake, we create branding as if it were our own.

The businesses began: 2011

Willow & Blake is a branding agency that creates brands from beginning to end. When a fledgling company comes to us, it's our job to take the idea from the founder's brain and turn it into a strategy, combine tone of voice with a visual identity, and create a rollout campaign to launch.

frank body is a global skincare business specialising in high-performance body care. We offer reliable and affordable skincare products that solve women's skin problems. Our core audiences are the two vastly different Gen Z and millennial consumer groups. More recently, we've developed anti-ageing products for women in their forties.

The common theme between my roles across both businesses is 'brand'. I describe myself as a writer – that's my roots – who grew into a marketer who grew into a brand strategist who specialises in consumer brands.

I didn't start out wanting to be an entrepreneur – I just found myself always starting 'projects' to follow my passions, which grew into work or business opportunities. I was only 23 when we started Willow & Blake, and I think youthful naivety is a powerful driver for believing you can do anything you want. The idea of flexibility and freedom has been continuous throughout my life and I knew I wouldn't be able to live in my core values if I had a traditional job.

I've done things because I believe so wholeheartedly in the idea rather than being led by a potential financial outcome. I think you need the belief in what you're doing to sustain you through what are inevitably going to be very tough times in business. That belief in what you're doing or that love for what you're doing (not that I've loved every moment of my job – I've hated some parts of it!) is what keeps you going.

As a business owner, you can't just specialise in one skill. Look to industries in which you have no experience and work out ways you could fix problems there. You also need an element of ego and self-belief, and

I mean that in the most positive way, because if you don't think you can do something, you'll never be able to do it.

Willow & Blake started as a copywriting agency. When we launched, we noticed a gap in the market. At the time, the written word for brands was a complete afterthought – everything was very design-led. But we were big believers in messaging and strategy being the foundation upon which you built a visual identity, so we started with that, then grew into a full-service agency.

Willow & Blake's value proposition is that we create brands as if they were our own. What makes us different to most other creative agencies is that we're running a consumer brand business, frank body, alongside. Our agency team are creatives at heart but we've trained them to think commercially. They work in the same office as frank body's finance, product development and retail teams, so they learn by osmosis what it takes to run a consumer-brand business and apply that thinking to their creative work, making sure it can stretch across a plethora of different applications for a business. I don't know of many other creative agencies that have that thinking and experience in-house.

I really like the idea of starting in a niche and owning it well, and then doing something else and doing that really well, and then adding something else, rather than trying to do everything from the get-go. It's easier in terms of your focus being singularly on one thing and trying to do that one thing well. I think word of mouth is still one of the most powerful forms of marketing for any brand – for people to be able to describe what you do, who you serve, what your services are and what your product is. If it's very niche, it becomes easier for them to explain. People tend to overlook how important that is. Build a solid base and then you can grow and expand that over time.

The great thing about our culture is that if I really want to start something or there's an idea I want to pursue, I can. We also try to have a very entrepreneurial nature within our organisation, so that we can make that happen for anyone who works for us who has a great idea and can put a business case together for it.

In terms of challenges, I find people management extremely taxing to do properly. I love the people who have worked with us, however you're not just someone's boss when you're their employer. You're their coach, therapist, mentor, mother, friend and employer, and that's a lot of hats to wear. I don't think people appreciate how much time and energy it takes to do people management well. It's become harder because employees increasingly have higher expectations of employers outside of the basic remit of their job, too. You don't always have to meet those expectations – some people are not meant to work within your organisation and it's okay for them to move on. Ultimately, you'll retain the people you're value-aligned with and have much longer working relationships with those people.

My best tip for managing staff is that clarity is kindness, in every sense of the word. Employees need to know where they're going. If you don't have clear job descriptions and pathways for progression, if you don't help them understand when and why pay rises happen and define their career evolution, you'll lose them, so spend time on doing that now. And don't set people up to fail. If you don't give them the feedback they need, you're not allowing them to grow as an individual or serve your organisation in the best way possible.

Running my businesses is a 24-hour job, because I'm always thinking about work. My subconscious is solving problems while I'm sleeping, in the shower, while I'm driving. I'll be sitting playing with my baby but 20 per cent of my brain will be locked into work. I think it's the inevitable curse of the founder that you're always working, but it's also what allows you to be in business. I need to learn how to switch my brain off, but then again, if I could easily switch my brain off.

I don't think work–life balance exists as a business owner, and to be honest I don't really like the word 'balance'. I think it assumes that there can be this perfect equilibrium of things, and that's just not life. I strive for rhythm and flow. Setting boundaries is important, but they need to have an element of flexibility for our own sake. Being too rigid is the thing that will drive us mad and create more stress.

The external support our business relies on has changed over time. We work with external accountants and regulators for both businesses, and although we have most of the skill sets we need in-house for our brand work, we still hire experts occasionally. At frank body, for example, we bring on experts for our retail fit-outs. We don't have permanent in-house talent for that because it would be insanely expensive. Same with photographers and videographers. Sometimes we'll pull something together internally, but it's really worth investing in specialists when the work is crucial to success.

While I'm a big believer in getting your hands dirty when you start a business (when I started both of my businesses, we didn't have any employees), I'd advise people to outsource once they get to the point where they feel like they're not doing a critical task well. In the beginning we were everything – we did every job and had no funding. And there's something really great about that, because you learn so much about your customers and the business. But eventually you get to a point where you can't do it all, so you look at what's on your plate and which tasks are limiting your ability to use your primary skill set to propel the business forward, and you reassign those first, either by hiring staff or outsourcing.

At frank body, the first thing we hired for was customer service, because we were spending so much time on that and wanted to do it really, really well because we believed so wholeheartedly in its importance.

People underestimate the amount of personal growth and self-understanding that comes with being in business. I wouldn't change any of the problems I've faced, just how I faced them – how I internalised so much stress and let it impact my health, my relationships, my friendships. That's the biggest piece of advice I could give to any potential founder. Invest in therapy, understand yourself, do a SWOT analysis on yourself and work out what you need to spend time working on.

You need adversity to get you to where you want to be and to shape who you are as a person, not just in work. I like that piece of advice. It's not about going back and changing what happened – it's about going back to times when you didn't have that self-belief and asking if you'd had it, could you have tackled a problem in a slightly different way?

A valuable lesson I was taught very young by my grandfather – and I wish I'd thought about it more when I started my businesses – is that you are worth whatever price you put on yourself. It can be interpreted in many different ways: in terms of the energy you're trying to protect, or the monetary value you place on your product or service – even the value you place on your ideas and your self-worth. Understanding that you're worthy in every sense will help you go far in times of those clusterfuck shit-fires that happen in all businesses. That's the lesson I'd go back and remind myself of.

Chapter Eight

Managing your business like a pro

Once you have your business up and running, there are several things you need to keep a constant eye on to ensure performance remains high. In this chapter we'll go through hiring and managing employees, as well as risk management, including insurance. While these subjects may feel a little dry, remember, this is your livelihood! Many small business owners throw their life savings behind their venture, so learning how to manage it well is essential.

It's about the people, people

Your team is the backbone of your business. As such, finding the right people and managing them effectively can make all the difference to your success. Hiring and managing employees involves finding the right talent, onboarding them effectively and creating an environment where they can thrive.

As Adam Jacobs, co-founder of The Iconic and now head of recruitment start-up Hatch, says, 'It's a widely known secret that second-time founders often focus on people and hiring problems, because what you learn when you build a business – and I saw The Iconic go from zero to 1000 people – is that the majority of the success of a business comes down to who's on the bus . . . And hiring is not easy.'[1]

I agree with many of the founders whose stories are featured in this book, that people management may well be the hardest part of managing a business. In fact, I might even go so far as to say it's the worst part of your business. But don't despair! I'm here to help you find and keep great staff.

Strategies for success

HIRE SLOW, FIRE FAST

One piece of advice I stick with is to hire slow, fire fast. My team knows I really test new employees at the start because I believe that people are rarely able to put their best foot forward in an interview. In a few short meetings you can't fully assess a person's capability or how they're going to interact with the rest of your team, with your customers or in tricky situations.

At first you won't have a lot of extra budget, so you'll probably start by hiring people for all-rounder roles. Make sure you set them up with clean processes and systems in the early days as it can be super annoying and time-consuming to break bad habits later. In the beginning I would hire with a specific role in mind, but I also needed the right personality. Personality fit in your first hire is really important. Often if it's technical in nature you can outsource that – get a freelancer who can help. As the business grows, you can bring in more specialised people.

What I concentrate on through the recruiting process is making sure the prospective employee has a level of attention to detail that

I find acceptable. I ask them to run through a few tasks so I can get an idea of the quality of their work, or if they're a creative, I ask for a portfolio so I can assess the types of things they've done. And then, in the interviews, I look for cultural fit because for me that's really important.

But it's not until a new employee comes on board that you can really test them. In those first few weeks it should be clear if they are up to standard, and if any part of you is feeling they're not the right person, you need to get rid of them quickly. While that might sound cruel, it's actually the kindest thing you can do for them and for you. You don't want someone getting six months into their employment and neither you nor them being happy. That's six months of butting heads. Your pre-existing internal culture sees that and sees you accepting that, and this can get the rest of the team offside. They're the ones who already have your back – so such a situation is neither productive nor constructive.

On top of that, if you fire an employee after six months, it will be hard for them to find a new job. It's much more palatable for somebody who's looking for a new job to go into another interview and say they spent a week with you and it wasn't the right fit so they're finding a new role. I'd have mad respect for a person who said that to me in an interview.

So hire slow, fire fast is definitely part of the way I work. I prefer to do an abundance of interviews than hire the wrong person. It's worked well for us. We haven't had to fire fast, but knowing that's where we're at puts everyone on the same page and sets expectations internally as well.

My hand therapy business is a specialised team of physiotherapists and occupational therapists who treat people with hand and upper limb injuries, including elderly people, sportspeople and post-operative patients. We're very community focused and care about our patients and their families.

Over five-and-a-half years the business has grown from two directors working part time to a team of eight therapists and two administrators. As we grew, we were unable to manage the caseload so gradually hired new hand therapists and then took on an administrator, which was the best decision ever. I've learnt that getting to know your team and finding out how best to support them helps people excel in their roles. It's also helpful to outsource HR advice and assistance when needed.

I recommend that aspiring business owners outsource as soon as they can afford it and that they get their brand and values consistent from the start. If I could have my time again, I would have outsourced a lot more of the tedious tasks a lot earlier to focus on my areas of expertise. On that note, I have the best accounting/advisory team ever. We outsource accounts payable and have a virtual assistant [VA] to help with out-of-hours phone calls from patients. In the past we have also invested in SEO services.

I'm a member of She Owns It, a women in business networking support group. I also recommend the Social Club Community for digital marketing and Instagram support.

I've managed to strike a good balance of work and personal time. I work in a clinical capacity 20 hours per week and run the business for approximately the same amount of time. In winter it's a lot busier, with all the sporting injuries we see.

Build your dream team

The ultimate guide to building a dream team who will drive your business forward starts with creating detailed and enticing job descriptions, using a mix of recruitment strategies to attract top talent, and acing the interview and selection process. Once you've found your people, proper onboarding is crucial, followed by training and development and positive performance management.

There's a range of tools and in-person activities and processes you can undertake during the hiring process, including interviews, online quizzes, in-person practical assessments and, of course, speaking with previous employers. Obviously, the role you're hiring for will somewhat dictate what you prioritise. If you're hiring a software developer, their programming abilities will be your top priority and working remotely will likely be okay, whereas if you're looking for a top sales performer, their in-person communication skills will be paramount.

Personally, unless it's a legal requirement, I don't necessarily think that a person's educational or past experience is the ultimate indicator of whether or not they're capable. Naturally our finance team have the qualifications they need to do their work, but most of our social media team haven't been to uni because it's not necessary. The best social media managers right now come from the chronically online Gen Z. They know how to get on a trend, how to tap it, how to talk. Those skills don't actually have anything to do with those assignments you might do at university. I prefer to hire for cultural fit and get the right person with the right ethics for my business rather than to hire someone for their technical capability and then put up with poor performance. To hire the right fit for your business:

DEFINE YOUR NEEDS

First, identify the skills, experience and qualities you require in your employees. Having a clear understanding of your needs helps you find the right fit for your business. For example, if you're running a café, you might be seeking baristas with excellent customer service skills.

CREATE A JOB DESCRIPTION

Writing a detailed job description that outlines the role, responsibilities and qualifications will help you attract the right candidates and set expectations.

RECRUITMENT STRATEGIES

There are several ways to recruit candidates, from using recruitment agents to posting ads on job boards such as Seek, to advertising in professional organisations, if your industry has them. Choosing the right methods and channels will help you find and attract better candidates from a more qualified talent pool.

INTERVIEW AND SELECTION

Once you receive applications, sort through them to create a shortlist of candidates to interview. Conducting assessments, such as running the applicants through simulated exercises, can help you evaluate their real-time skills and make better hiring decisions. Check their references, too.

ONBOARDING

This is the process whereby you introduce new employees to your business, culture and processes. Effective onboarding helps new hires integrate smoothly and become productive quickly.

TRAINING AND DEVELOPMENT

Providing ongoing training and development opportunities will enhance your employees' skills and knowledge, keep them engaged and improve their performance. For instance, if you're managing a fitness studio, offering regular training for instructors on new techniques can keep your classes fresh.

PERFORMANCE MANAGEMENT

Monitor and evaluate employee performance regularly to ensure alignment with your business goals. Effective performance management helps you identify strengths, address weaknesses and recognise achievements.

EMPLOYEE ENGAGEMENT AND RETENTION

Work hard to create a positive work environment that motivates and retains your employees. Engaged employees are more productive and loyal, and contribute to a healthy culture. Perhaps offer flexible work arrangements, and make sure to recognise your employees' achievements.

OVER TO YOU

Make a list of roles you'd like to hire for in the future. For each, write a job description that outlines the skills and personal characteristics you're looking for. Consider what formal qualifications the person might need, or even whether formal qualifications are essential. Make a list of daily, weekly, monthly and yearly tasks/goals you'd hope the applicant would achieve for you if you hired them, and work out roughly what value that would deliver to the business (including how much time it would free up for you to put into other things that would generate more income). Use this, along with published salary guidelines, to determine the salary range. Write up a job ad and have it ready to publish when the business can afford to bring a person on board.

Manage your dream team

Unfortunately, whether you like it or not, the bigger your business gets, the more people management you'll have to do. Today I do more people management than ever before, and it's really hard – not drama, just hard work. It's realising they might not know how to use your systems and you're the only person who has the capacity to train them in those systems. People management is always going to be a pain point. You can perfectly control your business on paper, but you can't control emotions or people getting sick or their career aspirations or goals.

Having HR policies in place will help guide everyone's expectations and set out standards to follow. They're hard to set up but will save you time in the end as you won't have to create new approaches each time someone presents with a question or issue. They'll also mean you're treating everyone fairly as the terms are the same across the board.

There's a bit to understanding and implementing HR policies and ensuring you're meeting your obligations without drowning in unnecessary paperwork. First and foremost, there are laws you need to abide by, so it's a matter of understanding which laws apply to your business and then tailoring policies to your unique environment. Of course, there's no point in having HR policies if they're not clearly communicated. Let's go through the basics and give you a head start.

KNOW THE LEGAL REQUIREMENTS

As an employer, it's important you know which employment laws and regulations apply to your business, including minimum wages and working conditions. In Australia these are outlined and managed by the Fair Work Ombudsman.[2] Compliance with legal requirements protects your business from legal issues and penalties.

IDENTIFY YOUR BUSINESS NEEDS

Tailoring your HR policies to your business needs ensures the policies are relevant and effective. So, once you broadly understand your obligations under the Fair Work system (see Chapter 4), it's important to assess the specific HR needs and challenges of your business. For instance, if you're managing a tech start-up, you might need policies on remote work, flexible hours and intellectual property.

DEVELOP CLEAR POLICIES

Next, it's important to create detailed and understandable HR policies that cover key areas such as recruitment, performance management, leave entitlements and workplace behaviour. Clear policies provide guidance and set expectations for employees and managers and remove any confusion. For example, if you're running a beauty salon, you need to have clear policies on dress code, client interactions and health and safety.

COMMUNICATE POLICIES EFFECTIVELY

Naturally, there's no point in having HR policies if no-one in your business is aware of them. As part of onboarding employees and in their ongoing performance management, make sure they are aware of and understand your HR policies. Effective communication will ensure they know what's expected of them and what they can expect in return. Many times, it can help with employee retention – for instance, if you have a policy that repays overtime with time off in lieu.

TRAIN YOUR TEAM

It's important to provide training in HR policies and procedures to employees and managers to ensure that everyone understands and can effectively apply the policies. For example, if you're running an online boutique, training customer service representatives in policies related to customer interactions and returns is essential.

There are a variety of tools and platforms available to help deliver training, such as:

» **HR software:** This can help to manage policies and employee information.

» **E-learning platforms:** Resources like Udemy, Coursera and LinkedIn Learning can provide training in HR policies.

» **Collaboration software:** Platforms like Slack, Microsoft Teams and Trello can help you communicate and collaborate on HR policies.

MONITOR AND UPDATE POLICIES

Be sure to regularly review and update your HR policies so they remain relevant and compliant with changes in laws and business needs.

SEEK PROFESSIONAL ADVICE

Consulting with HR professionals or legal experts can help to make sure your policies are comprehensive and compliant. Having the right systems and procedures in place can also help you scale quickly, and professional advice can help you avoid legal pitfalls. For example, if you're running a tech start-up, consulting with an HR consultant or employment lawyer can help you develop policies on intellectual property and data security.

Identify a list of HR policies that your business needs. Hint: many state government websites offer templates for HR policies and manuals. Tailor these to suit the specific needs of your business, taking care not to contravene Australian Fair Work laws. Your best bet is to check out the Fair Work Ombudsman's guide for small business.[3]

Risk management

Finally, let's talk about understanding and managing your risk. Understanding and managing risk and insurance obligations involves identifying potential risks to your business and ensuring you have the strategies in place to protect against those risks. It may sound a bit dull, but if you're putting your lifeblood into building your business, you absolutely want to know it's protected.

I have a friend who owned a big cosmetics company that had been running successfully for a while when they put through their biggest ever minimum order quantity. Having never insured their orders before, my friend didn't think to do it then, either. I don't even think she knew you could get sea insurance for your stuff if it fell off the side of a ship. And her entire order fell off the side of a ship and it wasn't insured. There's nothing the shipping company would do in this instance as it's deemed 'reasonable' that they might lose a container, and it's your responsibility to insure your goods. That's a lot of money down the drain!

Identify potential risks and challenges

Because I know you're too smart to find yourself in a similar situation, it's time to look at practical ways to help you manage the sometimes-bumpy road ahead. One of the most helpful things you can do is what the fancy-pants consultants like to call a 'risk mitigation plan' or what I prefer to call a 'let's avoid panic' plan.

As you know, I'm a planner from way back (literally – I'm a retired financial planner) and that means I love getting organised. Getting organised to avoid risk doesn't get everyone as excited as it does me, though. I know a lot of people will say, 'Hey Victoria, I'll deal with that problem when it comes.' That may be fine in your personal life, but when you're running a business that has regular bills to pay, including people's salaries, with which they pay their mortgages and kids' school fees, then you need to approach things a tad more seriously. If you'll allow me to get teachery for a minute here, there are some genuine business benefits to be had.

Proactive planning allows you to anticipate and mitigate issues before they become significant problems. It will likely help keep your business stable financially and operating smoothly even if it's hit with disruptions. Let's face it – we all want to be the good guy, not the baddie, when the world is falling apart. Being a good guy is also likely to keep building your brand and bring you more customers, and will help keep the boys in blue away. (Although it may be boring, some of the risk management stuff is about keeping you legally safe and compliant.)

Here's a useful series of steps you can run through to start planning ahead on managing risks for your small business. Ultimately you want to be able to sleep well at night, and knowing you've got even a basic plan for managing bad days and worst-case scenarios is a heck of a lot more useful than counting sheep.

CONDUCT A RISK ASSESSMENT

Conducting a risk assessment is a systematic process of identifying and evaluating potential risks to your business. It involves analysing each aspect of your operations to pinpoint vulnerabilities and assess the likelihood and impact of various risks. To begin with, it's important to understand the various types of risks that can impact your operations. They fall into the following categories:

» **Financial risks:** These include things such as cash flow issues and credit shortages. To counter these risks, regularly review your cash flow statements and financial forecasts. Use accounting software like Xero or MYOB to track your expenses and revenue in real time.

» **Operational risks:** These cover things like supply chain disruptions and equipment failures. To reduce them, conduct regular audits of your supply chain and equipment and implement standard operating procedures (SOPs) for key processes.

» **Market risks:** These include changes in consumer behaviour and economic downturns. To avoid them, stay updated on market trends and consumer behaviour through industry reports and market research. Use tools like Google Trends to monitor changes in consumer interest.

» **Compliance risks:** These relate to regulatory changes and legal issues. To stay in the know, subscribe to updates from regulatory bodies such as the Australian Securities and Investments Commission (ASIC) and the ATO. They'll keep you informed about changes to laws and regulations.

» **Reputational risks:** These are things like negative publicity and customer dissatisfaction. Monitor online reviews and social media mentions using tools like Google Alerts and Hootsuite.

Using the risk assessment categories above as prompts, list any risks that might impact your business. Rank them in order of how likely you think it is that they might happen, and then rank them again in order of severity. This will give you a risk matrix. Once you've identified the risks and their probability, you can decide how much time and effort you might put into finding a solution for them. The more specific you are, the more useful. For example, if you're running an ice-creamery, an operational risk would be a power outage; without electricity, your main product will melt. The likelihood is based on previous years' outages (in my area, unfortunately it's around three times a year, usually for at least 12 hours!). The impact is high, given you would lose all your stock and at least a day or two of trading, depending on how quickly you can get replacements. As such, if this were my business, I'd be investing in a serious backup generator to ensure I didn't lose all my precious stock in the event of a power failure.

Steps to safety and security

By quantifying risks and prioritising them based on their potential impact, you can develop a clearer picture of where your business stands and what areas require immediate attention. This enables you to allocate resources more effectively and implement measures to mitigate the identified risks. It might be helpful to organise a workshop with key team members to identify any potential threats to your business.

Following that, you'll want to draw up a risk matrix – basically a table that helps you categorise risks based on their likelihood and impact. Use this matrix to prioritise which risks need immediate attention. Developing different scenarios (best-case, worst-case, and most likely) can help you understand how various risks might impact your business.

KNOW THE LEGAL REQUIREMENTS

First, ensure you understand the legal requirements for insurance that apply to your business. Compliance with legal requirements protects your business from legal issues and penalties. For example, if you're running a retail store, you need to understand public liability insurance and workers compensation requirements.

IDENTIFY YOUR BUSINESS RISKS

Assess the specific risks that could impact your business so you can take steps to mitigate them. For instance, if you're managing a tech start-up, you'll need to consider cyber risks and data breaches.

DEVELOP A RISK MANAGEMENT PLAN

Once you've identified and assessed the risks, the next step is to develop a comprehensive risk management plan. It should outline specific strategies and actions to address each identified risk and may include measures such as diversifying suppliers to reduce dependency on a single source, implementing robust financial controls to manage cash flow, and investing in staff training to enhance operational efficiency. The plan should also establish clear roles and responsibilities, ensuring that everyone in the organisation knows their part in managing risks.

IMPLEMENT RISK MITIGATION STRATEGIES

Implementing risk mitigation strategies involves putting your risk management plan into action. This may include adopting new technologies to improve data security, establishing contingency plans for supply chain disruptions, and securing insurance coverage to protect against financial losses. Effective risk mitigation also requires ongoing monitoring and adjustment of strategies to ensure they remain effective. By proactively addressing potential risks, you can minimise their impact on your business and create a more resilient operation. Regular training and communication with your team are also vital to make sure everyone is aware of and committed to the risk mitigation efforts.

OVER TO YOU

Brainstorm ways in which you might be able to reduce risk in your business. You might consider diversifying your supplier base, investing in comprehensive insurance policies, implementing cybersecurity measures and writing out procedures to manage incidents, for instance.

TRAINING AND COMMUNICATION

Once you have determined your risk management plans and processes, you need to make sure all team members are aware of and understand them. Effective communication means that everyone will know what is expected of them and what they can expect in return.

People often remember by doing, so a helpful way to communicate these policies is to provide training for employees and managers, so that everyone fully understands and can effectively apply the policies. For example, if you're running a fitness studio, training instructors in health and safety procedures is essential.

MONITOR AND UPDATE

Regularly review and update your risk management plan to guarantee it remains relevant and effective. This involves regularly assessing your internal and external environment for new or evolving risks, and evaluating the performance of your risk mitigation measures. Setting KPIs and conducting regular audits can help track the effectiveness of your strategies. What's more, it can save you money – ensuring you only have insurance policies to cover you for what you need, for example. Keeping your plans and policies up-to-date also ensures ongoing protection and compliance. For instance, if you're managing a tech start-up, regularly reviewing your cyber risk policies is essential.

JES'S BUSINESS STORY

We specialise in product label printing and branding for small businesses. Before we started, professional printing wasn't accessible to small businesses, so we're super proud of the positive impact we've made on this community.

At the time of starting the business, we were in life's trenches. My husband had decided to go back to uni after ten years in the workforce, we'd moved back to my mum's and we were saving for our wedding. While my husband was working at night, I would play around with selling various products to make a bit of money on the side, and I realised there was a huge gap in the market for a business like mine – helping other sellers to brand and promote their products. I found an amazing designer who had a little desktop printer and I told her I would help her to market her business. One thing led to another and we now have a seven-figure turnover and employ multiple staff.

We scaled for the first three years. It was a really challenging time and it forced us to be smart and set up systems. Once they were set up, the workload felt easy no matter what our sales were for the month or how busy we got. Last year we had our first $200,000 month, which was exciting! We've also started purchasing our equipment with cash.

It's important to spend money in the right areas. We tell our customers all the time that they can use a 5-cent label on their product, but if they use a $2 label the product's perceived value could be $10 to $20 more. So it's not always about cutting costs.

I think paying staff fairly and what they deserve is really important to getting their best output and value. And I often review our costs and speak to suppliers to see if they can tighten up our pricing to be more competitive.

It's challenging for any small business owner to have a healthy work–life balance. It's hard not to take things to heart, and not to stress and feel anxious. Throw in the fact that I built the business while pregnant and raising my two little kids, and it's been really hard. But I can't imagine it any other way. It's 100 per cent worth it (most days)!

Business insurance

As a small business owner in Australia, safeguarding your entrepreneurial venture is like wearing a parachute when you jump out of a plane. Not that I'm going to be doing that any time soon, but if I did, I'd sure as hell want to have a parachute strapped to my back!

Insurance is quite literally your safety net when unexpected events jeopardise your hard-earned progress. The right insurance policies can protect your business from financial ruin and ensure continuity in times of crisis, from natural disasters to legal liabilities. While they're not all mandatory (some are by law), being an all-in kinda gal I like the full suite, but you have to balance your needs against your wants against your budget.

The type of insurance you need largely depends on your industry and specific business activities. A tech start-up might prioritise cyber insurance and professional indemnity insurance, while a retail store might focus on public liability and commercial property insurance. Understanding the risks associated with your industry and choosing the right mix of compulsory and optional insurance policies can provide comprehensive protection for your business. If it's all a bit overwhelming, I suggest speaking with a business insurance broker.

Choose the right insurance coverage

Select insurance policies that provide adequate coverage for your business risks. For instance, if you're managing a café, you might need public liability, property, and business interruption insurance. If it's just you and you're the main breadwinner in your family, you may want key person insurance. Some insurances are compulsory by law, such as workers compensation, depending on what type of business you are running. Others are optional to help protect your business and assets. The government's business.com.au website outlines these and provides helpful advice specific to each industry.[4]

COMPULSORY INSURANCE

These are the two types of insurance that I consider compulsory for every business, large or small:

Workers compensation insurance

This is mandatory for any business that employs staff. Workers compensation insurance covers medical expenses and lost wages for employees who get injured or fall ill due to their job. For instance, if you own a boutique and an employee injures themselves while setting up a display, this insurance will cover their medical costs and any required time off work.

Public liability insurance

While not legally required, public liability insurance is often essential due to contractual obligations or industry standards. It covers legal costs and compensation if your business activities cause injury or property damage to a third party. For example, if you run a café and a customer slips on a wet floor and sustains an injury, public liability insurance will cover any legal fees and compensation claims.

OPTIONAL INSURANCE

The options for insurance are plentiful. Anyone who knows me knows I'm a fan of insurance. As I always say – the best insurance is the one you don't need. But you don't want to be caught without it. That said, it costs, so spend some time reviewing your needs with a professional to get the best cover for what you need and can afford. Here are some you might consider:

Professional indemnity insurance

This is crucial for service-based businesses, such as consultants, designers and accountants. It protects against claims of negligence or breaches of duty arising from professional services provided. If a client claims your work caused them financial loss, professional indemnity insurance will cover the legal costs and any compensation awarded.

Business interruption insurance

This covers loss of income during periods when you can't operate your business due to an insured event, such as a fire or flood. If a natural disaster or other event forces you to close temporarily, business interruption insurance will cover your lost income and ongoing expenses like rent and salaries.

Product liability insurance

If your business manufactures or sells products, this insurance is essential. It covers claims of injury or damage caused by your products. For example, if you sell handmade skincare products and a customer has an allergic reaction, product liability insurance will cover legal fees and any compensation claims.

Cyber insurance

With our increasing reliance on digital platforms, cyber insurance is becoming more important. It covers losses from data breaches, cyber attacks and other cyber-related incidents. If you run an online store and your customer data is hacked, cyber insurance will cover the costs of managing the breach, legal fees and any compensation claims.

Commercial property insurance

This covers damage to your business premises and its contents due to events like fire, theft or natural disasters. For instance, if you own a retail store and a storm damages your building and inventory, commercial property insurance will cover the repair and replacement costs.

Vehicle insurance

If your business uses vehicles, commercial vehicle insurance is essential. It covers damage to your vehicles and third-party property in the event of an accident. For example, if you own a delivery service and one of your vans is involved in an accident, vehicle insurance will cover the repair costs and any third-party claims.

Business continuity

Okay, it's great that you have all those safety nets in place, but let's get practical. What happens if you hit a crisis? How do you deal with it when the proverbial hits the fan?

Business continuity planning and crisis management involve preparing for and managing unexpected events that could disrupt your business operations. Putting the right things in place, like insurance and a business continuity plan (BCP), will mean your business (and your income!) can keep going, even if you can't.

OVER TO YOU

Based on the risks you identified earlier, create a detailed plan to manage and respond to these crises should they arise — such as a power outage, or if you or a key team member gets sick and is unavailable to work.

COMMUNICATE

Once you have a plan mapped out, communicate this with your team. It's easier to hear and understand things when you're not in crisis mode, so go through this with them before anything goes wrong. Effective communication leads to transparency and buy-in from all parties involved, and means everyone is ready should the worst happen.

TRAINING AND DRILLS

Conduct training and drills so that your team is prepared to respond to crises. This means everyone will know their roles and responsibilities during a crisis. Key person backup is like training an understudy – who will take that critical place on stage if the leading woman is unavailable? The show must go on!

SEEK PROFESSIONAL ADVICE AND REGULARLY UPDATE

Consult with crisis management and business continuity professionals to help you avoid pitfalls and ensure your plans are comprehensive and effective. Insurance brokers are a great place to start. Regularly review and update your crisis management plans and BCPs so that they remain relevant and effective. This will lead to ongoing protection and compliance.

Principle 8: Plan to thrive

Set yourself up to succeed in every environment. You never know when the wind will change or how it will blow and you definitely can't assume that life in business will be all smooth sailing. Plan ahead and put your safety nets in place, so you're equipped to thrive in all conditions.

Meet the founder: Brittney Saunders

Brittney Saunders is an absolute go-getter in the entrepreneur space. You may have first heard of her when she was killing it as a beauty content creator. Now, Brittney is the founder of the successful inclusive clothing brand FAYT. She is also a podcaster and all-round source of positivity and inspiration.

Name: Brittney Saunders

Business: FAYT the Label

Industry: Fashion and retail

Product/service: Women's fashion, including capsule wardrobe pieces and the best-fitting denim styles through to active/leisurewear and pieces you can wear to special occasions. We are best known for our basics.

Target audience: Women aged 20 to 40, but women of all ages shop with us

Secondary audience: The people who haven't discovered us yet!

Unique selling point: Our size range, which spans from 6 to 26, and the quality of our clothes. We genuinely care about the fit of our styles and never cut corners when it comes to fit or fabric. We want women to be able to shop with confidence.

The business began: 2017

I've always had an entrepreneurial spirit. It started in my teenage years – I've had little businesses since the age of 17. At the time they felt more like hobbies (I guess I was too young and naive to realise that what I was doing was 'business'). People paid me for spray-tanning and doing their make-up for formals, weddings and special occasions, and I pretty much said yes to any opportunity thrown at me.

When it came to starting FAYT, I didn't see it as this big business idea, just another of the little hobbies I thought I'd try. I had no idea it would turn into even half the brand and business it's become! I think that's been the biggest beauty of my journey – I went into it completely clueless, and now, seven years later, it's booming!

I don't think I could stand working for someone else. I entered the workforce at the age of 14 at my local McDonald's because I was so keen to work and be independent. From age 14 to 21, I had over 20 jobs and tried it all – retail, fast food, waitressing, bartending, direct sales, beauty counters and various office roles. As soon as I didn't feel happy in a job, I quit and moved onto the next, constantly searching for the 'right one' to bring me happiness. Lo and behold, none of them did! It took becoming self-employed to realise it's what I was destined to do. I get so many personal joys out of being in business, but not having to answer to anyone is right up there.

FAYT has gone through many changes over the years. I started the business on my own, working from the garage underneath my house. Fast forward to now and we have five retail stores across NSW, Queensland and Victoria and thousands of customers. It's safe to say my business has changed in every way possible and is still changing every year. We are never not growing and improving the way we do everything – being in business has made me embrace constant change. I love it.

When FAYT started, I did everything myself. My role encompassed inventory management, stock sampling, paying invoices and payroll, all the social media and website management, packing and sending out orders, customer service and marketing. I would scout the models, do their hair and make-up, then run the photo shoot! As the business has grown, I've had to let go of a lot of these responsibilities so that my time can be put towards my main goal: growing this thing. I now do stock sampling, product development and ordering, running ad accounts and creating content for social media. I also work directly with my management team to support them in their roles.

My first casual employee came on board near the beginning as a bit of an all-rounder. We're now at over 60 employees. Staffing, in my opinion, is the hardest part of business (well, one of the hardest parts, anyway). In the early days, I felt constant pressure to make every employee happy at all times, but now I know you simply can't. Dealing with staff challenges you in ways you could never imagine. In saying that, it can also be a very rewarding part of your business journey.

These are my top five tips for managing employees:

1. Be kind, but also be mindful of becoming too close with staff. Be friendly, of course, but learn to draw a line and set boundaries.

2. Don't hire family or friends. (I know it works for some, but it's rare, which is why this has become general wisdom and my advice!)

3. Talk with your staff often. Ask them how they're going, let them know they're doing a great job, ask them if there's anything you can give them a hand with. Don't just talk to staff when you need to tell them they've done something wrong. Communication is *very* important.

4. Set out clear expectations when it comes to your employees' roles in your company.

5. Provide your staff with a nice environment to work in where they can show up every day and feel comfortable, relaxed, happy and supported.

I could say much more, but my overall advice when it comes to managing staff is to use your common sense. I treat my team in the way I would hope to be treated if I had a manager or boss.

Now that I understand the importance of having the right people working in my business, one of the main things I'd have done differently is to have made this an absolute priority from day one instead of wasting my time with the wrong staff. In saying that, I don't regret the decisions I made. But take this as my lesson and advice: the people you have working for your business will make it or break it, so find the right ones from the get-go.

The second thing I'd have done differently is be more ballsy, sooner, in all areas. In the first few years of FAYT, I was way too nice and soft. I played it safe and was a little scared to take risks, and I was completely shocked by how much this whole being-in-business thing costs! Running a business is the most expensive thing I've ever done and I'm learning that the bigger the business gets, the higher those costs become. But I've also learnt that you need to just go for it to see big results. You have to spend money to make money, right?

My other piece of advice to my past self is that there's no situation you can't handle – you'll always figure it out and everything will be okay.

I'm very lucky as I wake up every day and feel like I'm never working – and I think that's my definition of success. Running my business has me feeling like I've never worked a day in my life (even though I'm working harder than ever before) and I think that comes down to the fact that

I simply love what I do. Even though I work a lot, I'd say I have a healthy work–life balance. It's important to take time for yourself and your partner as a business owner, which I think I do well.

To any budding entrepreneurs out there, I'd say just go for it and don't hesitate when it comes to making those scary decisions, because that's when the fun *really* begins!

Chapter Nine

Handling growth and expansion

Up to now we've concentrated on getting your business established. But it's always important to keep one eye on the future, too, so this chapter focuses on growth and expansion. While you might think you don't need to worry about this now, ideally you'll have a concept of how you'd like your business to look from the get-go, and again in one, three, five and ten years' time. Being clear on your long-term vision will help you get your structure right in the early days, which will save you time, money and pain later on.

Whether you're a budding entrepreneur or a seasoned business owner, in this chapter you'll find everything you need to take your business to the next level. First up we look at strategies for business growth and scalability, then we venture into exploring new markets and opportunities. Third, we discuss franchising and licensing options, and finally, we tackle mergers, acquisitions and exit strategies, offering insights on how to navigate these complex processes to ensure a smooth and profitable transition.

Are you ready to supercharge your business growth? Then let's get started!

Grow and scale your business

After you've successfully been operating for a while, it's natural to start thinking about the next step. Do you want to expand – should you?

In terms of growth, what you want for yourself and your business will change over time, but your intrinsic personal values shouldn't (see Chapter 1). My goalposts have definitely changed, especially since becoming a mum and having gone through scaling up, shutting down and starting back up another business. I want a more sustainable operation now that focuses on lifestyle and creates the life I want to live, but I also want my team to go on that journey with me and have a business that people look at and can see we're doing good things.

A sound approach

Ultimately my motto is: do good, be good and everything will be okay. I'm very lucky that I work in a space where we have an impact. It's not like a product-based business where I have to convince people of our value. We teach financial literacy, which I believe people are desperate for and deserve. If you can find a similar core value in your business, the way in which you scale up or down over time might change but the essence of your business will remain the same. And if you can imbue your team with those same values, you'll have an entire organisation that lives and breathes that culture so it will carry it on even if your role changes over time. If you do decide that scaling is on your horizon, consider the following:

KNOW YOUR MARKET

Just as you did in the beginning, before you add to your business, it's important to continue reviewing it with fresh eyes to identify new opportunities. Examine your sales data to identify patterns, best-selling products and customer demographics. At SOTM we also like to run regular customer surveys to gather feedback from our tribe about their needs and preferences. In my businesses, we find social media a great place to do research – and it's fun, too. I can't tell you how many cool new products and ideas burst into my feed on a regular basis. I'm always thinking about how I could implement something similar for our SOTM community.

IDENTIFY GROWTH OPPORTUNITIES

As the world continues to evolve, it's important to schedule regular time to focus on identifying growth opportunities – often described as 'gaps in the market' – by assessing potential areas for business expansion; these could be new markets, products or services. Identifying such growth opportunities will allow you to capitalise on them effectively.

For my businesses, even though we operate in the financial space, I like to look outside the finance industry for new ways of doing things – in fact, that's where our best ideas have come from. Until *She's on the Money* came along, most business podcasts were delivered by boring men in suits talking about tax and balance sheets and indexation. While those things are important, I knew we could deliver that kind of information in a much more fun and interesting way. Also, looking internationally helped prompt our latest brand update. Once we realised we had a global vision, we knew we needed to update our look to reflect the business we had become.

DEVELOP A SCALABLE BUSINESS MODEL

Scaling is about creating efficient processes. If you're planning for growth, it's important to create a business model that can grow without a proportional increase in costs. That might be outsourcing certain tasks, such as accounting or customer service, to external resources. Or it might be using tools like Zapier or Hootsuite to automate repetitive tasks, freeing up your time for strategic planning. Some businesses use digital platforms especially designed for certain tasks and designed for scale, such as the e-commerce platforms Shopify or WooCommerce.

CAITLYN'S BUSINESS STORY

I am a business coach and mentor to the hair, beauty and barbering world. We offer a range of digital short courses, coaching programs, free eBooks, casual coaching and more.

My coaching business has been running for almost eight years. It has grown from my dining table with just little old me, to a small office-within-an-office with an assistant, to now me and my three interstate staff working remotely from home. I also have a coach working alongside me to take a load off, which has happened this year and is going SO WELL! My staff are all mums, so they can work when it works for them, too.

If I were to change anything, it would be three things:

1. Be choosier with clients. At the start I was very money focused and took on people I didn't love working with. Now I put all clients through a vetting process to ensure they will gel well with my business.

2. Put myself out there to speak on stages and do things that scare the shit out of me. I've been presenting at events, and my business has grown stacks because people are seeing more of me. Also, doing scary things has made me better equipped to deal with other uncomfortable situations that have arisen in life and business.

3. Run my own events and collaborated in-person with other businesses earlier! This was something I only started doing about

﹛ 18 months ago. Person-to-person interactions are so damn powerful for a mostly online business. Watching people transform is incredible.

CREATE A FINANCIAL PLAN

Implementing growth strategies generally requires some up-front investment. Develop a financial plan that outlines your future intentions, including budgeting, forecasting and funding. This will provide the resources you need for growth and ensure financial stability. First and foremost, I recommend working with an expert business adviser who can help you realise your business goals. They can assess your plans – such as whether it's worth investing in commercial real estate, for instance – for the short- and long-term impacts on your business, and the best way to go about making the plans a reality.

INVEST IN TECHNOLOGY

Designing for scale is made easier by leveraging technology to streamline operations, improve efficiency and support growth. If you think about it, most areas of your business could probably benefit from deploying a technology solution, whether that's using Canva templates to speed up content creation, online accounting systems to streamline your sales and reporting, or a CRM to build customer retention.

Which tools you use will depend on what kind of business you're running. Many tools are designed to work for specific industries, such as integrated bookings and customer service platforms for the beauty and hospitality industries. If your business delivers virtual products and services, digital marketing tools like Google Analytics, SEMrush and Mailchimp can be game changers. For service industries, it's often about using cloud-based solutions such as Google Workspace or Microsoft 365 for storage and collaboration.

Obviously, there's always a trade-off between the cost of implementing such technologies (not to mention the cost of ongoing subscriptions and maintenance) and what your budget can afford. Many have trial periods so you can test them out before making a longer-term commitment. You'll also want to set some time and budget aside for training yourself and your team so you can get the most out of whatever software you choose to use.

SURROUND YOURSELF WITH A STRONG TEAM

As we've heard now from several of our founders, the key to success is hiring and developing a team who can support your business growth. While many of us start out in business alone, surrounding yourself with a strong team is essential for executing growth strategies and maintaining quality, whether that means hiring permanent staff or developing a reliable freelance network or appointing trusted external advisers (or, for many of us, all three!).

MONITOR AND ADJUST STRATEGIES

As business owners, we need to adapt to changing market conditions. While it's important to be able to pay the bills today, we always need to have one eye on the path ahead. Taking time to develop and regularly review your growth strategies will ensure you have a thriving, sustainable business well into the future.

One way to do this is by setting benchmarks and regularly measuring against them to see how your business is tracking over time. Select a few key performance indicators (KPIs) that reflect the health of your business – for example, number of sales through a particular season or period, customer visits per store, and profit gaps on best-selling items.

Your customers can be the best source of information and give you an early warning system before declines show up on your business books. Implement feedback loops through surveys and reviews to continuously gather those customer insights.

Finally, it's important to remain nimble in today's volatile world, and that's one clear advantage we have as small business owners. Remaining open to change and adopting an agile approach to business planning allows for quick adjustments based on real-time data and feedback.

SEEK PROFESSIONAL ADVICE

No-one expects you to have all the answers – knowing where to go to get those answers is key. Consulting with business advisers or mentors can help ensure your growth strategies are comprehensive and effective. Especially when it comes to specialist knowledge, professional advice can help you avoid pitfalls and create effective growth strategies.

Depending on what business you're in, mentorship or incubator programs might be available. Generally headed up by titans of industry, these can be an invaluable source of helpful advice and encouragement. If they don't exist, find other ways to network – industry conferences, webinars and training events are all good spaces to connect with experts and peers.

Finally, you can hire business consultants for specialised advice and strategic planning. Make sure you do your homework, though – there are plenty of sharks out there willing to help you part with your money for little in return. If you do engage a specialist, map out what you want from your investment before you pay them for it. Setting goals and paying upon completion of those goals can be a good way to go.

Explore new markets

One path to growth is expanding into new markets. As founder Erin Deering explains later in this book, this is by no means an easy task as it involves identifying and entering unfamiliar and untested areas. The upside is that it could open up new places for your products or services to thrive. Obviously, the idea is to deliver business growth by expanding your customer base and increasing revenue. It also spreads your risks through diversification, because you reduce your dependence on a single market.

What to look for

Exploring new markets may be a foreign concept (boom-tish, see what I did there!), but let me walk you through a useful approach.

IDENTIFY POTENTIAL MARKETS

Review your current market and its strengths to identify new markets where your products or services could succeed. In the broadest sense, it's about spotting global trends. Social media helps here, but you can find a heap of industry reports and publications online as well.

You'll want to break down any potential new market into segments based on demographics, geography and behaviour to identify underserved areas. See where your business values, products and services might align with emerging or underserved trends in other areas. Look at where your competitors are expanding and identify gaps they might have overlooked, then see if there are any local operators serving the market and determine what you could do differently and better than them.

CONDUCT MARKET RESEARCH

Once you've made a shortlist, gather information about your potential markets, including market size, competition and customer needs. First, get an overview of each potential market. Read existing market research reports, government publications and industry studies to collate initial data. Ideally, next you'll undertake some primary research. For this you'll need to conduct focus groups, interviews and online surveys to collect firsthand insights. Finally, if feasible, visit the potential markets to get a real-world understanding of the local business environment.

OVER TO YOU } What trends have you noticed across the world. Is there something happening overseas that you think would go nuts here in Australia? Set a timer for 20 minutes and brainstorm all the coolest ideas that have popped across your socials lately.

ASSESS MARKET ENTRY STRATEGIES

Once you've identified prospective new markets, it's time to evaluate the feasibility of entering the playing field. Trade laws or export barriers could make one market virtually impossible, but another market might provide lucrative incentives. It's also good to look at the different ways to enter new markets to find the most effective approach and avoid potential pitfalls. For instance, from late 2020 to early 2024, China restricted Australian wine imports through punishingly high tariffs.[1] The options include exporting, franchising or joint ventures. You'll want to evaluate the costs and benefits of each. Once you've identified the best option(s), ideally you'll run a sample set or pilot program. This allows you to test your product or service in a smaller segment of the new market to gauge its potential.

IDENTIFY GRANTS AND FUNDING OPPORTUNITIES

The Australian Government has many grants and programs to help Australian businesses sell their products and services overseas.[2] These grants and programs provide financial support and help build your skills and knowledge. They include the Export Market Development Grants (EMDG) program, which provides grants to encourage Australian businesses to market and promote their goods and services globally, as well as offering landing pads, finance, customs duty refunds and endorsements.[3] The many opportunities available change all the time, so it can be hard to stay abreast of them. The best ways to do this are:

» **Visit government websites:** Regularly visit business.gov.au and state/local government websites for updates on small business grants and funding programs.

» **Join industry associations and chambers of commerce:** Become a member of relevant industry associations and attend networking events to stay informed about new funding opportunities.

» **Use grant databases and online platforms:** Use GrantConnect and commercial grant finder services to search for and receive alerts on available grants and funding.

LAWRENCE'S BUSINESS STORY

I am part of MDB Taxation & Business Advisors, which operates within the accounting industry and specialises in comprehensive financial solutions. Our target audience is entrepreneurs in the professional services and digital space. We've been in business for 38 years.

If I could go back, the advice I'd give my past self would be simple yet transformative: get a coach, get a coach, get a coach. Seek guidance from mentors who can help navigate the complexities of business and personal growth.

Invest in therapy, and do the inner work – this is essential. It's important to understand and resolve your fears and emotional baggage so you can approach your business from a place of inspiration and purpose and dive 100 per cent into what you love, leaving behind any unnecessary fears and doubts. The journey on the other side of this work is incredible. The people and opportunities I've attracted since embracing this approach have been beyond anything I could have imagined. Life in business is truly amazing when you're aligned with your purpose and passion.

DEVELOP A MARKET ENTRY PLAN

One you've completed your research, it's time to create a detailed plan for entering your new market, including goals, timelines and resources. As the famous saying goes, 'Luck is what happens when preparation meets opportunity'. A market entry plan provides a roadmap for successful expansion. Your plan will include the details you've researched above and such elements as:

The local market

» **Cultural sensitivity:** Conduct thorough research on cultural norms, values and consumer behaviour in the new market so you can create marketing messages that resonate with local audiences.

» **Language adaptation:** Ensure all your marketing materials, including websites, advertisements and customer service scripts, are translated accurately and are culturally adapted to the local language.

» **Local influencers:** Partner with local influencers or brand ambassadors who have a strong following and can authentically promote your product or service.

A local supply chain

» **Local suppliers:** Identify and vet local suppliers and manufacturers who can meet your quality and delivery standards, and establish contracts or agreements with them.

» **Logistics and distribution:** Set up efficient logistics and distribution channels by partnering with local logistics companies and understanding the local regulatory requirements for import/export.

» **Inventory management:** Implement an inventory management system that is adaptable to local market conditions, ensuring you can meet demand without overstocking.

Legal and regulatory requirements

» **Compliance checklist:** Create a comprehensive checklist of all legal and regulatory requirements for operating in the new market, including business registration, tax obligations and industry-specific regulations.

» **Local legal counsel:** Hire local legal experts who can provide guidance on compliance issues, help with contract negotiations and navigate any legal challenges that may arise.

» **Intellectual property protection:** Ensure your IP, such as trademarks and patents, is protected in the new market by filing the necessary applications and by monitoring for potential infringements.

If you incorporate these specific tactical steps, your market entry plan will be robust and better equipped to handle the complexities of entering your new market successfully.

BUILD STRATEGIC PARTNERSHIPS

Ideally, you'll spend some time forming partnerships with other businesses or organisations to support your market entry. Strategic partnerships can provide resources, expertise and market access. They may become a formal arrangement or be an ad hoc campaign. You could collaborate with local businesses, distributors or influencers who have a strong presence in the new market. You might join industry associations and networks to build connections and gain insights, and you could consider forming joint ventures with local companies to share resources and reduce risks.

SEEK PROFESSIONAL ADVICE

Consult with market entry experts or business advisers to ensure your strategies are effective and compliant with the multiple tax and legal frameworks you'll be navigating. Professional advice can help you avoid pitfalls and create successful market entry strategies. For example, if you're manufacturing in a foreign country, consulting with a market entry expert can help you navigate international expansion.

Using the above headings as prompts, write out a potential market exploration strategy for a new area into which you could expand your business. Even if you have no intention of doing so, the exercise can be worthwhile for inspiring you to think differently about your business. Imagine how it might look/work/operate/deliver in a foreign country. The ideas might surprise you and you could even implement some of them locally.

Franchising and licensing

Franchising and licensing are well-proven strategies for expanding your business. They can be a good option for helping you expand your brand, increase revenue and grow your business without the typical risks associated with opening in new locations.

Franchising and licensing involves allowing others to use your business model, brand or products in exchange for a fee or royalty. Franchising is granting a franchisee the right to operate a business under your brand and business model, while licensing is granting a licensee the right to use your intellectual property, such as trademarks or products.

These pathways can be a good way to scale your growth. They allow your business to expand across multiple locations without you having to personally manage each one and are a way to grow your business without the significant capital investment typically required if you are to retain solo ownership, as well as reducing the financial and operational risks associated with expansion. They can also generate revenue, as you generally receive franchise fees or licensing royalties. Having several stores trading under your banner increases your brand's visibility and market presence.

Exploring your options

Exploring franchising and licensing options can be a game changer for your business, but it's not a foolproof plan. As with any business idea, approach the concept with a healthy level of scepticism and engage expert advice before you commit large amounts of money, whether you're the person setting up a franchise or you're buying into one. If this is something you're interested in, here are some things worth considering.

WHAT'S YOUR BUSINESS MODEL

First things first – if you're thinking of franchising, you need to take a good, hard look at your current business model. Is it strong, scalable and replicable? This is crucial, because a business model that works well in one location should be able to succeed in others. Think about your USP and what makes your brand stand out. If you've got that secret sauce, you're already off to a great start!

DEVELOP A FRANCHISE OR LICENSING PLAN

Create a comprehensive plan that outlines how you'll franchise or license your business. What are the key elements that need to be standardised? How will you ensure consistency across different locations? Your plan should also cover financial projections, operational guidelines and marketing strategies. Remember, a well-thought-out plan is your roadmap to success.

CONSIDER THE LEGAL SIDE

Franchising and licensing come with a host of legal requirements and regulations. You'll need to draft detailed agreements that protect your brand and ensure compliance. This is where it's essential to consult with legal experts who specialise in franchising or licensing. They'll help you navigate the complexities and will safeguard your interests.

CREATE TRAINING AND SUPPORT SYSTEMS

For your franchisees or licensees to succeed, they'll need robust training and ongoing support. Develop comprehensive training programs that cover everything from day-to-day operations to customer service excellence. Additionally, set up support systems that provide continuous assistance and resources – tools like FranConnect, FranScape and Naranga can help you manage franchise operations and communications. Remember, your franchisees' success is your success!

MARKET YOUR FRANCHISE OR LICENCE

Once you've got everything in place, it's time to spread the word. Develop a marketing strategy to attract potential franchisees or licensees. Use various marketing channels, including social media, industry events and online platforms, to reach your target audience, highlighting the benefits of joining your brand and showcasing your success stories.

SUPPORT YOUR FRANCHISEES

Your role doesn't end once you've signed an agreement. Ongoing monitoring and support are crucial to ensure consistency and quality across all locations. Regularly check in with your franchisees or licensees, provide feedback, and offer additional training if they need it. Building strong relationships with them will foster loyalty and drive your collective success.

CONSIDER THE DOWNSIDES

Franchising sounds like the ideal path to growth, but it's not risk-free. Don't hesitate to seek professional advice throughout this journey. Whether it's legal counsel, financial advisers or franchising consultants, their expertise can be invaluable. They'll help you avoid common pitfalls and ensure you're on the right track.

ELLEN'S BUSINESS STORY

Despite having a decent-sized population, our town was 30 minutes' drive from the closest dentist. I was underpaid, working in public health, and saw the opportunity. Before we opened our dental surgery I discussed the idea with a colleague and crunched the numbers. We decided it was a viable business idea, and from that point we worked hard. Within four months we opened our clinic for trading.

In the first 12 months, we had a solid profit margin. We are now into our third year of business and continuing to grow. We started with one oral health therapist, one dentist and one dental assistant; we now have one oral health therapist, six dentists and four support staff.

Since opening, our business has been fortunate enough to go from strength to strength. Due to the location, convenience and our reputation in the town, we have been able to increase our profit margins. The business was able to self-fund an additional clinic room to enable us to expand and therefore increase our productivity and billings.

I'm 31 and I have a one-year-old. Being in business allows me to be able to afford to stay home with my little girl. In addition, I've been able to create a workplace I love, choose suitable individuals for positions in my clinic, build a dream team, and have the ability to change something in the clinic if it's not working.

Mergers, acquisitions and exit strategies

The final path to business evolution is . . . the end: mergers, acquisitions and exit strategies. These involve combining with another business, purchasing another business or planning your exit from your business. Some businesses begin with their end in mind, whereas others naturally progress to this point over time.

Navigating mergers, acquisitions and exit strategies can be daunting, but understanding the basics is crucial for a smooth transition, and I'm here to help! First things first: although they're often discussed together, there are three different approaches to business transformation:

- » **Merger:** When two companies combine to form a new entity.
- » **Acquisition:** Where one company purchases another company.
- » **Exit strategy:** Planning the process of selling or leaving your business.

No matter where you're at in your business journey, it can be a worthwhile exercise to consider your endgame. It can lead you to establish systems and processes in the early stages that will help your business grow and make for a smooth transition upon exit. If you end up staying with the business once you merge or sell, you want to be doubly sure that you have handed over something of quality you can be proud of.

My ultimate goal in business, because I'm a bit altruistic, is to make me redundant. I would love there not to be a need for my podcast. I'd love for a finance book to be like, 'Why would you bother? Everyone knows how to do that', but that's not going to happen in my lifetime. So realistically for me, I'm scaling back up again, this time to create a sustainable business but also to free up my time to do more meaningful work on the side. I would love to join more boards and do more work in that space, and I'd love to be able to work more closely with charities, but I don't have the capacity for any of that at this point. I need to understand what the next phase looks like before I can plan for those things.

Things to consider

When it comes to planning, here's what you need to do if you're considering a merger, acquisition or exit strategy.

ASSESS YOUR BUSINESS READINESS

Before diving in, take a step back and evaluate whether your business is truly ready for such a monumental change. Are your finances in order? Is your team prepared? This self-assessment will help you identify any gaps and ensure you're well prepared for what's to come.

IDENTIFY POTENTIAL PARTNERS OR BUYERS

Whether you're merging, acquiring or exiting, finding the right fit is crucial for a seamless transition and future success. Finding suitable businesses means scouting for potential partners or buyers who align with your business values and goals. For example, if you have built a piece of tech that solves a critical market problem, look for a large player in the industry who may want to use your technology to advance their business.

CONDUCT DUE DILIGENCE

Due diligence is all about doing your homework. Thoroughly investigate potential partners or buyers to ensure they are financially stable, reputable and a good match for your business. Likewise, do this if you're the one doing the buying. This step is essential to avoid any unpleasant surprises down the road. Due diligence ensures you make informed decisions and avoid potential pitfalls.

DEVELOP A STRATEGIC PLAN

A well-thought-out strategic plan is your roadmap to success (I know I keep saying this, but it's true!). Outline the goals, timelines and resources needed to execute the merger, acquisition or exit strategy. Early identification of the elements you'll need – such as the specific business financials, or industry certifications – can help you prepare them in advance. Such things may take months or even years to complete, so planning is really important here.

CONSIDER THE LEGAL SIDE

Legal matters can be complex, so it's crucial to consult with legal experts to navigate the intricacies of mergers, acquisitions and exit strategies. In some cases, competition laws may come into play – though generally these pertain to the larger end of town. Use lawyers to help you draft agreements, understand regulatory requirements and protect your interests.

COMMUNICATE WITH STAKEHOLDERS

Transparent communication with your stakeholders – employees, customers, investors – is vital. Keep them informed and engaged throughout the process to maintain their trust and support. Clear communication will also help manage their expectations and mitigate any potential concerns.

MONITOR AND EVALUATE PROGRESS

Once the process is underway, continuously monitor and evaluate its progress. Are you meeting your milestones? Have any unforeseen challenges come up? Regular check-ins will help you stay agile and make necessary adjustments to keep things on track.

SEEK PROFESSIONAL ADVICE

Finally, don't hesitate to seek professional advice. Whether it's financial advisers, legal counsel or industry consultants, their expertise can provide invaluable insights and guidance to ensure a successful transition.

Principle 9: Level up

Should I stay or should I grow? Knowing when and how to scale is a constant challenge for entrepreneurs. Instinctively we think we should be aiming ever upward, but sometimes staying lean is the smartest option. Review your decisions in line with your values not your ego, and you'll have the answer.

Meet the founder: Sarah Davidson

Thanks to a series of fortuitous timings, Sarah Davidson describes her transition from law to entrepreneurship as a happy accident. These days, through her podcast Seize the Yay, *she teaches others how to follow their dreams while still managing to pay the bills.*

Name: Sarah Davidson

Business: Matcha Maiden

Industry: Health and wellness

Product/service: High-quality matcha (powdered green tea)

Target audience: Discerning tea drinkers, health-conscious eaters

Secondary audience: People looking for alternative beverages

Unique selling point: High-quality, affordable, accessible matcha powder

The business started in: 2014

I was a mergers and acquisitions lawyer who became an accidental entrepreneur. These days I'm primarily a media personality with a particular interest in the wellness space. I guess that's always been my interest – it's the common theme across everything I've done.

My transition out of corporate was a happy accident. It might sound clichéd, but it wasn't on my vision board. I had a very traditional corporate legal career that was going really well. Despite my podcast, *Seize the Yay*, being something of a poster child for corporate refugees, I was never that person who left because I hated it or because it was oppressive.

I would happily have stayed there a few more years, but I accidentally stumbled upon a gap in the market for matcha powder. My husband and I bought some for ourselves (I was using it as a coffee replacement for health reasons) from a beautiful organic wholesale farm in Japan. When it turned up, it was 2 million serves too many for the two of us to consume by the use-by date – we'd received a full pallet! Instead of throwing it out, we figured we'd try to recoup some of the cost by selling it as a fun little side project.

Luck and timing played a major part in our success. At the time, matcha was only available at a very high-end, high-quality ceremonial grade. It was starting to be known as a product, but no-one had branded it. There was no online frank body type of availability – no easily bought, beautifully packaged, accessibly priced version of matcha.

Our matcha hit the market just as everyone knew what it was. The Kardashians were drinking it and posting about it on their socials. People would see others drinking green matcha smoothies but they couldn't buy the powder anywhere. We swooped in and started making it available. Nic is a techie and very handy (I knew I kept him around for a reason!). He knocked up a website and helped with logo design, and we put up an online store.

Matcha Maiden became that garage-to-global cliché story, but I think if we hadn't started at that DIY level, we'd have been too overwhelmed to even begin. We started out creating our packs in a friend's commercial kitchen – like *Breaking Bad* but with healthy green powder! We hand-packed for about six months, while I was still at the law firm.

Back then, the social media algorithm was less complicated. We got onto the radar of Urban Outfitters in the US and they emailed us wanting a supply contract for every Urban Outfitters store in America. I thought their initial email was spam, but when it proved to be real I had to quit my job so we could fulfil the order. We had no packers – we'd never expected to scale so much so quickly!

The momentum of being first to market carried us for a couple of years without really needing to do anything other than wing it. No-one else had time to catch up. After about three years we started to see big competitors pop up, like T2 and Blackmores, and at that point the self-doubt kicked in hard. The stakes were so much higher, and I almost bowed out voluntarily. We'd had a great run, but I thought we couldn't possibly compete with those giants.

That was when I really learnt about 'knowing your market'. I quickly discovered that the people who bought matcha from Blackmores in a supermarket were not the same people who were buying our boutique family-run matcha powder. If you're buying off the shelves of Urban Outfitters, you're probably not after the discounted supermarket version. It took a long time, but I eventually realised that even if those guys could outprice us, we had our market and it was very different to what they were aiming for. So we doubled down on holding our position.

It was about year six when our next evolution arrived: getting into the major retailers. At that point we had about 1000 stockists around the world, which was amazing. But the next stage was getting our stock onto supermarket shelves, as in white labelling for Coles and getting into that huge FMCG [fast-moving consumer goods] level of production. Although it seemed counterintuitive to our early positioning, we knew we couldn't grow any bigger unless we got into the major retailers, and we knew that would make us more attractive to sell later on if we wanted to make an exit.

That was a really difficult period, because of everything it took to even pitch to those retailers. We did a Chobani incubator program, which was an amazing opportunity to learn about scaling and the FMCG landscape, and we took on some investment from them. We saw what it took to streamline your factory processes and go from purchase orders of 1000 to purchase orders of 100,000.

Through that process I realised that to take Matcha Maiden to that level would mean me going full circle back into a corporate business with a board and the kind of accountability demanded by my old law firm, just in a different forum. Such big changes to the business would mean I'd pretty much become a factory worker – we'd have our own factory and I'd be in high-vis all day. That was my first realisation that bigger isn't always better.

I'd started to think that scaling for the sake of scaling was the goal, but then I remembered that I'd got into this business for flexibility, community, creativity, a dynamic fast pace, and the ability to roll out ideas and products. I loved getting there before the competitors, but if we got into Coles we couldn't do that anymore. It was a real ego moment of 'I want to get bigger and bigger' because that's what I thought we should do, but realising that the bigger we got, the more I'd hate it, because my role would become something I never wanted it to be. I had to put my ego aside and say, 'I think this is where we either say goodbye to being the guardians of this business or we say goodbye to the aggressive upwards scaling and instead continue to serve the customers we have at this middle band.' People talk quite often, too, about the fact that you actually don't make that much money when you're in Coles. Even though your purchase order value and your revenues might be huge, you don't end up taking home that much more than you do at the middle level because the margins and costs of doing business are so tight. I decided it wasn't actually what I wanted, even though my ego wanted it.

So we started looking at whether we might sell the business. We had conversations with T2 and Unilever reps – bigger brands that I thought would be good guardians if Matcha Maiden went to that next level. But none of the conversations went in the direction I wanted for it. I decided I didn't want our beautiful family business to become really corporate.

On top of that, we had to review our supplier because of costs, to meet the margins. The tea farm we'd been using the entire time, which was our differentiating factor in terms of taste and quality, was Japanese and USDA Organic certified, but we'd reached a point where we couldn't use them anymore because it wasn't cost-feasible. And if it's not the same matcha, then it's not the same business. It's a different product. It might as well be called something else.

I realised I would rather just close altogether and say goodbye and do something else than sell it. So we stopped looking for a buyer and started looking for partners instead. At that point we took on some invest-ment from a family fund that is an expert in taking businesses from that five- to seven-year itch to the ten-year, and then they sell from the ten to 20. They seemed like a much better fit than a big conglomerate. After six months they loved it and wanted to buy it completely, which wasn't the plan at the beginning.

Through all this, I realised, *Oops, I did it again* – I'd gone and made the business my identity. I'd done that when I was working in law, too. My whole identity had been 'lawyer' and I hadn't known who I was outside of that. Then with our business I became 'the matcha lady'. People would literally call me 'the matcha chick', and it became really hard to disen-tangle myself from all that.

I'd patted myself on the back so much for leaving my law career, for taking a big leap, for getting out of my comfort zone to go into business. I'd thought I'd never have to do such a big scary leap ever again – that I'd ride on the coat-tails of this matcha thing for the rest of my life. But then I realised that everything's a chapter, and Matcha Maiden had been a seven-year chapter. It's not like I'd done the millennial thing and just done it for a year and then got bored. I had given it a good go. And in the background the podcast had started and I had hosting gigs and public speaking gigs. I realised that I'd be of more use to the universe if I moved further into that space.

I was never meant to just be selling tea. It was an amazing means to an end – it helped me discover that my skill set is helping other people to make the jump.

Chapter Ten

Overcoming challenges and setbacks

Welcome to our final chapter, where we tackle a topic that's close to every entrepreneur's heart: how to overcome challenges and setbacks. If there's one thing I can guarantee you about running your own business, it's that things will never go perfectly. And you have to accept that. You can either get really upset and bogged down in the fact that something's gone wrong, or you can roll up your sleeves and go, 'Alright, great. How do I fix it?'

This plays into that thing called grit – when you have to knuckle down and just get shit done. You can't be all 'Woe is me!' That'll just make it worse. And honestly, if you're going to succeed in running your own business, you have to be good at being tough and getting on with it. Frankly, you won't have a choice – or you will, but that choice will be to shut up shop and go work for the man. If you choose to stay running your own business, when (not if) a problem comes rolling in, you have to solve it.

In this chapter, we'll learn how to embrace challenges and see them as opportunities. First we'll look at emotional resilience, and then we'll look at some practical approaches to setting yourself up to ensure the road ahead is a little less bumpy.

Build resilience

Embracing setbacks and turning them into stepping stones to success can make you stronger, wiser and more prepared for future challenges. It involves recognising setbacks, understanding their causes and using them as opportunities for growth. I love this stuff – which might explain why I did both a master's in psychology and a business degree! Personally, I think that one of the most valuable things to come out of running your own business is the incredible personal growth it brings.

For instance, what happens if your business partner tells you they're leaving? You can go to bed and cry about it, or you can just get shit done so the business keeps moving and you avoid impacting the rest of your team. Yes, you could get bogged down in it, but you have to remember that business itself is not inherently personal. So you need to be able to separate the two. When a business partner leaves, of course it feels personal, but you have to say nah, this is business. You have to put your business hat back on and really pull it down over your eyes and just push forward. If you're not doing that and you become emotional, you'll start making bad decisions – decisions that are not in the best interests of your team or your business.

I'm sure I'm not the only person who writes salty emails to get things off my chest – it feels good! But do you know what I do then? I don't send them. As a business owner, I don't send those emails because that's not the best and most constructive thing to do. Instead, I find alternative outlets that allow me to vent, whether it's therapy or having a glass of wine or going to a quiet room with my entire team and getting loud! When we're having a challenging time at SOTM and have no choice but to accept what's happening, we get on with it – but we also say, alright, if we get this done, we'll then go and do this other fun thing. That's cathartic.

It's really important to find what works to help keep you in balance. As a small business owner, setbacks are going to feel personal, but you need to pull yourself out of that. If you don't, it will ruin your business.

The nine stages of growth

It can help if you see your business journey mapped out along stages of personal growth. If you're a small business owner in Australia, especially in the SOTM community, you'll already know that the journey is filled with highs and lows. But guess what? Those lows, those failures, are actually golden opportunities to learn and grow. Here, we're all about how you can turn setbacks into set-ups for an even stronger comeback.

I've identified nine stages of growth on the entrepreneurial journey.

1. ACKNOWLEDGE AND ACCEPT FAILURE

First things first, it's crucial to acknowledge and accept failure. Pretending it didn't happen or brushing it under the rug won't help anyone. Embrace the fact that failure is a natural part of the business journey. Whether it's a product that's not selling or a marketing campaign that has flopped, accepting it allows you to move forward with a clear mind. Remember, every successful entrepreneur has faced failure at some point. It's not the end of the road; it's just a detour.

2. ANALYSE THE CAUSES

Once you've accepted the failure, it's time to dig deep and analyse its causes. Understanding the root cause is essential for preventing similar issues in the future. This step is about turning a critical eye inward and being brutally honest with yourself. What went wrong? Was it a lack of market research, poor timing, or maybe inadequate resources? Use tools like SWOT analysis to break down the situation.

3. EXTRACT VALUABLE LESSONS

Now that you know what went wrong, it's time to extract valuable lessons. Think of each failure as a teacher. What can you learn from the experience? Maybe you need to improve your financial planning, or perhaps your team needs better training. Write down the lessons and keep them handy. They are your roadmap for future success. Remember, every failure brings you one step closer to getting it right.

4. DEVELOP AN ACTION PLAN

Armed with your newfound knowledge, it's time to develop an action plan. This plan is your blueprint for turning things around and making sure you're better prepared next time. It's where you turn the lessons into actionable steps. Create a detailed plan outlining how you'll address the issues that led to the failure. Set SOTM goals (Specific, Optimistic, Time-bound, Measurable) to keep yourself on track.

5. CULTIVATE A GROWTH MINDSET

A growth mindset is your best ally in overcoming failure. Embrace the belief that your abilities can be developed through dedication and hard work. This mindset encourages resilience and a love for learning. Surround yourself with positive influences and keep reminding yourself that failure is not a reflection of your worth but an opportunity for growth. Stay curious and open to new experiences.

6. SEEK SUPPORT AND MENTORSHIP

Don't go it alone! Seek support and mentorship from those who've been there and done that. Join networking groups, attend industry events and don't be afraid to ask for help. Mentors can provide invaluable insights and guidance to help you navigate through tough times. Their experience can offer you a fresh perspective and practical advice you might not have considered.

7. IMPLEMENT STRESS MANAGEMENT TECHNIQUES

Running a business can be incredibly stressful, especially when dealing with failure, so it's important to implement stress management techniques to keep your mental health in check. Practices such as mindfulness, meditation and regular exercise can make a world of difference. Remember, taking care of your mental health is just as important as managing your business. A healthy mind leads to better decision-making and increased resilience.

8. CELEBRATE SMALL WINS

In the hustle and bustle of running a business, it's easy to overlook the small wins, but celebrating these victories, no matter how minor, can boost your morale and keep you motivated. Whether it's landing a new client, completing a project on time or simply making it through a tough week, take the time to acknowledge and celebrate these achievements. They are proof that you're making progress.

9. CONTINUOUSLY REVIEW AND IMPROVE

Finally, make continuous review and improvement a part of your business strategy. Regularly assess your performance, gather feedback and make any necessary adjustments. This ongoing process ensures that you're always learning and evolving. Use tools like customer feedback surveys and performance metrics to keep track of your progress. As I've said many times in these pages, continuous improvement is the key to long-term success and resilience.

Stay competitive in a changing market

Overcoming challenges isn't all about avoiding misadventure. Some of the realest pain small businesses face is having their ideas stolen by competitors or their offerings going out of favour, perhaps due to new technology or just plain old changing tastes and fashion. So how do you stay competitive in a changing market? Essentially, you need to continuously adapt to new trends, technologies and customer preferences. It may seem exhausting to have to reinvent yourself constantly, but we're not talking about whole makeovers – just a little glow-up every now and then to keep your business looking cute.

Stay true to yourself

I know you probably don't believe it, but back when I started, I was a shy little thing. Pushing myself out of my comfort zone to meet people and make connections transformed my business growth. Being in business can be a lonely game, so it's important to build connections that give you support and can help you thrive.

That said, be careful of those you connect with, and stay true to your brand values. Over the years I've been approached with many opportunities that at first glance looked like quick wins for the business, would pay a lot and open up opportunities. But when I looked at them properly I realised that, long term, they didn't align with my values, so I said no.

In essence, one of my core business values is to do good and be good. It's our brand DNA, and it sounds like a no-brainer, but once you get into business it can be very hard to maintain. There are so many temptations, so many opportunities that pop up that feel like easy wins. Stop. Make sure you always review them and think about people's ulterior motives. No-one's ever going to do something for you for no return. So when an opportunity pops up, is it an opportunity for you or more for them? Critically evaluate it, asking what, ultimately, does it look like.

Stay connected

One of the reasons small businesses fail is because they get locked into their own echo chamber. If you get too isolated, that lack of connections and support can lead to missed opportunities, and sometimes you really need to bounce ideas around or vent with someone outside your business. While nothing beats a good face-to-face chat over a cuppa, staying connected with like-minded people and businesses on social media can also help. Though it may not be your favourite pastime, it's important to have a social presence for your brand's visibility and customer reach, too.

JOIN LOCAL BUSINESS NETWORKS

Joining your local business networks is a game changer. They offer a platform to connect with other business owners, share experiences and even collaborate on projects. Look for local chambers of commerce, industry-specific groups or social media communities. Being part of a network not only provides support but also opens up opportunities for partnerships and referrals.

ACCESS GOVERNMENT PROGRAMS AND GRANTS

The Australian Government offers a variety of programs and grants designed to support small businesses. Whether you need funding for a new project or assistance with training, there's likely a program that can help. Check out Chapter 5, as well as resources like Australian Small Business Advisory Services (ASBAS), to find out what you're eligible for. Applying for these grants and programs can provide the financial boost you need to take your business to the next level.

COLLABORATE WITH OTHER LOCAL BUSINESSES

Collaboration is key in a thriving business community. Partner with other local businesses for mutual benefit by co-hosting events, sharing marketing efforts, or even bundling products and services. Collaboration not only helps you reach a broader audience but also fosters a sense of community and support among local businesses.

ENGAGE WITH LOCAL CHAMBERS OF COMMERCE

Engaging with your local chamber of commerce can provide numerous benefits. These organisations offer resources, networking opportunities and advocacy for small businesses. By becoming an active member, you can gain access to valuable information, training programs and even discounts on services. Chambers of commerce are also great advocates for local businesses, helping to create a supportive environment for growth.

LEVERAGE SOCIAL MEDIA PLATFORMS

Social media platforms are invaluable for creating meaningful connections with customers and building a robust support network. Engage directly with your audience through comments, Q&A sessions and live streams to foster trust and loyalty. Use Facebook groups for customer interaction and support, share customer stories to create community, and collaborate with influencers to broaden your reach. Leverage social media analytics to tailor your content effectively, ensuring you meet your audience's needs and interests. By using social media to build genuine connections, you can foster a supportive and engaged community around your business.

Stay current

The business world is constantly evolving, and staying updated with the latest trends, technologies and best practices is crucial.

KEEP LEARNING!

Continuous learning not only enhances your skills but also keeps you motivated and inspired. Enrol in online courses, attend webinars, read industry blogs and listen to podcasts.

Platforms like Coursera and LinkedIn Learning offer a wealth of online courses to help you upskill and stay ahead of the curve. Whether you want to learn more about digital marketing, financial management or leadership, these platforms provide access to courses from top universities and industry experts. Investing in your education is one of the best ways to grow your business and stay competitive.

ATTEND WORKSHOPS AND EVENTS

Workshops and events are fantastic for learning new skills and staying updated on industry trends. Many organisations offer free or low-cost workshops on topics ranging from digital marketing to financial planning. Attend these events to gain valuable insights and network with like-minded entrepreneurs. Plus, they're a great way to break the routine and get inspired!

SEEK MENTORSHIP AND ADVICE

Being mentored can be incredibly valuable for small business owners. Seek out experienced entrepreneurs who can offer guidance and advice. Many organisations provide mentorship programs specifically designed for small business owners – one is the Small Business Mentoring Service (SBMS). A mentor can help you navigate challenges and set realistic goals, and provide a fresh perspective on your business.

OVER TO YOU

> Make a list of skills and knowledge you know you need to build upon your business success. Now, order them in terms of priority – the ones you're most interested in and which would make the biggest difference to your results. Now, find the courses, mentors or training that will help you upskill.

STAY ALERT

Keep an eye on what other businesses in your industry are doing – what is and isn't working for them. To ensure you never miss important updates, set up Google Alerts for keywords related to your industry. That way, you'll receive notifications whenever there's news or developments on topics that matter to your business. Additionally, subscribe to industry-specific newsletters and podcasts. Platforms like Feedly can help you organise and manage your subscriptions, making it easy to stay on top of the latest information without feeling overwhelmed.

Stay flexible

A flexible business strategy is essential in a rapidly changing market. Be prepared to pivot and adapt your plans as needed. Regularly review your business goals and strategies to ensure they align with current market conditions. Flexibility allows you to respond quickly to new opportunities and challenges, keeping your business resilient and competitive.

MONITOR FINANCIAL PERFORMANCE

Keeping a close eye on your financial performance is non-negotiable. Regularly review your financial statements, track your KPIs and conduct cash flow analyses.

SEEK FEEDBACK AND CONTINUOUS IMPROVEMENT

Always seek feedback and strive for continuous improvement to make sure you're always evolving and meeting the needs of your market.

FOCUS ON QUALITY AND CUSTOMER SERVICE

Never compromise on quality and customer service. These are the cornerstones of a successful business. Ensure that your products or services consistently meet high standards and that your customer service is top-notch.

INVEST IN MARKETING AND BRANDING

Investing in marketing and branding is crucial for staying competitive, making your business memorable and attracting loyal customers.

Embrace technology

Innovation and technology are your best friends in a changing market. Stay open to new ideas and be willing to adopt technologies that can streamline your operations and enhance your customers' experience. Whether it's implementing a new CRM system, using AI for customer service or exploring e-commerce platforms, embracing innovation can give you a competitive advantage and keep your business agile.

FINANCIAL MANAGEMENT

Naturally, the first tools I'm keen to talk about are money tools! Managing your finances is crucial, and this is where platforms and tools like Xero and

MYOB are absolute game changers. Xero offers a cloud-based accounting solution that's perfect for small businesses, allowing you to manage your invoicing, payroll and expenses all in one place. MYOB is another fantastic option, with features tailored to Australian businesses, including GST management and BAS reporting.

These tools not only help you stay on top of your finances, but also save you heaps of time so you can focus on growing your business. If your accountant is anything like mine, they'll probably insist on you using one of these resources. They do come with a subscription fee, though, so unless your business is big enough to afford it, a lovely old-fashioned spreadsheet can help you keep track of the basics just as well. Many of our SOTM sole traders are fine with that!

MARKETING AND SOCIAL MEDIA

Next, let's get your marketing game on point. Tools like Canva and Hootsuite are super useful for creating and managing your marketing campaigns. Canva is a user-friendly graphic design tool that lets you create stunning visuals for your social media, website and marketing materials. Hootsuite, on the other hand, allows you to schedule and manage all your social media posts from one dashboard. This means you can plan your content in advance and ensure a consistent online presence without stress. Of course, there are quite literally hundreds of other tools out there, so do your research and find the ones that suit your needs.

E-COMMERCE

If you're selling products online, e-commerce platforms like Shopify and WooCommerce make it all possible. Look for an all-in-one e-commerce platform with built-in wizards that will make setting up and running your online store a breeze. Ideally, they'll also help you take care of inventory management and payment processing. Shopify is really simple to use, but WooCommerce, a customisable, open-source e-commerce platform, is another excellent option, especially if you're using WordPress for your website, as it will integrate seamlessly with your existing site. Again, there are plenty of options around, so take a few for a test drive to see which of them aligns best with your business.

CUSTOMER RELATIONSHIP MANAGEMENT (CRM)

Building strong relationships with your customers is key, and that's where CRM tools like HubSpot, Mailchimp and Zoho CRM come in. These platforms help you track customer interactions and manage leads, and can even automate your sales process. Many were originally built around email marketing and have developed to include analytics that will help you understand and engage with your customers better. These tools ensure you never miss an opportunity to connect with your audience.

PROJECT MANAGEMENT AND COLLABORATION

Staying organised and on top of your tasks is essential, especially if you're juggling multiple projects. Tools like Trello and Asana are perfect for project management and team collaboration. Trello uses boards, lists and cards to help you visualise your tasks and workflow, making it easy to track progress and stay organised. Asana offers a more comprehensive project management solution, with features like task assignments, due dates and project timelines. Both tools are fantastic for keeping your team aligned and avoiding anything falling through the cracks.

Meet the founder:
Mia Klitsas

Mia Klitsas's period care company, Moxie, turned the industry on its head when she launched nearly 20 years ago, and it's been doing things differently ever since. Though surrounded by a powerful team, Mia keeps a hand in all aspects of the business to ensure she stays in touch and makes the best decisions for the business and its customers.

Name: Mia Klitsas

Business: Moxie

Industry: Period care

Product/service: Products that help you manage your period – anything from pads, tampons and period cups to mini hot water bottles, chocolate, intimate wipes and even a naturopathically blended tea specifically made for period feels

Primary audience: Women aged 18 to 30

Secondary audience: Anyone with a period!

The business began: 2005

Moxie offers progressive cycle care for down there. We are 100 per cent Australian-owned and female-led, and we consciously create our products using materials that are gentle on your body and the environment but strong for your flow, giving you confidence and comfort when you need it most. We also champion open, uncensored and unfiltered menstruation conversations.

I went into business because I felt driven to address a missing personal and product-related pain point. I saw a gap in the period care market, which was largely dominated by huge multinational companies offering products that, in my view, didn't truly reflect a woman's experience with menstruation. My idea was to repackage period care products – starting with tampons – originally in cute, refillable, recyclable tins. Not only did I want to solve the problem of tampons rolling around in the bottom of our bags, but I also felt the packaging needed a design refresh. That's how Moxie was born.

The best thing about being in business for myself is having the autonomy to execute my own ideas without being told they're not worthy. Sometimes those ideas work out well and sometimes they don't, but that's all part of the journey – and also how you know you're pushing the envelope and challenging yourself and the norms within your industry.

The worst thing is not having someone to tell you when your ideas are rubbish. We do have transparency and a very open and honest policy within our team and no 'hierarchy' as such, so the team do voice their opinions, which I appreciate, but sometimes being a business owner can feel isolating and stressful as it all starts and ends with you. As an owner, every decision, whether it is your own or not, is ultimately your responsibility, as are the consequences.

Initially I underestimated the importance of resilience and its crucial role in overcoming the obstacles and setbacks inherent in running a business. Resilience, much like a muscle, strengthens over time. While having a great idea is a strong starting point, it's persistence through challenges that truly drives evolution and helps you discern what matters most in the broader context.

Ultimately, our primary focus is serving our audience, which means we're heavily influenced by market dynamics, including competitive trends, consumer buying habits and evolving market trends. As a result, our business continuously adapts to these factors. For instance, we've revised our tampons and pads to eliminate plastic wrappers. While much of our supply chain remains consistent, we value the strong relationships we've built with our suppliers over time, which we hope will endure as the business evolves. I'm always open to change and willing to adjust our strategies if they no longer serve our business or audience effectively. I truly believe flexibility and adaptability are essential to any business's success.

I've been really hands-on in the business since day one, and I don't think that will ever change. While I'm officially 'director', I'm also a marketing manager, customer service support, warehouse packer, sales rep – just to name a few. I think it's crucial as a business owner to really understand each facet of your business to be able to effectively lead and make informed decisions. This hands-on involvement not only keeps me connected to the day-to-day operations but also ensures that I can address challenges and opportunities from a comprehensive perspective.

If I could go back and do things differently, I might scale up more gradually in export markets and invest more time and research in those markets rather than diving in headfirst in such a big way (we launched overseas around 18 months after launching in Australia). That may have allowed us to manage growth more effectively and adapt to challenges in a more controlled manner. That said, each experience has been a valuable lesson, and I believe that navigating those early challenges has ultimately strengthened the business.

We use a bunch of external support services. I'm a huge advocate for engaging with experts and advisers as consultants as I think it's a great way to seek and invest in expertise for your business when you may not be able to afford them (or have the need for them) as a full-time resource. We call on various experts depending on our needs at any given time, from accountants to creative directors to product formulators, strategic advisers, social media agencies – the list is long! If you need support with a facet of your business, guaranteed there is someone out there who can assist you. You don't necessarily need to hire your own staff to bring those skills into your business.

The most impactful support has come from connecting directly with other founders, business owners and industry experts. Building a close-knit network of trusted friends and advisers over time has proven invaluable. Being able to call on each other for support, share experiences and exchange contacts has made a significant difference in navigating the challenges of running a business. I also try to keep on top of emerging trends by following various social media accounts that are aligned with my target audience. This combination of personal connections and trend awareness has been pivotal in our ongoing success.

We also have a great team. I learnt very quickly that you can't do everything on your own – nor do you have the expertise to execute every facet of your business. Hiring staff has been both a wonderful and not-so-wonderful decision at different times.

I like to empower my team with autonomy. I really let them take ownership of their projects and make decisions without micromanaging them, giving them the freedom to experiment with new approaches, ideas and initiatives. This often leads to creative solutions and a boost in morale and motivation.

We also foster a culture of transparency: I've always been open about company goals, challenges and successes, and I believe this helps build trust and engagement in a team. We have a weekly team 'huddle' where everyone shares updates and feedback, which helps create a sense of shared purpose and accountability.

I aim to lead by example. As a founder (and even as a manager), this is a no-brainer for me. Model the behaviour you expect from your team. Demonstrating qualities such as integrity, dedication, a positive attitude and respect for others sets a standard for your team to follow. And it can really help set the tone for the culture.

I think I have a relatively good work–life balance. I actually enjoy working into the evenings and so tend to leave the office last as I like to do much of my creative thinking/strategy work when it's quiet. But once I leave, work stays at work. When I first started the business, I made a promise to myself that I wouldn't work weekends, because I was conscious of my family and personal relationships suffering as a result, and of losing my sense of self outside of my business. I do feel like that sometimes (as my work life and business are such a huge part of my identity), but to this day I've kept my promise to not work on weekends. Unfortunately, it's difficult as a business owner to switch the mind off, so while work may not physically come home with you, it's tricky for stressful situations not to consume you sometimes.

I'd be lying if I said there weren't days when I wonder if it would've been easier to work nine to five for someone else . . . ha-ha! But looking back, I would tell my younger self not to sweat the small stuff. Once you make a decision, trust in that decision. Don't procrastinate and question whether or not it was right – trust that it was the right decision with the information you had at the time. Put all your energy into that chosen course of action and do what you can to make it successful. If it doesn't work out, just make another decision!

Become a joiner

There are many incredible business associations and networks out there designed to support you, connect you with like-minded individuals, and provide valuable resources to help your business thrive. Here is a bit of basic information about some of the more useful ones that every modern small business owner should know about – visit their websites for more details of what they do and how they can help you.

BUSINESS COUNCIL OF AUSTRALIA (BCA)

The BCA is a powerful network that brings together the CEOs of Australia's largest businesses to work on public policy issues. While it might seem geared towards larger corporations, the BCA's initiatives and research can provide valuable insights for small business owners, too. They advocate for economic policies that benefit the entire business community, including small enterprises. By staying informed through the BCA's publications and events, you can gain a deeper understanding of the broader business environment in Australia.

AUSTRALIAN CHAMBER OF COMMERCE AND INDUSTRY (ACCI)

ACCI is the nation's largest and most representative business network. It offers a wealth of resources, from policy advocacy to business tools and templates, and also hosts a variety of events and training programs designed to help you grow your business. Joining ACCI can provide you with access to a vast network of business professionals, and opportunities to influence policy decisions that impact your industry.

BUSINESS ENTERPRISE CENTRES (BEC) AUSTRALIA

BEC Australia is a national network of not-for-profit organisations that provide support to small businesses through advice, training and mentoring. The centres are located across the country and offer services tailored to the needs of local businesses. Whether you need help with business planning, marketing or financial management, BEC can connect you with experienced advisers who can guide you every step of the way. Plus, their workshops and events are fantastic for networking and learning new skills.

WOMEN'S NETWORK AUSTRALIA (WNA)

Ladies, this one's for you! WNA is a vibrant community specifically designed to support female entrepreneurs. It offers networking events, professional development opportunities, and a platform to share your business journey with other women. It also provides access to a wealth of resources, including business articles, webinars and a member directory. Joining WNA can help you build valuable connections, gain inspiration from other successful women, and grow your business in a supportive environment.

SMALL BUSINESS ASSOCIATION OF AUSTRALIA (SBAA)

SBAA is dedicated to representing and supporting small businesses across the country. It offers a range of services, including advocacy, networking events and educational resources, as well as a platform for small business owners to voice their concerns and influence policy decisions. By joining SBAA, you can stay informed about the latest developments affecting small businesses and connect with other entrepreneurs who share your challenges and goals.

LOCAL CHAMBERS OF COMMERCE

Don't underestimate the power of your local chamber of commerce. From networking events to business expos and training programs, local chambers of commerce provide valuable opportunities to connect with other business owners in your area. They also advocate for local business interests and can help you navigate local regulations and opportunities.

INDUSTRY-SPECIFIC ASSOCIATIONS

Consider joining industry-specific associations relevant to your business. These organisations provide specialised resources, networking opportunities and advocacy tailored to your industry. For example, if you're in the retail sector, the Australian Retailers Association (ARA) offers resources and support specifically for retailers. Similarly, the Australian Marketing Institute (AMI) provides resources and networking opportunities for marketing professionals. These associations can help you stay updated with industry trends, best practices and regulatory changes.

Principle 10: Keep strong

In small business, the challenges your business faces can feel personal. Develop resilience and adopt a growth mindset to push through the hard times and use your 'mistakes' to make you stronger. Let your inner strength shine.

Meet the founder:
Erin Deering

Erin Deering is the co-founder of swimwear brand Triangl. She launched the Instagram-famous line in 2012 with her then-partner, Craig Ellis. The brand catapulted to success and counted Bella Hadid, Kendall Jenner and Hailey Bieber as early fans. At its height in 2015, it achieved a whopping US$60 million in sales![1] Deering exited the brand in 2018, but it still operates under the leadership of her former business partner.

Name: Erin Deering

Business: Triangl

Industry: Consumer goods

Product/service: Swimwear

Unique selling point: Swimwear that stands out

Target audience: Teenagers, and women in their twenties up to their forties

Secondary audience: Essentially an extension of our primary audience, given the broad appeal of our products

The business began: 2012

Triangl Swimwear began with an idea to create unique, eye-catching swimwear pieces. At the time I was progressing well in my career in fashion, working in marketing, e-commerce and customer care. However, the ceiling felt low, and at 26 I felt that the only way to achieve the career growth and creative freedom I desired was to start my own business. It was a somewhat naive yet exciting decision, driven by the belief that working for myself would provide unparalleled freedom and fulfilment.

I set up the business in 2012, and by January 2013 we had made our first sale. Our designs were distinctive – I bet lots of you couldn't escape Triangl on your Instagram feed back then! We used neoprene, a material that hadn't been commonly used in swimwear since the 80s.

Leveraging social media is a big part of what made our business successful. We gifted products to celebrities in a unique way that wasn't typically done with influencers back then. For aspiring business owners now, it's a reminder that innovation and creativity are important to make your product stand out.

I'll be honest, being a business owner is not so glamorous at times. I loved the freedom and flexibility working on my own business provided, but there was a catch. Although I initially thought I would have more free time, the reality was the opposite. Yet there was something thrilling about being in control and pushing myself beyond the boundaries of a typical career.

Running a business is all-consuming. It occupies your thoughts 24/7, and there's no separation between personal and business time. However, this level of obsession is necessary for success and should be embraced if you truly love what you do. For me, it manifested in an immense fear of failure. Running a business means a lot of it relies solely on you. It was daunting to realise my shortcomings and face the reality that if the business failed, it was my failure. However, this fear also made the experience exciting and ultimately contributed to my personal and professional growth.

As the business grew, we brought others on board, including tax advisers to navigate the complexities of operating in Hong Kong, accountants, translators for our work with China, and external customer care support. We also outsourced some creative tasks like image retouching and logistics. We hired a merchandiser and built a supply chain team in Hong Kong who proved to be very loyal and effective. Hiring staff was a necessary decision to manage the growing demands of the business, and in hindsight it was a positive move that contributed to our success.

My main tip is this: hire slowly and fire quickly. It's crucial to take your time finding the right person so you can maintain a positive company culture, and if someone isn't the right fit, it's important to address it quickly to avoid potential damage to the business. Additionally, leading by example, setting boundaries and maintaining professionalism while being approachable are key aspects of effective staff management.

Having a business isn't just about being the boss. I also advise prioritising self-development and working on yourself. Understanding your strengths and weaknesses and investing in personal growth through therapy, spirituality or other means is crucial. This self-awareness not only enhances personal wellbeing but also makes you a better leader and entrepreneur. Investing in yourself pays off in the long run and contributes to overall business success.

While starting Triangl afforded me financial freedom, it also led to burnout that I took years to recover from. But despite the challenges, I'm grateful for the experience as it has led to who I am today and provided me with the means to achieve my current happiness and success.

Looking back, I wish I'd handled challenges with less stress and been less reactive. The difficulties deeply affected me at the time, but I recognise that every experience, good or bad, led me to where I am now – and I wouldn't change that journey.

Own it!

As we come to the end of this book, I hope you have learnt so much more about yourself and the kind of business you want to develop. As you've heard, from my stories and many others', although this wild ride can be exhausting at times, it is also exhilarating and there's no other way I'd choose to live.

The five Business Bible commandments

The journey of entrepreneurship is filled with ups and downs, and as we've discussed multiple times in *The Business Bible*, having a solid plan can help you navigate through it all. Planning for the future and long-term success involves setting strategic goals, anticipating challenges and creating a roadmap to achieve sustained growth and stability.

Along the way, I've delivered one key principle at the end of each chapter. But if I could summarise the five most important things you need to start and thrive in small business, they are these: my five Business Bible commandments.

1. SET SAIL STRATEGICALLY

Setting a clear strategic direction is like plotting your course on a map – it gives your business a vision and a plan for where you want to go. With a well-defined strategy you can focus your efforts on the right opportunities, align your team and make decisions that drive your business forward. It's all about having a roadmap to success and sticking to it, even when the going gets tough.

2. DON'T RISK IT FOR THE BISCUIT

While risk management may not be the most glamorous part of running your business, it's absolutely essential. Identifying potential risks and developing strategies to mitigate them can save you a world of trouble down the line. Whether it's financial, operational or market-related risks, having a plan in place means you're ready to tackle challenges head-on and keep your business on solid ground.

3. RESOURCE IT RIGHT

Efficient resource allocation is your secret weapon for achieving your business goals without burning out. It's about making sure your time, money and people are all working towards the same objectives. By prioritising and distributing resources wisely, you can maximise productivity, reduce waste and ensure every dollar and hour spent is moving you closer to your vision.

4. BE ADAPTABLE

In the fast-paced world of business, adaptability is your best friend. Being able to pivot and seize new opportunities as they arise can set you apart from the competition. It's about staying flexible, embracing change and continuously learning so you can navigate the ever-evolving market landscape with confidence and agility.

5. AIM TO SUSTAIN

Sustainable growth is the holy grail for any business owner. It's not just about scaling quickly, but doing so in a way that's manageable and long-lasting. By focusing on sustainable practices and steady progress, you can build a business that not only thrives today but stands the test of time. It's about creating a legacy, not just a flash in the pan.

Before I go

Dear aspiring entrepreneurs,

As you stand on the brink of your entrepreneurial journey, remember that every great business started with a dream, a spark of an idea and the courage to pursue it. The road ahead will be filled with challenges, triumphs, learning experiences and opportunities for growth. But know this: you are capable, resilient and equipped with the tools to succeed.

Your passion and vision are the heartbeats of your business. Embrace your entrepreneurial spirit with confidence and let it guide you through the ups and downs. Stay true to your values and let your 'why' be the driving force behind every decision you make.

Surround yourself with a supportive network of mentors, advisers and peers who believe in you and your vision. Seek out knowledge, stay informed and never stop learning. The business environment is ever-changing, and your adaptability will be your greatest asset.

Remember, setbacks are not failures but stepping stones to success. Each challenge you overcome builds your resilience and brings you one step closer to your goals. Celebrate your achievements, no matter how small, and learn from every experience.

Your journey as an entrepreneur is a testament to your bravery, creativity and determination. You have the power to create something extraordinary, to make a difference and to leave a lasting impact. Believe in yourself, trust the process and keep moving forward.

You've got this. The world is waiting for your brilliance.

Stay fabulous and unstoppable,

Victoria

Notes

INTRODUCTION

1   G. Gilfillan (2015), 'Definitions and data sources for small business in Australia: A quick guide', Parliamentary Library, 1 December 2015.

CHAPTER 1

1   Australian Bureau of Statistics (2023), 'Counts of Australian businesses, including entries and exits', reference period: July 2019 to June 2023, released 22 August 2023.

2   Australian Small Business and Family Enterprise Ombudsman (ND), 'Number of small businesses in Australia' [report], August 2023.

3   Australian Taxation Office (2023), last updated 25 May 2023.

4   McCrindle (ND), 'Australia, the small business nation', [website].

5   E. Barron, L.E. Ruiz and E. Robles (2018), 'What drives an entrepreneur: Motives and the influence of institutions at different development stages', paper given at XXIII International Congress of Accounting, Administration and Information Technology, 3–5 October 2018, Ciudad Universitaria, Mexico City.

6   Y. Redrup (2021), 'How a cleaning product company became a $40m viral hit', *Australian Financial Review*, 10 February.

7   T. Page (2021), 'Why Steve Jobs' 2005 commencement speech is the most watched in history', *CNN*, 7 June.

8   G. Kawasaki (2004), 'Make meaning in your company' [video], Stanford University Entrepreneurial Thought Leaders, 20 October.

CHAPTER 2

1   Australian Small Business and Family Enterprise Ombudsman (ND), 'Number of small businesses in Australia' [report], August 2023.

2   Australian Small Business and Family Enterprise Ombudsman (2023), 'Contribution to Australian gross domestic product' [report], June 2023.

3   MYOB (2024), 'Business Monitor report', January.

4   ibid.

5   R.M. Ryan and E.L. Deci (2000), 'Self-determination theory and the facilitation of intrinsic motivation, social development, and well-being', *American Psychologist*, 55(1), pp. 68–78.

6   Australian Small Business Commissioner (2016), 'A submission by the Office of the Australian Small Business Commissioner to the House of Representatives Standing Committee on Education and Employment, Inquiry into Innovation and Creativity: Workforce for the New Economy', 9 March.

7   'SMH (2017), "World's happiest animal", the quokka, becomes the most popular tourist attraction at Australia's Rottnest Island', *SMH Traveller*, 1 March.

CHAPTER 4

1   business.gov.au (ND), 'Business structures: Types of business structures'.

2   Small Business, Big Marketing (2023), 'How to create an untouchable business by doing less' [podcast episode #660], 5 December.

3   Australian Business Register (2024), 'ABN entitlement', last updated 29 February 2024.

4   business.gov.au (2024), 'Patents', last updated 18 January 2024.

5   Australian Copyright Council (2024), 'Fair dealing: What can I use?' [fact sheet], 7 August.

6   Australian Consumer Law (2024), 'Australian Consumer Law', 18 January [website].

7   Office of the Australian Information Officer (2018), 'Australian entities and the European Union General Data Protection Regulation', 8 June.

8   Ben Wolford (ND), 'Does the GDPR apply to companies outside of the EU?', GDPR.EU.

9   business.gov.au (2024), 'Work health and safety', last updated 2 May 2024.

10 Department of Climate Change, Energy, the Environment and Water (2024), 'EPBC Act reform' (updated 5 July 2024) and 'National Environmental Standards' (updated 8 August 2024).

11 Australian Competition and Consumer Commission (ND), 'Environmental and sustainability claims' [website].

CHAPTER 5

1   See 'Business and organisations' on the ATO website.

2   Y. Redrup (2021), 'Atlassian's Scott Farquhar tells founders not to bootstrap', *Australian Financial Review*, 6 May.

3   Parliament of Australia (2016), 'Inquiry into innovation and creativity: workforce for the new economy' [parliamentary business], 9 November.

4   business.gov.au (ND), 'Grants and Programs Finder'.

CHAPTER 6

1   CyberWardens (2023), 'Small business urged to bridge the gender equality gap on cyber security' [media release], 23 March.

CHAPTER 7

1   M. Bouris (2024), '#451 Girls With Gems: Rewriting the rules of fashion with Lia Georgantis', *The Mentor with Mark Bouris*, 9 July, [podcast].

2   J. Dent (2023), 'Five minutes with Geoff Ramm, author of *Celebrity Service*', Meon Valley Business Travel, 18 October.

CHAPTER 8

1   A. Santoreneos (2022), 'Who's on the bus': The Iconic co-founder Adam Jacobs on the lead indicator of success', *Forbes*, 28 October.

2   For more information, see 'Fair Work system' (ND), Fair Work Ombudsman website.

3   Fair Work Ombudsmen (ND), 'Small business and the Fair Work Act', Fair Work Ombudsman website.

4   business.gov.au (2024), 'Business insurance', 18 January.

CHAPTER 9

1   ISWR (2024), 'How China's tariffs on Australian wine changed the market landscape', IWSR, 5 February.

2   For more information, see 'Export grants and programs' at business.gov.au.

3   For more information, see 'Export Market Development Grants' (ND) at the Austrade website.

CHAPTER 10

1   L. Mega (2024), 'Why Erin Deering sold swimwear sensation Triangl',
     Foundr, 15 May.

Acknowledgements

Congratulations, my friend, you've made it to the end of *The Business Bible*! I hope you feel empowered to take bold steps in your business journey and inspired by the wisdom and experience shared throughout these pages. Writing the acknowledgements is always one of my favourite parts of the process because it gives me the opportunity to express my deepest gratitude to those who have helped bring this book to life – because, let's be real, it takes a team to build something this special.

To Stephen. As we grow together, each chapter of life has brought new meaning and here I am thanking you yet again. From being my partner, to my fiancé, to my husband, and now the most cherished role of all, being an incredible father to Harvey. Watching you thrive in this new chapter of fatherhood continues to amaze me. Your unwavering support and belief in me and my ever-growing ideas means more than I can put into words. I couldn't imagine doing this without you and I feel incredibly lucky to share both this life and this journey with you. You're the very patient backbone of this family and Harvey and I are so lucky to have you.

To my son, Harvey. Every time I sit down to write I'm reminded of why I do what I do and why it's so important to me to build a thriving business that leaves a strong legacy – because I want to help create a world where you can chase every dream that crosses your mind. You've brought a new dimension of joy, purpose and motivation into my life.

I am endlessly proud to be your mum and I'm excited to see the incredible person you're becoming. Keep dreaming big.

To my parents, Judi and Eric Devine. Your love and belief in me have shaped everything I am today. You've always encouraged me to follow my dreams, no matter how audacious, and that unwavering support is something I carry with me every day. Seeing you both as grandparents has been one of the greatest joys of my life and Harvey is so fortunate to have you as role models. Thank you for everything.

To Isabelle Yates. Five books! Can you believe it? Your support and guidance have been nothing short of extraordinary. Thank you for your patience, encouragement and always being in my corner. I am beyond grateful to you and to the entire team at Penguin. Charle Malycon, your dedication to helping me craft the perfect book for our readers is truly inspiring. Working with all of you has been a privilege and I look forward to many more collaborations in the future!

And finally, to you, my readers. This book is for you. You are the reason I continue to write and create. *The Business Bible* is a testament to the strength, courage and resilience of those embarking on their entrepreneurial journeys. I hope these pages serve as a guide, a companion and a reminder that success in business is possible for all of us, no matter where we begin. Your support of my work is a gift I never take for granted and I am so proud to have you as part of this community. Let's continue to build something incredible together.

She's
on the
M●ney

Take charge of your
financial future

Victoria Devine

Creator of Australia's #1 finance podcast

Winner of the ABIA General Non-fiction Book of the Year 2022
Winner of the Best Personal Finance & Investment Book of the Year
at the 2021 Business Book Awards

Through her phenomenally popular and award-winning podcast **She's on the Money**, Victoria Devine has built an thriving community of women finding their way to financial freedom. Honest, relatable, non-judgemental and motivating, Victoria is a financial adviser (now retired) who knows what millennial life is really like and where we can get stuck with money stuff. (Buy now, pay-the-price-later schemes, for one!) So, to help you hit your money goals without skimping on brunch, she's put all her expert advice into this accessible guide that will set you up for a healthy and happy future. Learn how to be more secure, independent and informed with your money – with clear steps on how to budget, clear debts, build savings, start investing, buy property and much more. Along with all the practical information, Victoria will guide you through the sometimes-tricky psychology of money stories and habits, so you can establish the values, good practices and confidence to help you build your wealth long-term. Just like the podcast, the book is full of real-life money stories from members of the **She's on the Money** community who candidly share their experiences, wins, and lessons learned, to inspire others to turn their stories around, too. With templates and activities throughout, plus a twelve-month plan to get you started, you can immediately put Victoria's recommendations into action. You are not alone on your financial journey, and with the money principles in this book you'll go further than you ever thought possible.

From the bestselling author of *She's on the Money*

Investing with She's *on the* Money

Build your future wealth

Victoria Devine

Creator of Australia's #1 finance podcast

Shortlisted for ABIA General Non-fiction Book of the Year 2023

The ultimate millennial investment guide from the award-winning, number one bestselling author of **She's on the Money**. Through the **She's on the Money** podcast and online community, and her bestselling first book, financial adviser (now retired) Victoria Devine has helped thousands of Australians take charge of their financial futures. Investing is a huge part of building wealth, which is why Victoria's second book is all about learning how and why to invest and taking confident action to create an investment portfolio that will set you up for security and prosperity later in life. Start by understanding your money mindset, risk profile and why you can't afford not to invest – especially if you're a woman (thanks, gender inequality!). Dive deep into the various ways you can invest in the stock market and learn more about property investment. Discover how your superannuation has already made you an investor and get the low-down on ethical investing before creating your own investment strategy that reflects your goals and values. Covering all this and more, Victoria's straightforward guidance and practical activities in **Investing with She's on the Money** will have you feeling educated, empowered and ready to grow your future wealth in no time. Everyone has different starting points, but it's never too early or too late to begin your investing journey – so let's do this!

The ultimate first
home buyer's guide

Property
with
She's
on the
Money

Victoria Devine

AWARD-WINNING AND BESTSELLING AUTHOR

Smash your property goals with Victoria Devine's informative guide – whether you're getting your first foot on the ladder, hunting for your dream home or planning for an investment property. Even with the challenges involved (interest rates and crazy-high house prices, we're looking at you!), so many of us still really want to own property. Whether it's the security and financial perks of owning your home or the benefits of having an investment property, the appeal and rewards are many. But buying a property can also be one of the biggest decisions you'll ever make, so you want to get it right – right? Luckily, Victoria Devine has written **Property with She's on the Money** to equip you for the whole process – from establishing your property values and truly under-standing *why* you want to buy a home, to saving for the all-important deposit, the right key experts to speak to, all things mortgages, what to buy and when, and how to make every stage of the process as smooth as possible – right through to renovating and selling. It's packed with practical advice, innovative ideas and real-life stories from members of the **She's on the Money** community who have achieved their home ownership goals. With this game-changing guide, property is no longer confusing, overwhelming and out-of-reach. It's clear, inspiring – and totally within your power.

Powered by Penguin

Looking for more great reads, exclusive content and book giveaways?

Subscribe to our weekly newsletter.

Scan the QR code or visit penguin.com.au/signup